The rise of financial capitalism

International capital markets in the Age of Reason

Larry Neal
University of Illinois at Urbana-Champaign

CAMBRIDGE
UNIVERSITY PRESS

Published by the Press Syndicate of the University of Cambridge
The Pitt Building, Trumpington Street, Cambridge CB2 1RP
40 West 20th Street, New York, NY 10011-4211, USA
10 Stamford Road, Oakleigh, Melbourne 3166, Australia

First published 1990
First paperback edition 1993

Printed in the United States of America

Library of Congress Cataloging-in-Publication Data available.

A catalogue record for this book is available from the British Library.

ISBN 0-521-38205-X hardback
ISBN 0-521-45738-6 paperback

To Peg, Kathy,
Liz, and Chris

Contents

Acknowledgments

The origins of this book date back to 1975, when Robert Eagly told me of his data source for a paper on the integration of the London and Amsterdam capital markets: the then elusive *Course of the Exchange,* by John Castaing. I acquired my own copy of the microfilm made by the British Library during a sabbatical leave in 1976. Since then, various research assistants have toiled at the task of transcription: Barry Stregevsky, Eugene White, Rick Cheney, Eric Schubert, Xiao-Lei Zuo, David Wheelock, Esther Ogden, Daniel Barbezat, and Alan Dye. Each research assistant has benefited from the programs and files created by his or her predecessor, but the major advances have come from the improved computer technology achieved over the past decade. From a portable Texas Instruments terminal with an external modem to link with a CYBER mainframe computer using a series of FORTRAN programs to enter and clean data to an IBM-AT with VGA monitor using dBase III+ customized screens and programs for entry and cleaning is a revolution in scholarly technology that has to be experienced to be appreciated. Financial support from the University of Illinois Research Board and from the Bureau of Economic and Business Research in the College of Commerce and Business Administration was essential to get the project under way and to bring it to the productive phase, when it became funded by the National Science Foundation (grants SES 83-09211 and SES 85-20223).

Several of these chapters have appeared in abbreviated form in various journals or edited volumes: Chapter 2 as "The Rise of a Financial Press: London and Amsterdam, 1681–1810," *Business History,* 30(April 1988), pp. 163–78; Chapter 5 as "How the South Sea Bubble Was Blown Up and Burst," in Eugene White, ed., *Financial Panics in Historical Perspective* (New York: Dow-Jones-Irwin, 1990); Chapter 6 as "The Dutch and English East India Companies Compared: Evidence from the Stock and Foreign Exchange Markets," in James Tracy, ed., *The Rise of Merchant Empires* (Cambridge University Press, 1989); Chapter 7 as "The Integration and Efficiency of the London and Amsterdam Stock Markets in the Eighteenth Century," *Journal of Economic History*, 47(March 1987), pp. 97–115; Chapter 8 as "Integration of International Capital Markets: Quantitative Evidence from the Eighteenth to Twentieth Centuries," *Journal of Economic History*, 45(June 1985), pp. 219–26.

Preliminary versions of these papers and the remainder of the chapters have been presented at various conferences and numerous seminars, including workshops at Bielefeld University, the University of Chicago, Colby College, Columbia University, Harvard University, Indiana University, Northwestern University, University of South Carolina, University of Trier, Vanderbilt University, Washington University at St. Louis, and Yale University. Participants at those workshops helped improve the current version as much by their puzzled questions as by their interest in the topics.

The help of various archivists and librarians has been critical at various stages in acquiring supplemental materials, especially Cora Gravesteijn, then at the Economische-Historische Bibliotheek in Amsterdam, Henry Gillett, archivist at the Bank of England, John Hodgson, chief of the Roehampton repository for the Bank of England, and P. Balachandran in the Commerce Library of the University of Illinois. Counsel and encouragement from members of the hardy band of historians who study the eighteenth century have been very important also, especially Jan de Vries, P. G. M. Dickson, John McCusker, James C. Riley, and James Tracy. Advice and tutoring on principles of finance were freely provided by my colleagues in finance: Josef Lakonishok, Louis Scott, and David Whitford. It is always a pleasure to acknowledge the generous support of other economic historians that was tendered at various stages: Charles Calomiris, Lance Davis, David Galenson, Henry Gemery, Charles Kindleberger, A. J. H. Latham, Peter Lindert, Donald McCloskey, Philip Mirowski, Joel Mokyr, Douglass North, Herman van der Wee, Eugene White, Jeffrey G. Williamson, and especially the editors of this series, Michael Bordo and Forrest Capie. A special word of thanks is due to Stanley Engerman, who read the first draft in its entirety with his usual care and intelligent advice and is responsible for some major improvements in argument and exposition. Finally, I have to acknowledge the contributions of my colleagues and students in the Economic History Workshop at the University of Illinois, who endured and critiqued most of the chapters in their imperfect early form: Lee J. Alston, Jeremy Atack, Royall Brandis, John McKay, Salim Rashid, Thomas Ulen, and Paul Uselding. No doubt errors and deficiencies remain, but these friends and colleagues have done their best to protect the reader.

1. Historical background for the rise of financial capitalism: commercial revolution, rise of nation-states, and capital markets

The decade of the 1980s saw the emergence of international capital move-ment as a dominant feature of the economic relations among nation-states. The resulting pressures on exchange rates, balances of payments, and trade patterns have disconcerted all participants – those who make national economic policy, as well as international financiers and ordinary citizens. Perhaps the most striking episode was the collapse of the world's stock markets during the week of 19 October 1987, the suddenness, sharpness, and inclusiveness of which took all observers by surprise. Some, trying to determine if computer-driven sales in New York or in Tokyo had led to the collapse of international stock markets in 1987, were disoriented on find-ing that Tokyo prices for 20 October preceded, rather than followed, New York quotes for 19 October. They were forced by this circumstance to confront once again the mystery of the international date line, a phe-nomenon first detected by the chronicler of Magellan's voyage to circle the earth.

Antonio Pigafetta recorded his amazement that, according to the Por-tuguese inhabitants of the Cape Verde Islands, it was Thursday, 10 July 1522, when his ship returned to the European settlement there, not Wednesday, 9 July, as indicated in his diary.[1] He finally reasoned correctly what had happened,[2] but nearly two centuries later the English buccaneer and explorer William Dampier remarked on the discrepancy of dates in East Asia. The Portuguese, Dutch, and English who settled in the Pacific islands by going east from Asia were a day ahead of the Spanish settlers who arrived by going west from the Americas. The accidents of European

---

[1] Derek Howse, *Greenwich Time and the Discovery of the Longitude* (Oxford University Press, 1980), pp. 160–1.

[2] ". . . as we had always sailed towards the west, following the course of the sun, and had returned to the same place, we must have gained twenty-four hours, as is clear to any one who reflects upon it." Antonio Pigafetta, "Diary," quoted by Lord Stanley of Alderley, ed., *The First Voyage round the World* (London: Hakluyt Society, 1874), p. 161, and Howse, *Greenwich Times*, p. 161.

settlement, whether from west or east, in the Pacific Basin during the Age of Exploration have determined to this day the zigzags of the international date line, which is not embodied in a formal agreement but is merely a way to show the differences in dates that exist among the islands of the Pacific.[3]

Perhaps each age has to discover certain fundamental truths such as the international date line in its own way, but historical precedents for such discoveries are reassuring evidence that the patterns revealed are indeed fundamental truths. Moreover, they usually are more easily discerned in a historical context rather than a contemporary context. In the case of financial markets, for example, in the eighteenth century there were many fewer well-organized marketplaces and fewer groups of active traders than now. Moreover, government regulations and taxes were much less onerous and diverse. The financial trauma of 19 October 1987 reaffirmed that we live in a new era of closely integrated international bond, equity, and money markets. The financial innovations, as well as the technological innovations, that have led to this new era are still being put into place. It is already clear that they will not be adopted and perfected smoothly. The remainder of this book argues that eighteenth-century Europe provides a historical precedent that can be examined to give us some useful perspective, a sense of the potential dangers as well as the possible advantages of our new financial system.

In the course of investigating the origins of international capital markets in Europe in the late seventeenth century and their operation throughout the eighteenth century, I have become increasingly impressed with the modernity of their operations. Whereas the capital flows and price movements of that era have no direct bearing on today's events (although they can be used to test and refine modern economic and financial theories), the background conditions that led to the development of the international capital markets of the eighteenth century do have some striking similarities to our modern adventures. There were wars, revolutions, religious persecutions, political upheavals, and displacements of wealthy elites at the end of the seventeenth century as there are at the end of the twentieth. There were also investments (and disinvestments) on a large scale by foreigners in the government debts of the leading nations, changes in trade patterns that yielded immense profit opportunities for the most knowledgeable international entrepreneurs, and insider trading, takeover attempts, and financial

---

[3] Howse, *Greenwich Times*, p. 163.

disturbances that destroyed and created private fortunes in apparent chaos. Because the eventual outcomes in these early markets were largely beneficial for the participating countries and their private citizens, it is encouraging to review their history. Encouragement is always welcome in times of rapid change and uncertainty, and history may give its students a sense of confidence and even direction when they turn to coping with the demands of the present.

The history of financial capitalism begins, it now appears, with the "price revolution" of sixteenth century in Europe, which could more aptly be termed the "first financial revolution." Traditionally, the price revolution has been associated with the influx into Europe first of gold from the Portuguese trade with Africa and then silver from the Spanish mines in Peru and Mexico. Price levels throughout Europe more than doubled and remained at the higher levels through the next century of economic crisis.[4] The classic work of Earl Hamilton offered powerful evidence that the increase in silver imports into Spain and from there to the rest of Europe led to the increase in prices.[5] He further argued that in countries where profit inflation occurred because money wages lagged behind the rise in final prices, there was a powerful impetus for the rise of capitalism.[6] Later historians have disputed almost every aspect of Hamilton's famous thesis, but two points are particularly pertinent to the case for a financial revolution. First, prices rose more rapidly than did the supply of specie, implying that it was used ever more efficiently. Moreover, nominal rates of interest appear to have fallen in the most active commercial centers, whereas persistent inflation alone would have tended to raise them. Second, the major units of account throughout Europe tended to depreciate in terms of silver over the sixteenth century, whereas the influx of silver alone should have led them to appreciate. This indicates that governments' supplies of bullion, rising more rapidly than ever before, still did not keep pace with governments' demands. Their demands depended on the rise in prices, as well as more grandiose military goals, whereas their supplies depended on

---

[4] The standard treatment of the price revolution is Fernand Braudel and Frank Spooner, "Prices in Europe from 1450 to 1750," in E. E. Rich and Charles Wilson, eds., *The Cambridge Economic History of Europe*, Vol. 4 (Cambridge University Press, 1967), pp. 374–486.

[5] Earl J. Hamilton, *American Treasure and the Price Revolution in Spain, 1501–1650* (Cambridge, MA: Harvard University Press, 1934).

[6] Earl J. Hamilton, "American Treasure and the Rise of Capitalism (1500–1700)," *Economica*, 9(November 1928), pp. 338–57.

their taxing power, as well as the greater numbers of tax sources becoming available.

What were the main elements of the financial revolution that was responsible for these anomalies of sixteenth-century inflation? The Portuguese and Spanish discoveries in the East and West Indies at the end of the fifteenth century required merchants throughout northwestern Europe to develop new financial techniques in order to exploit the opportunities of long-distance trade. The new profit opportunities were realized only after protracted waiting periods, and the longer delays before receiving returns on overseas investments required new forms of finance. The greater variety of trade goods available for Eastern merchants and the increased dispersion of their markets required financial intermediaries capable of mobilizing larger sums, waiting for longer periods, and dealing with greater numbers of clients spread over greater distances than ever before. The increased demand for financial intermediation arising from the possibilities of profit was met in large part by the projection of power by the emerging nation-states of Europe. Especially influential was the Habsburg Empire of Charles V and Philip II. These two Habsburg monarchs, in their imperial endeavors, stimulated the rise of financial intermediaries throughout Europe – individuals and firms who could operate across market boundaries, whether defined by geography, language, religion, or political authority.

Corresponding to the stocks of fixed capital embodied in the thousands of oceangoing vessels constructed during the sixteenth century and to the stocks of inventory capital carried in their cargo holds, then, were transferable and negotiable claims on these physical stocks – financial capital. As markets developed for the exchange of these financial claims independent of the markets for the exchange of goods, the possibilities for shifts in ownership, use, size, location, and composition of physical capital were enlarged enormously. This phenomenon of financial markets directing the outcome of goods and factor-of-production markets has been termed financial capitalism. The origins of the term appeared at the end of the nineteenth century, when it was clear that the capital markets of the industrial world were directing the course of the second industrial revolution associated with automobiles, chemicals, and electricity.[7] But it is clear that capital markets with many of the characteristics of those of the late nineteenth century arose much earlier in western Europe. And it may well be,

---

[7] Rudolf Hilferding, *Finance Capital: A Study of the Latest Phase of Capitalist Development*, translated by Morris Watnick and Sam Gordon, edited by Tom Bottomore (London: Routledge & Kegan Paul, 1981).

as argued at the end of this book, that they directed the course of the first industrial revolution as well.

The origins of financial innovations

The first financial revolution in early modern Europe, according to James Tracy, arose from the wartime demands that Charles V levied on the provinces of the Habsburg Netherlands in 1542.[8] The imposition of provincewide excise and property taxes pledged to service annuities, both life annuities (for the duration of one or two lives, nominated by the purchaser) and heritable annuities (perpetual, but redeemable by the States-General), led to the creation of a large and growing market for these long-term securities. They were heritable, transferable, and therefore suitable for resale, although the resale market seems to have been limited.[9] It is noteworthy in light of subsequent developments that a large part of the annuities sold by the County of Holland went to "foreigners," primarily residents of the surrounding provinces in the north.

Herman van der Wee believes that a financial revolution arose in late-sixteenth-century Antwerp.[10] The key innovation was the perfection of the negotiability of the foreign bill of exchange in this multinational, multilingual marketplace of the emerging world economy. Domestic bills were less flexible, because they had a more limited number of potential clients and because they were typically repaid in installments, so that the backs of domestic promissory notes were devoted to recording the repayments. Foreign bills of exchange were paid in full at the time stated, and so the back of the bill was available for a series of endorsements to third parties.

The foreign bill of exchange took advantage of offsetting balances that merchants accumulated with each other in different ports, so that local currency could be used only for local payments, whereas bills drawn against balances held abroad would be used for foreign payments. The

---

[8] James D. Tracy, *A Financial Revolution in the Habsburg Netherlands: Renten and Renteniers in the County of Holland, 1515–1565* (Berkeley: University of California Press, 1985).

[9] Tracy mentions notes in the inscription lists concerning annuities that had been transferred, but not to transfer books. Tracy, *A Financial Revolution*, p. 90, fn. 50.

[10] Herman van der Wee, *The Growth of the Antwerp Market*, 3 vols. (The Hague: Nijhoff, 1963), and "Monetary, Credit and Banking Systems," in E. E. Rich and Charles Wilson, eds., *The Cambridge Economic History of Europe. Vol. 5: The Economic Organization of Early Modern Europe* (Cambridge University Press, 1977), pp. 290–392.

LONDON   AMSTERDAM

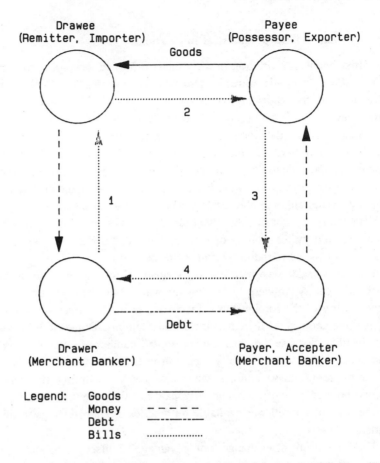

Figure 1.1. The foreign bill of exchange and the international flows of money, goods, and capital.

buyer of a bill (drawee, or remitter) purchased it from the drawer, a merchant with foreign correspondents, paying in local currency (Figure 1.1, London side). He could then remit it to pay for imports he had received from abroad. So the bill was drawn in foreign currency to be paid out by the acceptor of the bill in the foreign city to the final possessor of the bill (the payer and payee on the Amsterdam side, Figure 1.1), who either was the foreign exporter or had been assigned it. The ability of the London importer to pay the Amsterdam exporter in a bill of exchange depended, of course, on the willingness of the Amsterdam merchant banker who had to accept the bill to extend credit to the London merchant banker. In place of a shipment of bullion in payment for the goods imported, the existence of the bill of exchange allowed payment to occur by an export of short-term capital from Amsterdam to London. So there were typically four parties to the bill, shown in Figure 1.1 as the drawer and drawee on the London side and the payer and payee on the Amsterdam side, although the eighteenth-century usage was to refer to the drawee as the remitter of the bill, the payee as the possessor of the bill, and the payer as the accepter.[11] The payee could assign the bill to another party, but in so doing assumed responsibility for its eventual payment along with the drawer and accepter. Multiple assignments or endorsements therefore increased the security of this negotiable instrument and its liquidity.

This revolution in means of payment originated in Antwerp, where the negotiability of the long-established foreign bill of exchange was created by introducing serial endorsements. This innovation was transferred to Amsterdam with the Portuguese Jews and various Protestants expelled from Antwerp in 1585 and was perfected with the establishment of the Amsterdam Wisselbank in 1609. Using the Wisselbank, merchant bankers could transfer payments denominated in bank money (called *banco*) rapidly and securely among themselves without the delays and uncertainties caused when a bill was extinguished by sending it back to the original drawee. For example, the flow of new debt from the London merchant banker to the Amsterdam merchant banker shown at the bottom of Figure 1.1 could occur by transfers from one account to another within the Wisselbank, as could the subsequent extinguishment of the bill. This actually improved the negotiability of the bill, because the time delay in protesting bills refused by the designated accepter was then reduced, as was the risk to the accepter of default by the drawer. Moreover, it allowed so-called dry bills, or short-term lending by merchant bankers to local merchants, to become more efficient, reducing the rate of interest on short-term credit. Under this variant, the flows shown in Figure 1.1 were reversed: The merchant banker bought a foreign bill from the local merchant as the basis for lending him money (Figure 1.2, London side) and sent the bill to his correspondent, who had it accepted by a colleague by promising immediate "rechange" – purchase of a bill drawn on London with the

11 Malachy Postlethwayt, *The Universal Dictionary of Trade and Commerce*, 2 vols. (London: 1774; reprinted New York: Augustus M. Kelley, 1971), s.v. "Acceptances," "Accepter," "Bills of exchange," and "Drawer."

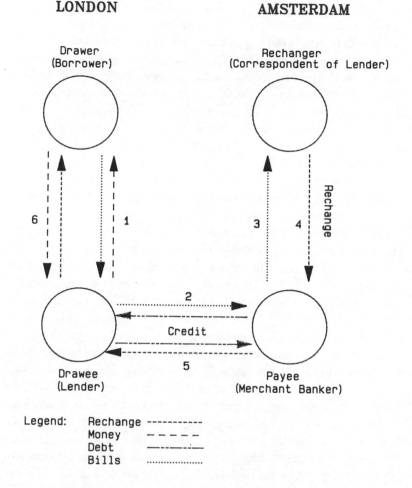

Figure 1.2. The foreign bill of exchange as a means of credit.

proceeds of the bill drawn on Amsterdam (Figure 1.2, Amsterdam side). This bill then would be sent to the merchant banker in London and accepted by the local merchant there, who in paying it off two months later would also have repaid his original loan from the merchant banker, including an undisclosed amount of interest.

The key features of these early financial innovations – safe and rapid international movement of funds in the bill of exchange, and safe and liquid long-term investment in the perpetual annuity – were successfully blended by 1609 in the shares of the Dutch East India Company (VOC hereafter, from the initials for Vereenigte Oost-Indische Compagnie). At that time, the directors of the company (known as the Heeren XVII) converted the initial investments that had been made into the first three voyages into a permanent capital fund. Investors could not recover their capital from the company, but were entitled only to whatever dividends might be declared each year, as well as the right to transfer their shares to another investor. The dividends were made high and stable, however, and so the resale market was made attractive. Operating control of the Heeren XVII was independent of shareholders, because it derived from the political compromise among the six cities written into the original charter. This allowed, indeed encouraged, foreign investors, because their participation would increase the working capital available to the Dutch without infringing on their power to control the far-flung enterprise.[12] The combination of a permanent capital and the separation of operating control from ordinary stockholders made these shares ideal for active trading in the secondary market that arose on the Amsterdam Beurs. That they were inscribed in the ledger books at each city chamber made them secure, and transfers could be made very quickly and cheaply in special transfer books.[13]

These features of the Dutch company were only gradually adopted by the English East India Company (EIC). The EIC made its capital permanent in 1650 and allowed foreign ownership at the time of renewal of the charter in 1698. Throughout the eighteenth century the management of the EIC was liable to stockholder revolt and pressure, even though foreigners were excluded from positions as directors. Whereas trade in Dutch shares was active at dividend time as shrewd investors moved in to strip the dividends,[14] trade in English shares was especially active during the election of new directors.[15]

Diffusion of financial innovations

The origins of these assorted financial innovations in western Europe derive fundamentally from the overseas discoveries and the emergence of

---

[12] J. R. Bruijn, F. S. Gaastra, and I. Schöffer, *Dutch-Asiatic Shipping in the 17th and 18th Centuries,* Vol. 1, *Introductory Volume,* Grote Serie of *Rijks Geschiedkundige Publicatien,* Vol. 165 (The Hague: Nijhoff, 1987).

[13] This is described in detail by M. F. J. Smith, *Tijd-Affaires in Effecten aan de Amsterdamsche Beurs* (The Hague: Nijhoff, 1919), pp. 30–7.

[14] Ibid., p. 27. This is Smith's interpretation of the observed increase in activity, but the point deserves further research, because a cosmopolitan pool of share owners and the requirement to be present locally to receive dividends could create the same phenomenon.

[15] Lucy S. Sutherland, *The East India Company in Eighteenth-Century Politics* (Oxford: Clarendon Press, 1952), pp. 144–6.

long-distance trade. Not only were the mental horizons of Europeans broadened by the discoveries, but also their time horizons were lengthened by the duration of the voyages. Moreover, the pursuit of the conflicting goals of power by the monarchs and profit by the merchants forced innovations by each. But equally important to our story was the process of diffusion. The innovations described earlier were adopted only fitfully by other European states over the course of the seventeenth century. In the case of Holland and England, the innovations were implemented in improved, more efficient form, because the process of transplantation eliminated the legal restrictions and encumbrances that had been imposed in the country of origin. This was especially true for the bill of exchange when brought to Amsterdam from Antwerp at the end of the sixteenth century and perfected in the first decade of the seventeenth. It was true also of the transferable share when brought from Amsterdam to London at the end of the seventeenth century and perfected, in the decade after the South Sea Bubble, with the transferable annuity obligation of the state.

The initial impetus for the spread of these particular innovations derived from the wars and the underlying religious conflicts that led to mass migrations and countermigrations of religious minorities. The forced displacement of merchant elites began with the expulsion of the Sephardic Jews from Granada in 1492 by Ferdinand and Isabella. It continued in the sixteenth century with the persecution of Ashkenazic Jews in central Europe, as well as the emerging Protestant groups, and culminated in the seventeenth century. In that century, the flight of refugee elites began with the Spanish expulsion of the Moors from Valencia,[16] spread through central Europe with the Thirty Years' War,[17] and climaxed in the 1680s with the expulsion of the Huguenots from France,[18] the importation of Dutch Jewish communities and other religious dissidents into England with William III,[19] and the "flight of the wild geese" from Ireland (which included Richard Cantillon).[20] All these groups took with them their tal-

---

[16] Earl J. Hamilton, "The Decline of Spain," *Economic History Review,* 8(1937–8), pp. 168–79.

[17] Geoffrey Parker, *The Thirty Years' War* (London: Routledge & Kegan Paul, 1984).

[18] Warren Scoville, *The Persecution of the Huguenots and French Economic Development, 1680–1720* (Berkeley: University of California Press, 1960).

[19] William Cunningham, *Alien Immigrants in England,* 2nd ed. (London: Cass, 1969), and Harold Pollins, *Economic History of the Jews in England* (London: Associated University Presses, 1982).

[20] Antoin E. Murphy, *Richard Cantillon: Entrepreneur and Economist* (Oxford: Clarendon Press, 1986).

ents and skills and as much of their treasure as they could; they left behind
them contacts that could be called on again and again.

From the time of Henry VIII (1509–47), England benefited from receiving numbers of the most skilled and adept of these religious minorities who
had been persecuted in their homelands, although England was never the
dominant destination of any group, and it constrained those who arrived to
live in well-defined settlements and limited them to trades and skills that
were noncompetitive with those pursued by the native English.[21] Edward
VI (1547–53) continued his father's policy of protecting these dissident
communities, but Mary (1553–8) expelled all of them. Many went to
Frankfurt, where they mingled with Huguenot refugees from Wallonia.
German Anabaptists and Arians who had been established at Austin Friars
in the City of London by Edward VI were also dispersed by Mary. All these
groups were encouraged to return by Elizabeth (1558–1603), and their
numbers were augmented by an influx of Spanish Netherlanders. Cromwell (1648–58) was responsible for allowing the reentry of Jews into
England, for a price, of course. The encouragement of these refugees to
alight in England with their flight capital was continued in the Restoration
(1660–88). Lucy Sutherland reported that "in 1681 those managing the
affairs of the French Protestant refugees petitioned the Company to help
those who had fled bringing their fortunes with them by 'accepting such
monies as they should pay into the Company's Cashier at moderate interest
. . . until they could find out other ways of improving their estates.' The
Company agreed to accept any money so offered at 4 per cent. for three
months and then at 3 per cent. until the owners wished to withdraw it,
when they undertook to pay capital and interest without waiting for the
bonds to mature."[22]

But it was William III (1689–1702) who first raised foreigners to high
status. Daniel Defoe is credited with authoring a piece of doggerel that
lamented the dominating role of Dutch advice in guiding William's affairs:

> We blame the King that he relies too much
> On Strangers, Germans, Huguenots, and Dutch
> And seldom does his just affairs of State
> To English Councillors communicate.[23]

---

21 Cunningham, *Alien Immigrants*, pp. 140–1.
22 Sutherland, *The East India Company*, p. 11. She cites as her source the company's Court
Book (32, p. 179, 16 December 1681).
23 Quoted in David Ormrod, *The Dutch in London* (London: HMSO, 1973), p. 17.

These forced movements of tightly knit communities repeatedly along well-established routes of trade can be seen as movements of flight capital as well as of skilled labor. Such movements also resulted in the establishment of a network of correspondents who repeatedly conveyed information about political conditions and, more important to them and to economic history, economic and commercial circumstances. That laid the groundwork for the future transfers of technology, labor, and capital that would benefit England and Holland enormously.

The dispersions of religious and political communities because of repeated persecutions also provided the basis for the continued flow of financial capital in response to investment opportunities. In the first instance, this was a matter of necessity for the immigrant groups. They had to liquidate their capital stocks at their places of origin into portable form to be carried with them to their eventual destinations. Once there, they had to invest quickly to establish themselves anew in their trades. But these stringencies placed on flight capital were quickly relieved by opportunities for war profiteering that arose in the wake of the persecutions. Starting with the Thirty Years' War (1618–48), the wars of the seventeenth and eighteenth centuries were increasingly international in their scope, even worldwide, because armed conflicts could occur anywhere that citizens of the warring nations came into contact. Within Europe, men and arms on a large scale had to be moved quickly to distant battle sites, and military success usually depended on the success of merchant bankers in moving funds to purchase and sustain mercenaries near the enemy's strongpoints. These wartime needs, climaxing with the War of the League of Augsburg (1688–97) and the War of the Spanish Succession (1702–13), gave emigré bankers opportunities for large profits. The introduction of the Dutch system of finance to Britain by Gilbert Burnet, bishop of Salisbury, made British public securities at last favorable objects of investment by emigrés throughout Europe,[24] and the volume of these securities outstanding was enlarged enormously during the war years from 1689 through 1713. The Protestant refugees ensconced in Geneva as early as 1730 probably held 30 million livres tournois in the public funds of France, chiefly in the form of rentes, and another 30 million livres tournois (£1.35 million) in the "stock" of England, primarily the transferable shares of the Bank of En-

---

[24] Jonathan Swift, *Works*, Vol. 8, edited by H. Davis (Oxford: Clarendon Press, 1951), p. 68, gives credit to Burnet, but ascribes to him far baser motives; cf. P. G. M. Dickson, *The Financial Revolution in England: a Study in the Development of Public Credit, 1688–1756* (London: Macmillan, 1967), p. 17.

gland, the EIC, and the South Sea Company. These all enjoyed a high reputation, were easily negotiable, and were always quoted above par.[25]

The large scale of these turn-of-the-century wars encumbered both France and England with their first major national debts,[26] mostly in the form of annuities at high rates of interest ranging from 8% to 10%. The rate of interest implicit in these annuities, issued during the wars and especially at their conclusion, was much higher than the rates of 5% to 6% that prevailed in the peaceful years of recovery that followed. Because of the awkwardness of transferring title on these securities from one owner to another, however, annuity holders could not easily realize their implied capital gains. Both governments, in making the annuities irredeemable at the time of issue and thereby guaranteeing potential investors that their annual payments would continue undisturbed for up to 99 years, gave up the possibility of reducing their debt service after the wars by issuing replacement debt at lower, peace time interest rates. The Mississippi Bubble and South Sea Bubble arose precisely from the competing efforts by France and England to convert fixed-interest irredeemable debt into variable-yield securities that could be more easily traded and retired. The premium paid by investors for the improved liquidity of these alternative financial assets translated into lower debt service for the government. Both the English and French governments seized on the weakened position of the once mighty Spanish Empire after the War of the Spanish Succession to convert their annuity debts into equity in large monopoly trading companies that would exploit the riches of the Spanish Empire. In this endeavor they took inspiration from the success of the VOC and the EIC in their successful exploitation of the riches of the Portuguese Empire in the Far East.

Placing the shares of these huge new companies on the relatively small stock markets of the time led to the famous bubbles of 1719 and 1720. In these episodes, the promises of financial gains from implementing proven innovations on a truly grand scale led to speculative excesses in which the prices of all shares rose quickly to unsustainable heights, collapsed, and left the markets in a disarray that invited political intervention and recriminations.[27] Whereas those bubbles traditionally have been seen as

---

[25] Herbert Luethy, *La Haute Banque Protestante en France de la Révocation de l'Edit de Nantes à la Révolution. Vol. 2: De la Banque aux Finances* (Paris: SEVPEN, 1961), p. 57.

[26] Earl J. Hamilton, "Origin and Growth of the National Debt in Western Europe," *American Economic Review*, 37(May 1947), pp. 118–30.

[27] These are analyzed in Chapters 4 and 5.

disasters that effectively forestalled the rise of financial capitalism for over a century,[28] they had an important effect in internationalizing the European investment community of the eighteenth century to an unprecedented and irreversible extent.[29] Instead of equity in perpetual joint-stock companies or debt in the form of annuities, however, the new financial instrument became the perpetual and redeemable annuity: the "Three Per Cent Bank Annuity" of 1726, the precursor of the "Three Per Cent Consol," created in 1751. Financial investment activity thereafter focused on this nearly ideal security, which essentially gave the holder an equity position in the financial fortunes of the state. But its attractiveness to the investing public depended on the relative ease by which it could be acquired and disposed of, the clear terms of the interest payments, and the readily available information about its current price and the military and political events likely to affect its price.

The financial revolution in England

This achievement in financial innovation in English government securities took over 30 years from the first issue of government-backed annuities in 1693 and 1694. These turned out to be not as popular as prior experience with them in the Netherlands and France had led William III's advisors to expect. Indeed, rather than annuities, the most successful financial innovations proved to be the state lotteries, beginning with the Million Lottery of 1694. This built on the triumphs of private lotteries, in which prodigious numbers of tickets at relatively low prices had been made available from reasonably large numbers of outlets. For example, Thomas Neale's lottery of 1693 had £25,000 of 10s. tickets available at 11 different goldsmiths, with 250 prizes at stake.[30] The success of the Million Lottery must be traced in large part to the low denominations in which the lottery tickets could be purchased, their ease of transfer, and the clear-cut (if uncertain and unfavorable) terms on which their returns were gained. They were sold in large numbers by ticket offices set up at major pubs.

All this stood in contrast to the restrictive conditions for purchasing, trading, and receiving the income of the annuities. The transfer of annuities

---

28 William R. Scott, *The Constitution and Finance of English, Scottish and Irish Joint-Stock Companies to 1720*, Vol. 1 (Cambridge University Press, 1910), pp. 436–8.

29 Dickson makes this point for England (*The Financial Revolution*, pp. 311–12), and it is made as well for Holland by F. P. Groeneveld, *Economische Crisis van het jaar 1720*, (Gröningen: Noordhof, 1940).

30 Dickson, *The Financial Revolution*, p. 45.

was entrusted to the Exchequer and remained very cumbersome until the process was taken over increasingly by the Bank of England through issuance of its own annuities after the South Sea Bubble. The subscriber to an annuity made his payment to the Exchequer and named the nominee whose life was being insured. In return, he received a tally of receipt and a paper "Standing Order," which was assignable, for the future payment of the annuity.[31] At each semiannual payment of the interest, the annuitant, his agent, or his assignee had to present proof that the nominee was still living. This usually was an affidavit signed by the parish rector of the nominee, or, after 1694, simply a declaration by the annuitant notarized by a justice of the peace. But because the Standing Orders were liable to every imaginable vicissitude over the course of the term of the annuity, transfers were made very elaborate. Titles to annuities had to be examined as carefully as titles to land. As a consequence, transfers were much less frequent than were transfers of shares in the joint-stock companies.[32]

Transfers of these shares, though still cumbersome by modern standards, were effected much more quickly and inexpensively. The companies used a double-entry system with two sets of books: the transfer books equivalent to the journal or flow accounts of merchants of the time, and the ledger books equivalent to the ledger or balance sheets in mercantile accounting. Each proprietor's initial holding was recorded in the ledger book on the left-hand side under the "Per" heading. Proprietors were arranged alphabetically and under each letter by size of holding. Additional shares purchased would be entered on successive lines under the initial entry. New proprietors would have entries created for them in rough alphabetical order at the end of the folios devoted to the original proprietors. Sales of stock by any proprietor would be entered under a "Contra" heading on the right-hand side. At the time of semiannual dividend payments, the Per entries would be totaled, and the Contra entries subtracted, and the balance would be the basis for payment of the dividend. Each entry in the ledger book, Per and Contra, was initiated by a transfer-book entry. Here printed forms, three to a page, were filled out in sequence and numbered so that each ledger entry, Per for the buyer and Contra for the seller, could be identified by a uniquely numbered transfer. On the transfer forms were entered the folio numbers for the ledger accounts of the seller (top) and of the buyer (bottom) to complete the cross-referencing. The transfer form itself was filled in by a clerk, who also witnessed the transfer and gave, in order, the

31 Ibid., p. 76.
32 Ibid., pp. 458–9.

name, status, and place of residence of the transferor, the date of the transaction, the nominal amount of shares in pounds sterling being transferred,
and the name, status, and place of residence of the transferee. The transfer
was complete when signed by both parties, witnessed by the clerk, and its
margin embossed on payment of the required nominal transfer fee.[33]

According to Dickson, these transfer and ledger books used by the Bank
of England were virtually identical with those of the VOC.[34] The transfer
books of both were available four to five days each week for transfers to be
made, and the transfer fees were quite low in both cases. But it appears that
transfers were nevertheless more cumbersome and difficult for the Dutch.
Complaints were made about the sloppiness of the clerks, the need to have
two witnesses, and the delays in verifying that the seller had full title to at
least the number of shares being transferred. Moreover, three-sevenths of
the shares of the VOC could be transferred only in the six chambers of the
other VOC cities. The registration of transfers was continuous and reliable
in the English case, tedious and uncertain in the Dutch, and that difference
accounted for the prevalence of spot transactions in the London stock
market as opposed to the dominance of term or futures transactions in the
Amsterdam market.[35]

The origins of international capital markets

The first treatise on speculation, futures contracts, hedging, "bulls,"
"bears," options for puts and refuses – in short, all the paraphernalia of
viable markets in contingent claims – was Joseph de la Vega's *Confusion
de Confusiones*, published in Amsterdam in 1688.[36] That work, written in
Spanish and translated into German only in 1919, into Dutch in 1939,[37]
and into English in 1957, was clearly intended for the edification of the
Jewish community of Amsterdam, largely Portuguese, who had become
active in trading shares of the VOC after 1650.[38] De la Vega ascribed the

---

[33] This describes the original transfer books and ledgers of the Bank of England, which were
used to detail the speculative transactions during the South Sea Bubble (see Chapter 4).
[34] Dickson, *The Financial Revolution*, p. 459, fn. 6.
[35] Smith, *Tijd-Affaires*, pp. 37–45.
[36] Joseph de la Vega, *Confusion de Confusiones*, translated by Hermann Kellenbenz (Amsterdam: 1688; reprinted Cambridge, MA: Harvard University Press, 1957).
[37] Otto Pringsheim, trans., *Confusion de Confusiones van Josseph de la Vega (Die Verwir-
rung der Verwirrungen: Vier Dialoge über die Börse in Amsterdam)* (Breslau: 1919), and
M. F. J. Smith, trans. *(Verwarring der Verwarringen)* (The Hague: Nijhoff, 1939).
[38] Johann de Vries, *Een Eeuw vol Effecten, Historische schets van de Vereiniging voor de
Effectenhandel en de Amsterdamse Effecten beurs, 1876–1976* (Amsterdam: Vereniging
voor de Effecten handel, 1976), p. 22.

rise of an active, well-organized stock market in Amsterdam to the nature of the VOC. With its capital of nearly 6.5 million florins divided into transferable shares of 3,000 florins each, and with dividends that averaged 22.5% annually on the original share capital for the next 120 years,[39] the VOC provided continuing opportunities for investment and profit taking for shareholders. An envious French author in 1664 claimed that, indeed, "there are few years, wherein they get lesse, then [sic] 30 per Cent."[40] The authoritative modern reckoning is that even after the disastrous years of the 1780s, by the time the company wound up its affairs as a private enterprise in 1796, it had averaged an annual payout of 18% on its original capital for nearly two centuries.[41]

References in the secondary literature to the financial innovations brought into England by the Dutch financiers and advisors who flocked into London with William of Orange after the Glorious Revolution of 1688 all seem to derive from the remarkable description of London's stock market by John Houghton in 1694.[42] Houghton, a fellow of the Royal Society, determined to bridge the gap between pure science and applied technology in all fields of human endeavor in a weekly series of pamphlets entitled "A Collection for Improvement of Husbandry and Trade," which began to appear in 1691. Between a series on wheat and another on cattle, Houghton decided to relax from his Augean labors by describing the techniques of trading shares in joint-stock companies in the coffeehouses of Exchange Alley. His description of "refuses" is a model of clarity and merits reproduction:

. . . when India shares are at seventy-five, some will give three guineas a share, action, a hundred pound, down for refuse at seventy-five, any time within three months, by which means the acceptor of the guineas, if they be not called for in that time, has his share in his own hand for his security and the three guineas . . . so in plain *English*, one gives three guineas for all the profits if they should rise, the other for three guineas runs the hazard of all the loss if they should fall.[43]

[39] Jean-Pierre Ricard, *La Négoce d'Amsterdam: contenant tout ce que doivent savoir les marchands et banquiers etc.* (Rouen: J. B. Machuel, 1723), p. 400.

[40] *A Treatise touching the East-Indian Trade* (London: 1664), p. 17, [Hollander 169; Massie 797]

[41] J. P. de Korte, *De Jaarlijkse Financiele Verantwoording in de Verenigde Oostindische Compagnie* (The Hague: Nijhoff, 1983), p. 93.

[42] John Houghton, *A Collection for Improvement of Husbandry and Trade,* 9 vols. (London: Randall Taylor et al., 1692–1703; republished Westmead, Farnborough, Hants.: Gregg, 1969), p. 264.

[43] Ibid., p. 264. The terms "action" and "hundred pound" were used interchangeably with "share," because "action" was the French term, and share prices were quoted as the number of pounds needed to purchase a nominal value of 100 pounds in the capital stock of the company.

Houghton appended copies of a "Course of the Exchange" (22 May 1694) sheet, which showed prices of shares for 52 joint-stock companies, as well as exchange rates on various European cities and prices of gold in various forms. W. R. Scott reproduced one of these lists, but he stated that Houghton's venture lapsed after a few issues.[44] In fact, it was but the precursor of one of the most remarkable instances of a continuously published periodical known to scholars: John Castaing's *Course of the Exchange*. This unsurpassed data source began publication in March 1697 and continued to appear twice weekly, on Tuesdays and Fridays, through the entire eighteenth century under a variety of publishers.[45] Each issue gave the closing exchange rates on the major European cities at the Royal Exchange in London on Tuesdays and Fridays just before the mail for the foreign packet boats was posted from the London Post Office. That was followed by prices of gold and silver in various forms. Then came price quotations for the past three trading days on each of the major securities traded by the brokers in Exchange Alley. The list was headed by the shares in the three leading joint-stock companies, but included the other chartered companies, as well as quotations on various issues of government debts and annuities. It concluded with a listing of the numbers of the various short-term government bills that were in the course of being paid off at the Exchequer.

The major statistical findings reported in the remainder of this book are derived from analysis of data encoded directly from Castaing and supplemented by price quotes from contemporary newspapers in London and Amsterdam for the early eighteenth century and by *Lloyd's List* and the *Amsterdamsche Effectenpryslist* for the early nineteenth century. This unique data base provides many opportunities for a fresh approach to important questions posed by historians about the operation of the governments and joint-stock companies of the eighteenth century. We shall see, for example, how intertwined were the Mississippi and South Sea bubbles of 1719–20, what determined the outcome of the continued competition among the East India companies of the English, French, and Dutch, the effects of the major wars of the century on international economic activity,

---

[44] Scott, *The Constitution and Finance, Vol. 1*, p. 329.

[45] John J. McCusker, *Money and Exchange in Europe and America, 1600–1775: A Handbook* (Chapel Hill: University of North Carolina Press, 1978), p. 31. A full history of the publication can be found in Larry Neal, "The Rise of a Financial Press: London and Amsterdam, 1681–1810," *Business History*, 30(April 1988), pp. 163–78. In 1811, when the *Course* was published by Wetenhall, it became the official price list of the London Stock Exchange.

and the intricate economic and financial interplay between the French Revolution and the British industrial revolution. For modern finance scholars, the data provide unusual opportunities to examine the operation of capital markets unencumbered by income taxes or direct regulation and to explore the properties of various time-series modeling procedures when applied to an unusually long run of data. These issues will all be covered in the chapters that follow. We begin by taking a closer look at the origins and development of our primary source of data: John Castaing's *Course of the Exchange*.

2. The development of an information network and the international capital markets of London and Amsterdam

The religious and dynastic wars that convulsed Europe in the quarter century 1688–1713 were fought on a larger scale than the earlier wars of the seventeenth century, and arguably with less result. Moreover, in the course of the War of the League of Augsburg (1689–97) and the War of the Spanish Succession (1702–13), communities of religious and political minorities, not to mention deposed dynastic households, were dispersed in greater numbers than ever before. These dispersed communities kept in touch with one another through regular correspondence, facilitated during wartime by the movements of troops and supplies for those troops and during peacetime by the packet boats and stagecoaches that were regularly carrying post among the ports and capital cities of Europe.

The emerging network of information in Europe in the seventeenth century centered on Amsterdam. The various reasons for this were well analyzed by Woodruff Smith, who focused on the reporting innovations made by the Dutch East India Company in order to maintain central control of its far-flung operations.[1] From this invaluable internal source of information were derived the linkages to merchants dealing with the Dutch East India Company and even to the rival English and French companies and to the governments of all the European powers. As more merchants, consular agents, and newspaper publishers congregated at Amsterdam, the amount of information available increased, and the bits of information being exchanged increased geometrically. Amsterdam's natural monopoly as an information center was confirmed.

London, however, grew rapidly in importance both as a commercial center and as an information center. It very likely rivaled Amsterdam by the end of the eighteenth century and surpassed both Amsterdam and Paris during the Napoleonic Wars. Smith's analysis, based on a combination of

---

[1] Woodruff D. Smith, "The Function of Commercial Centers in the Modernization of European Capitalism: Amsterdam as an Information Exchange in the Seventeenth Century," *Journal of Economic History*, 44(December 1984), pp. 985–1005.

Douglass North's theory of transactions costs and George Stigler's theory of information,[2] does not explain how one center can eventually be displaced by another. Some exogenous change in technology or in trade patterns is required that will establish a new and more vigorous network with greater potential than the existing network. The success of the Dutch East India Company clearly was the exogenous shock that led to the rise of Amsterdam. What was the comparable force that promoted the rise of London as a competing center of an information network? There are many possibilities, but one that seems worth exploring is the greater proliferation of newspapers and other periodicals that occurred in England under William and Mary. Despite the earlier origins of both newspapers and a stock exchange in Amsterdam, it was in London, as far as we can now tell, that the first regularly printed stock price list appeared.

The earliest stock price lists in London

For the London Stock Exchange, the earliest printed evidence of price quotations of which we are aware comes from a weekly price list: Whiston's *The Merchants Remembrancer,* for 4 July 1681. That date is not likely to be pushed back much further in the British press. The Printing Act of 1663 had eliminated all newspapers in England, except for the official *London Gazette*. When that act, also known as the Licensing Act, lapsed in 1679, a number of newspapers arose "to arouse and exploit the passions of the dreaded London mob."[3] The emergence of a free press also encouraged experiments with new forms of business news periodicals. It is likely that Whiston was thereby encouraged to produce a "price current," a sheet listing current prices of goods available from abroad in the London market, in competition with a price current already being published by Robert Woolley.

Woolley did not include any information on the stock market in his price current; so Whiston's inclusion of this additional information may have given him a competitive edge. But Whiston did not give the actual prices for the shares of the East India Company and the Royal African Company (the only two listed), but rather symbols denoting that the East India shares

---

[2] Douglass C. North, *Structure and Change in Economic History* (New York: Norton, 1981), pp. 33–44; George Stigler, *The Organization of Industry* (Homewood, IL: Irwin, 1968), p. 176.

[3] S. R. Cope, "The Stock Exchange Revisited: A New Look at the Market in Securities in London in the Eighteenth Century," *Economica,* 45(February 1978), p. 5.

were at their highest level and the Royal African shares at their lowest. A marginal note stated that "the author, J. W. will buy or sell." The first listing of actual prices came in the 3 January 1682 issue of Woolley's price current. Jacob Price considered this to be Woolley's innovation, one that he introduced in his French-language edition of 25 October 1681.[4] It was very likely introduced by Woolley as a response to the new competition he was facing from Whiston.

It is striking that we should find not one but at least two competing price currents that began at nearly the same time to print information on the markets for financial assets in their infancy. It appears that both did this for the benefit of overseas merchants, who found these assets to be an interesting means of investing their trade credits in England while awaiting return cargoes. In fact, a third publication, John Houghton's *A Collection for Improvement of Husbandry and Trade,* also began in 1681.[5] It quickly failed, but 10 years later Houghton began again, at a time when the new government of William III was considering the possibility of passing a new printing act. In his first issue of this second run, Houghton explained his intention to give weekly accounts of agricultural prices, London shipping movements, London bills of mortality, and, "for whom it might concern, it was design'd to give weekly from hence an Account of the value of Actions of the East-India, Guinea, Hudsons-Bay, Linnen, and Paper Companies."[6] In his next issue, he felt it necessary to explain further the inclusion of stock prices:

Altho they that live at London, may, every Noon and Night on Working days, go to Garraway's Coffee House, and see what prices the Actions bear of most Companies trading in Joynt-Stocks, yet for those whose Occasions permit not there to see, they may be satisfi'd once a Week how it is, and thereby the whole Kingdom may reap Advantage by those Trades: Also they may learn hence some of the Cunning of Merchandizing, and have this Advantage, by laying their Monies there, in one or two days time they may sell, and have their Money to supply their wants at any time. Without doubt, if those Trades were better known, 'twould be a great Advantage to the Kingdom; only I must caution Beginners to be very wary, for there are many cunning Artists among them.[7]

---

[4] Jacob M. Price, "Notes on Some London Price-Currents, 1667–1715," *Economic History Review,* 2nd series, 7(1954), p. 244.

[5] This has been reprinted in full. John Houghton, *A Collection for Improvement of Husbandry and Trade,* 9 vols. (London: Randall Taylor et al., 1692–1703); republished Westmead, Farnborough, Hants.: Gregg, 1969).

[6] Houghton, *A Collection* (30 March 1692).

[7] Ibid. (6 April 1692).

Houghton made it clear that his primary audience lived in London or nearby, and he was only hoping to interest readers who lived in the provinces. No mention of foreign readers was made. So this price list was clearly intended for the domestic market.

Houghton tried several devices in an effort to supplement his London audience with a provincial profit margin, but none succeeded; so Houghton ceased publication of the weekly at the end of June 1692.[8] When he resumed publication of his weekly on 20 January 1693, he reduced the price from 2d. to 1d. and announced that his papers "may be had as easy as Gazettes."[9] The new run of Houghton's weekly continued to include the paragraph with the stock prices, and the issue for Friday, 11 May 1694, suddenly expanded the number of companies listed from 10 to 55. Prices of the shares, however, still were given only for the original 10, but a note was inserted stating that "a great many desire a list of Stocks; and those that desire the Values of them to be published may have them on very reasonable terms." The remainder of the year 1694 saw a number of articles inserted by Houghton on the history and current practices of the London Stock Exchange, and in the issue for 17 August 1694 appeared the first quotation for the Bank of England. The year 1694 apparently was quite favorable for printers of specialized stock price lists.

In Houghton's initial issue of 1695 appeared for the first time an advertisement stating that "John Castaing at Jonathan's Coffee-house, or Exchange, buys and sells all Blank and Benefit Tickets; and all other Stocks and Shares." That advertisement continued to run until the issue for 11 December 1696, when it disappeared. Houghton's next issue, 22 January 1697, then consolidated the Exchequer funds table, the exchange-rate table, and the list of share prices and placed them all on the front page, top right. That version of the consolidated "Course of the Exchange" continued through his last issue: 10 September 1703. But the dates for prices were no longer for the preceding Wednesday of that week; rather, they varied, but were always for a preceding Tuesday or Friday. That makes it appear that during that period they were merely copied from what was by then the definitive stock price list: John Castaing's *The Course of the Exchange* (Figure 2.1), which began publication in March 1697.[10]

The first issue of Castaing's publication that appears in the microfilm copy used in this study is that for 4 January 1698. At the bottom appears

[8] Ibid. (27 June 1692).
[9] Ibid. (10 February 1692).
[10] According to the *British Union-Catalogue of Periodicals*.

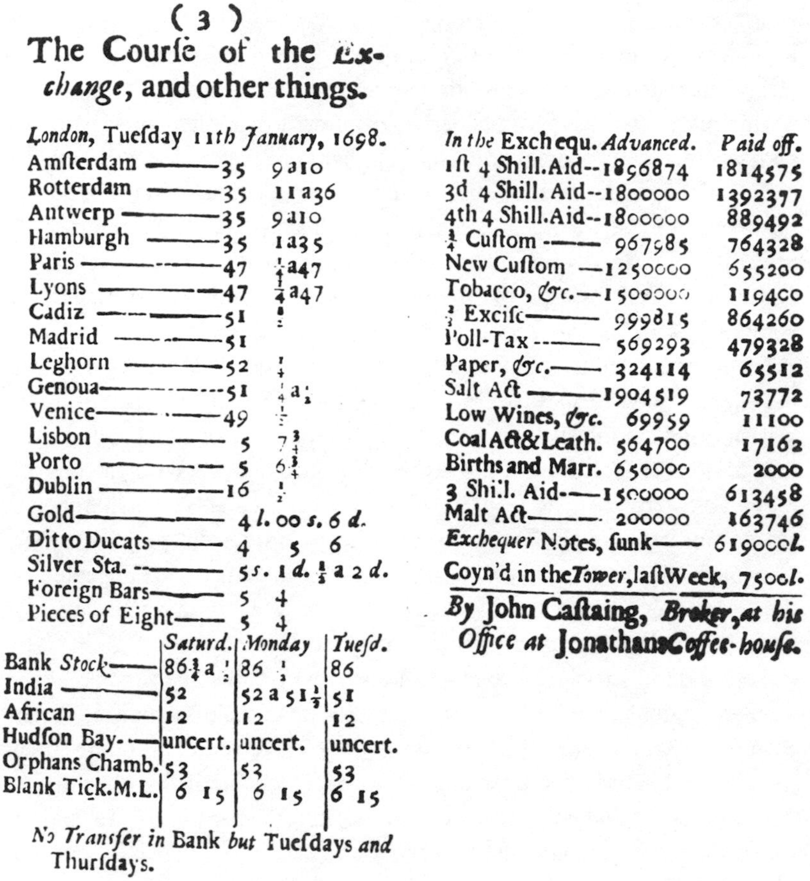

(3)

The Courſe of the *Exchange*, and other things.

London, Tueſday 11*th January*, 1698.		
Amſterdam	35	9 a 10
Rotterdam	35	11 a 36
Antwerp	35	9 a 10
Hamburgh	35	1 a 35
Paris	47	$\frac{1}{4}$ a 47
Lyons	47	$\frac{1}{4}$ a 47
Cadiz	51	$\frac{1}{2}$
Madrid	51	
Leghorn	52	$\frac{1}{4}$
Genoua	51	$\frac{1}{4}$ a $\frac{1}{2}$
Venice	49	$\frac{1}{2}$
Lisbon	5	7$\frac{3}{4}$
Porto	5	6$\frac{3}{4}$
Dublin	16	$\frac{1}{2}$
Gold	4 *l*. 00 *s*. 6 *d*.	
Ditto Ducats	4 5 6	
Silver Sta.	5 *s*. 1 *d*. $\frac{1}{2}$ a 2 *d*.	
Foreign Bars	5 4	
Pieces of Eight	5 4	

	Saturd.	*Monday*	*Tueſd.*
Bank *Stock*	86$\frac{3}{4}$ a $\frac{1}{2}$	86 $\frac{1}{2}$	86
India	52	52 a 51$\frac{1}{2}$	51
African	12	12	12
Hudſon Bay	uncert.	uncert.	uncert.
Orphans Chamb.	53	53	53
Blank Tick. M.L.	6 15	6 15	6 15

No Transfer in Bank *but* Tueſdays *and* Thurſdays.

In the Exchequ.	*Advanced.*	*Paid off.*
1ſt 4 Shill. Aid	1896874	1814575
3d 4 Shill. Aid	1800000	1392377
4th 4 Shill. Aid	1800000	889492
$\frac{1}{4}$ Cuſtom	967985	764328
New Cuſtom	1250000	655200
Tobacco, *&c.*	1500000	119400
$\frac{2}{3}$ Exciſe	999815	864260
Poll-Tax	569293	479328
Paper, *&c.*	324114	65512
Salt Act	1904519	73772
Low Wines, *&c.*	69959	11100
Coal Act & Leath.	564700	17162
Births and Marr.	650000	2000
3 Shill. Aid	1500000	613458
Malt Act	200000	163746

Exchequer Notes, ſunk —— 619000*l.*

Coyn'd in the *Tower*, laſt Week, 7500*l.*

By John Caſtaing, *Broker, at his Office at* Jonathans *Coffee-houſe.*

Figure 2.1. Castaing's *Course of the Exchange*, 11 January 1698.

this notice: "By John Castaing, Broker, at his Office at Jonathans Coffee-House." In the last half of the year 1699, that simple notice underwent a series of experimental changes that very likely reflected Castaing's efforts to develop sources of income complementary to his earnings from sales of the *Course of the Exchange*. The first expanded on his brokerage business: "He Buys and Sells Bank Stock and other Stocks or Shares, &c. and Daily attends at his Office for the Same" (5 May 1699). That was shortly dropped and replaced with an effort to expand circulation of the price list itself: "Any Body that will have this Paper, it shall be deliver'd every Tuesday and Friday, within the City of London, and as far as Whitehall, for 3 s. per quarter" (26 May 1699). He also mentioned a complementary publication: "The Copies of the East-India Sales are also sold at the said Office." That proved successful, but the longest-lived and most successful publication proved to be his interest book:

Note, There is a Convenient Interest-Book, not Five Inches Long, from 10001. to 11. for 1 Day to 92 Days, and 3, 6, 9, 12 Months, at 4, 5, 6, 7, 8, per Cent. Sold by John Castaing, Broker, at his Office at Jonathans Coffee-House.[11]

The interest book went through many editions over the following decades, adding tables for lower interest rates of 3% and 3.5% in 1732. Other items that were advertised from time to time included sales lists of the East India Company, tables for calculating premiums and discounts, and, for only a brief period in 1704, a "choice of Orange-Trees"![12]

From these various notices and the format of the price list itself we may infer the nature of the market for Castaing's publication. The emphasis on foreign exchange rates implies that the primary market was composed of merchants engaged in foreign trade, either foreigners themselves or British merchants dealing with foreign traders. This observation also holds for the commodity price currents discussed by Jacob Price, who noted that they were "not primarily for immediate use by the City merchant, who had more exact ways of determining the prices of goods in which he was seriously concerned, but rather as a convenience for those City merchants who wished to keep their country and foreign correspondents informed of the general state of the London market with the least possible trouble and expense."[13] The publication of copies of the East India sales by Castaing, goods destined in large part to be reexported to the European continent, strengthens this supposition. Even the mention of an exotic product such as orange trees implies a cosmopolitan clientele for the stock price sheet. Moreover, all the securities listed by Castaing could be owned by foreigners, although they usually could not participate in governing the company in the case of shares in joint-stock companies. So Castaing's listing, like Houghton's, was not intended to be complete but to concentrate on those he thought useful for his potential subscribers. The lists of subscribers for the two publications overlapped in London, but Houghton's extended to the provinces, whereas Castaing's went overseas.

Castaing's practice of giving daily prices for the securities, but only semiweekly quotes for exchange rates, is striking. According to Duguid,

[11] Castaing, *The Course of the Exchange* (London: 4 June 1700).
[12] Castaing, *Course* (23 June–29 September 1704).
[13] Price, "Notes," p. 243.

the Royal Exchange set its exchange rates only on Tuesdays and Fridays,[14] which were also the days when the mail left London for the packet boats at Harwich that went to Holland. So this explains the frequency of the exchange rates, as well as the days when the *Course* itself appeared. But why give daily prices for the past three days in each issue? Even when Houghton apparently was copying his data from Castaing, he found it useful to give only one day's quotations. The answer may be that foreign merchants, as well as British merchants dealing with foreigners, wished to have an independent record of the prices of securities in which their agents invested temporarily or which they accepted as means of payment. Because they did their business daily, they needed daily prices, whereas Houghton's country gentlemen invested only periodically and would have been content with weekly information. If these gentlemen were accustomed to a lag time of three days or more in receiving reports on the activities of their agents, the twice-weekly summary of daily trading results would have sufficed. More active speculators in the securities as such, on the other hand, would have required daily, or even hourly, updates, and they would have had to be located in London City. And because they were many fewer in number, the likelihood is much less that their demands for information would have made a regularly printed daily publication profitable. Further, speculators would have been most interested in prices of options to put or refuse, and the exercise dates for these varied from broker to broker. So the most likely explanation is that the daily prices in Castaing's *Course* were intended as an independent record against which could be checked the terms on which foreign and domestic merchants' or investors' contracts were made. It was this growing clientele of foreign merchants and English merchants with foreign clients who gave Castaing's price list the subscriber network of the critical size needed to make it the eventual monopolist.

The earliest stock price lists in Amsterdam

A similar history may remain to be told for an Amsterdam price list of securities. Castaing's network of foreign merchants and investors certainly included the Dutch, given their preeminence in European finance and their influence in England at that time, and it most likely included as well

---

[14] Charles Duguid, *The Story of the Stock Exchange* (London: Grant Richards, 1901), p. 29; Cope, "The Stock Exchange Revisited," p. 18.

Huguenots throughout the Continent, given Castaing's origins.[15] It is possible that Castaing's price list was modeled on a preexisting Dutch list. There is no hard evidence for this, but according to Folke Dahl, the first English newspaper was printed in Amsterdam and sent to London. Thereafter, each succeeding periodical, coranto, gazette, or price current that appeared in England was modeled directly on a Dutch antecedent.[16] Why should that not have been the case as well for the British stock list? Dahl also makes the interesting observation that the most characteristic difference between English and Continental periodicals was the large number of "editorial notices" that appeared in the English versions, but were unknown in Dutch periodicals.[17] That was precisely the striking contrast between Houghton and Castaing.

As attractive as the hypothesis may be that Castaing's publication was modeled on a Dutch precursor, the indications are merely circumstantial; there is no firm evidence that such a Dutch publication existed. The official price list for the Amsterdam stock exchange first began publication in August 1796.[18] That was in the second year of the Batavian Republic and was no doubt an expression of the desire of the new, revolutionary government to control, rather than to inform, the market for securities and its participants.[19] It was printed by Nicolaas Cotray, a Huguenot (like Castaing a century earlier in London), whose office was next to the General Post-Comptoir, and it was available from booksellers in Amsterdam, The Hague, Rotterdam, and Dord, as well as booksellers and post offices in the remaining provinces. The large quarto sheet printed on both sides listed securities of the Batavian Republic, the individual cities and provinces, and foreign countries, as well as exchange rates, prices of English funds (but in

[15] I owe this point to François Crouzet, who noted that Castaing is a common surname in the Bordeaux region. John McCusker has discovered the naturalization papers for the elder Castaing, confirming indeed that he came from Bordeaux.
[16] Folke Dahl, *A Bibliography of English Corantos and Periodical Newsbooks, 1620–1642* (Stockholm: Almqvist & Wiksell, 1953), p. 18; cf. his "Amsterdam – Cradle of English Newspapers," *The Library*, 4(1949), pp. 166–78.
[17] Dahl, *A Bibliography*, p. 20.
[18] Johann de Vries, *Een Eeuw vol Effecten, Historische schets van de Vereiniging voor de Effectenhandel en de Amsterdamse Effecten beurs, 1876–1976* (Amsterdam: Vereiniging voor de Effectenhandel, 1976), p. 2.
[19] Johann de Vries makes this argument. It is developed in detail by H. J. Hoes, "Voorgeschiedenis en Ontstaan van het Financieele Dagblad, 1796–1943," *Economisch- en Sociaal-Historisch Jaarboek*, 49(1986), pp. 4–5. But it may as well have been part of the breaking down of the power of the printing guild in Amsterdam, whose monopoly of Dutch-language printing could be infringed only by printing a periodical in another language.

London, two weeks earlier), and prices of American securities (but priced in New York, 10 weeks earlier). The Amsterdam publication, like the London *Course of the Exchange,* appeared semiweekly on Tuesdays and Fridays.[20]

There is some circumstantial evidence that earlier versions of a price list, not officially sanctioned, may have appeared regularly. In the 1720s there appeared printed forms for the use of Dutch brokers on which the names of all the traded securities were given, but the actual date and the prices were left blank to be filled in for each client. Many of these have been preserved in the Amsterdam archives. Van Dillen has reproduced a form with space for price quotes for each of the next two rescounter dates for both receiving and delivering the given stock.[21] It seems unlikely that this would have been the general form used for a regularly published price list. But van Dillen was not justified in inferring that this was the preferred form of price lists and that no lists were published regularly. It is more likely that this was a special form used by a few brokers to give particular price information to special clients. The price list forms that van Dillen thought that Dutch brokers used as substitutes for printed price lists had their counterparts in forms originating from London brokers and sent to customers in Holland. Cope, for example, cited one case in which prices for puts and refusals for 12 months, 6 months, and 3 months were given for East India and South Sea stocks and another in which prices of these and Bank of England stock were given for money and settlement in one month's time, as well as prices in guineas for three- and six-month refusals of the same stocks.[22] This clearly was very specialized information worth presenting to only a very important and active customer. In general, personalized and specialized services were complements, not substitutes, for general information sources.

In 1747, two issues of a fully printed price list appeared, 9 October and 6 November (exactly 28 days apart), giving prices for short-term annuities, shares in the Dutch East India Company and West India Company, all the English securities listed by Castaing, and then a number of life annuities. Van Dillen believed that these were specially published on the occasion of

[20] From the copy in the library of the Amsterdam Economic History Institute. Nicolaas Cotray's father, Pieter Cotray, was the owner and publisher of the French courant *Gazette d'Amsterdam.* Hoes, "Voorgeschiedenis," p. 6.

[21] J. G. van Dillen, "Effectenkoersen aan de Amsterdamsche Beurs, 1723–1794," *Econo-mische-Historische Jaarboek,* 17(1931), p. 3.

[22] Ibid., p. 19.

the "Liberale Gift," a voluntary capital levy, of that year.[23] It is at least as likely that these were copies of a regular publication that were specially preserved for that year because of the continued relevance of their contents for both tax collectors and taxpayers. Hoes noted two lists published by H. Diederiks in Amsterdam, 30 September 1788 and 3 April 1793.[24] And he cited another five copies of lists published by assorted printers from 1 May 1793 to 19 August 1796. In fact, in the years 1797–1804, another dozen imitators of Cotray's official publication appeared in other Dutch cities.[25]

Evidence from the Dutch newspapers also indicates the possibility that there had been earlier price lists of stocks in Amsterdam. The *Maande-lijksche Nederlandsche Mercurius* began publishing an abbreviated price list in 1792, and by September 1792 it had grown to half a page. Hoes thinks their figures came from the newly formed Collegie tot Nut des Obligatiehandels,[26] but they could have been taken from a specialized publication. The long-term experience of the price quotes printed in the *Amsterdamsche Courant* indicates the existence of such a source. The *Courant* began to print a short paragraph of financial news in July 1723 that continued throughout the eighteenth century. The *Courant* appeared three times each week, Tuesday, Thursday, and Saturday, and every issue in the last three months of 1723 contained the financial paragraph. The paragraph was always for the preceding day, and it concluded with prices of the Dutch shares traded on the Amsterdam Effectenbeurs. In August, the prices of the leading English stocks – Bank of England, East India Company, and South Sea Company – were included as well. In the later years of the 1720s, the paragraph typically appeared only once a week, in the Saturday issue, and often was irregular in appearing. In the early 1730s, however, the financial paragraph began to appear once again in each issue,

---

[23] Ibid., p. 2.

[24] Hoes, "Voorgeschiedenis," p. 40, fn. 9. Unfortunately for my thesis that these might be random examples of a regular periodical, the first date is a Tuesday, the second a Wednesday.

[25] Ibid., p. 7. I have also found in the card catalogue of the Erasmus University library in Rotterdam an entry for a serial publication, *Prijs-Courant der effecten*, for Amsterdam, 1741–1809. The card notes that three numbers are present for 1741 and 1788, two for 1801; some numbers are missing for 1808, and one number is present for 1809. None of the issues can be found on the shelves. But the catalogue card is important because it shows that at one time three issues did exist in the library for 1741 and 1788, years that were not mentioned by either van Dillen or de Vries, and Hoes mentioned only 1788.

[26] This "Group to Benefit the Trade of Securities" was in existence by at least 1787. Hoes, "Voorgeschiedenis," p. 4.

perhaps reflecting the renewed interest by Dutch investors in English securities that developed in the 1730s.[27]

The question must be raised whether the *Courant* gathered this information on its own or took it from a general trade publication distributed from
the Beurs itself. The English experience with financial paragraphs or tables, described earlier in connection with John Houghton, was that special-
ty sheets distributed as ephemera for the mercantile and trading community
were the sources for these features. Houghton's experience was replicated
by a growing number of English periodicals and newspapers over the
course of the eighteenth century. Cope mentions that in addition to
Houghton, the *London Post* was giving share prices by the start of 1699.[28]
Gentleman's Magazine gave monthly prices for an extensive list of stocks
from its first issue in 1731. In the mid-1730s, *Lloyd's List* began duplicat-
ing its version of the entire *Course* on the front page. Why should that not
have been the case for Dutch newspapers as well? It makes sense that the
Amsterdamsche Courant, a general newspaper devoted to foreign political
news, would extract price information from a specialized source. The
previously cited examples of price lists that appeared sporadically through
the eighteenth century may be the remnants of such a regular, but
ephemeral, publication. But unless runs of it are found, scholars will have
to be content with the coverage provided by the *Amsterdamsche Courant*
and perhaps the courants of other Dutch cities.

The rise and fall of competing price lists in London

The logic of one source becoming the center, or monopolist, of commercial
information, used earlier to explain the rise of Amsterdam and then its
displacement by London, may also be applied to competing sources of
printed information within a given information center. That logic would
predict that competition among several printed sources of the same information should eventually lead to the emergence of a single, authoritative,
"standard" source: a monopoly. The logic depends on the costs and benefits of information to different users. Users who are frequent investors
demand the latest information and consider the widest range of possibilities. For them, specialized information delivered quickly is valuable,
and their needs can be met by a variety of fairly expensive services, such as

[27] P. G. M. Dickson, *The Financial Revolution in England: A Study in the Development of
Public Credit, 1688–1756* (London: Macmillan, 1967), pp. 321–4.
[28] Cope, "The Stock Exchange Revisited," pp. 1–21.

market newsletters and investment services tailored to specific groups of investors. In the seventeenth century and especially the eighteenth century it was common practice for merchants to send letters by ship, just before sailing, in order to convey the latest commodity prices to their correspondents in the next port of call. Users who are less frequent investors, by contrast, are concerned only about making occasional trades and so are content with older information, if it is reliable. They are not willing to pay nearly as much as are the active traders for this information, and they will stay with the most reliable source. Their needs can be met by a fairly limited, standard set of prices as long as these appear regularly.

But such a standardized and regularly updated set of information also serves a very useful function for the active traders. It helps them to calibrate and confirm the specific data they are receiving from a variety of sources, some of which may be tapped only one time. The implication is that both sets of users may be served by the same standardized source of information. If the information is supplied by a firm, that firm is likely to be a monopoly, not because of declining average costs for the firm but because its product, the "standard" information, faces fewer and less suitable substitutes the more people are using it. When a new group of participants comes into a given market, there may arise temporarily two or more competing firms, supplying much the same information. But because there can be only one standard, eventually one must win out over the other. This is a characteristic of "network technologies," where the usefulness of a given technology or product depends in large part on how many consumers are using it.[29]

Standards for comparison, or, more precisely, standards for calibrating one's evaluation of a product, arise wherever consumption requires knowledge, and the purchase of financial assets on an active stock market such as those in Amsterdam and London in the eighteenth century certainly required knowledge on a daily basis by the participants, and more frequent information the more frequent their participation. Because it is expensive

[29] The conditions for adoption of a particular standard for networks of users have been analyzed by Paul David for a variety of new technologies, including electric power and typewriter keyboards: "Clio and the Economics of QWERTY," *American Economic Review*, 75(May 1985), pp. 332–7; *Some New Standards for the Economics of Standardization in the Information Age*, Center for Economic Policy Research Publication No. 79, Stanford, CA, 1986; and (with Julie Bunn) " 'The Battle of the Systems' and the Evolutionary Dynamics of Network Technologies," unpublished manuscript, Stanford University, 1986. But no one, to my knowledge, has applied the network technology theory to an "information product," as discussed here.

to acquire knowledge, consumers are likely to concentrate on one kind of financial asset and to evaluate it with a consistent source of information. Moreover, if the information is to be used to enforce contracts made with other investors or with one's broker, it is important that the source be accepted as a standard by other participants. So a given stock price list has the addictive quality of increasing marginal utility with increased use. Investors will want to keep informed on the values of their holdings, but will not want to keep increasing the resources they devote to gathering information.

The choice of a particular stock price list as the standard may be largely a matter of luck once the basic qualities that a price list must have are established.[30] If any version of a stock price list has a market share just a bit larger than the share of any other, the share of the former should increase steadily. Consumers of the "wrong" price list may continue to use it for some time because of its original addictive qualities, but eventually, if they continue to trade in financial assets, they will find it beneficial to switch to the medium used by the larger number of traders or investors. This pattern helps explain the rise of printed price lists for the earliest stock exchanges. The form and speed with which information on prices was transmitted for any financial market at any time in history also tell us something about the nature of the market in that period, particularly who might have been the most active participants.

In the year 1714, Castaing's *Course of the Exchange* made a number of changes in delivery and subscription policy, probably in response to the emergence of a competitor: John Freke. At this remove, we can only speculate why a competitor should have arisen well after Houghton had ceased publication. Because Freke was a lawyer and secretary and a "hot whig," which caused him to be selected as one of the objects of the ironical Tory tract *The Taunton-Dean Letter, from E.C. to J.F. at the Grecian Coffee-House* in 1701,[31] it is probable that he was appealing to the City brokers associated with the South Sea Company and the new political constituency that they, and Robert Harley, were trying to develop. Freke's price list was called *The Price Of the Several Stocks, Annuities, And other*

---

[30] This is similar to the argument made by Robert A. Jones, "The Origin and Development of Media of Exchange," *Journal of Political Economy*, 84(August 1976), pp. 757–75, regarding what particular form of money arises as the standard currency in the absence of government fiat.

[31] J. A. Downie, *Robert Harley and the Press: Propaganda and Public Opinion in the Age of Swift and Defoe* (Cambridge University Press, 1979), p. 50.

Publick Securities, Ec. with the Course of Exchange, and it lasted at least until 1722, its demise coinciding with the breakup of the South Sea Company, described in Chapter 5. In 1714, the original *Course of the Exchange* was published by John Castaing, Jr., and his office had been moved from Jonathan's to Garraway's coffeehouse. The only change that had been made in delivery and subscription policy to that date was the announcement in 1706 that the *Course* would no longer be delivered any farther than Temple-Bar.[32] The first change made by Castaing Jr. in response to the competition posed by Freke was to include a note that "Gentlemen, &c. may have this Paper deliver'd at their Houses at 3s. per Quarter" (2 April 1714). That was shortly after the appearance of Freke's first issue (26 March 1714), which had contained the same offer. The next change by Castaing was to reduce the price at the beginning of 1715 from 3 shillings to half a crown (2.5 shillings), a belated response to Freke, who had already dropped his price to 2.5 shillings at the end of April 1714.[33] Castaing's notice of a matching price continued to run throughout that year, and then was dropped. The next printed mention of the delivery price in the *Course* was at the beginning of 1721, when it was raised again to 3 shillings. In January 1722, delivery was again limited to only as far as Temple-Bar, and it appears that, the competitor Freke having been dispatched, Castaing could again exercise premium pricing and restricted service.[34] The last issue of Freke's *The Price Of the Several Stocks* was 22 June 1722.

By that time, Castaing's price list was available at his office "at the Stationer's, next the General Post-House in Lombard Street" (13 and 20 January 1719). From there it could be quickly mailed to both country and foreign subscribers. This combination of low price, inexpensive delivery, and rapid posting to the countryside and abroad must have made Castaing the natural monopolist of the business of publishing stock price lists.

With his rival safely out of the way, Castaing's *Course of the Exchange* continued to be published on Tuesdays and Fridays for the remainder of the eighteenth century as a family enterprise. Various new names appeared as the primary publisher, but under each new publisher reference was always

[32] "This Paper, after New-years-day will be delivered no further than Temple-Bar at the Rainbow Coffee-House: Where any Body may send for them Tuesdays and Fridays" (24 December 1706).
[33] Castaing, *Course* (30 November 1714), and John Freke, *The Price Of the Several Stocks, Annuities, And other Publick Securities, Ec. with the Course of Exchange* (London: 23 April 1714).
[34] Castaing, *Course* (6 January 1721, 19 January 1722).

made, directly or indirectly, to Castaing or his brother-in-law, Edward Jackson, or Castaing's sister, who was Jackson's wife.

The first new name to appear was that of Edward Jackson, who joined John Castaing, Jr., with the issue of 4 May 1725. In the first issue of 1730, the name of Castaing was dropped, and "Edward Jackson, Broker," alone was cited as the publisher. In 1735, a new publisher, Richard Shergold, appeared, and the next issue explained as follows:

By Richard Shergold, Broker, And the Widow, Sister of the late Mr. Castaing, Administratrix to Mr. Edward Jackson, deceased. At the Stationers, next the General Post-Office in Lombard Street. Where all Persons may have a Reference to the Papers published by Mr. Castaing and Mr. Jackson. [24 October 1735]

The year 1735 marked the emergence of a major competitor, and perhaps other lesser competitors. It was in mid-March of that year that *Lloyd's List* enlarged its format from being merely a "marine list" to including as well the full contents of the *Course of the Exchange*.[35] John McCusker has reported the existence of several copies of another competitor in the years 1736–9, *The London Course of the Exchange,* published by Francis Viouja and Benjamin Cole, found in the library of the Economic History Institute in Amsterdam.[36] No copies of Castaing's paper have been turned up by McCusker in the Dutch archives; so it appears that he was serving the Huguenot community on the Continent, whereas Viouja and Cole may have been supplying the needs of the Low Countries. It does appear that the price quotes for securities in *Lloyd's List,* though presented in the same format as in Castaing, were taken from different brokers. Often there were small differences in prices for a given security, and occasionally there were days when one had quotes for a security and the other did not. Those differences persisted into the nineteenth century.

In October 1749 the *Course* was published by George Shergold, "son of Richard Shergold, deceased" (24 October 1749), and, of course, the sister of Mr. John Castaing, who continued to be identified as Castaing's sister rather than Jackson's widow. Early in 1751, George Shergold was able to add to his name the title "Broker," and the price list became available both at the stationer's office and at his broker's office, back in Popes-Head Alley. In 1753, however, all business was transferred to Shergold's brokerage office. It appears that in this period the authoritative status of the

---

[35] John J. McCusker, *European Bills of Entry and Marine Lists: Early Commercial Publications and the Origins of the Business Press* (Cambridge, MA: Harvard University Library, 1985), pp. 62–4.

[36] Ibid., p. 63, fn. 99.

Course was eroded, but it does not seem to have been supplanted, or even seriously challenged, by any competitor.

This situation continued through the Seven Years' War and the American War for Independence. The first issue of 1764 replaced George Shergold with a new name: "Peter Smithson, Broker." However, the long-lived sister of the late John Castaing continued to be listed as co-publisher. This arrangement endured another 16 years, until 1780, when the publishing notice was dropped entirely, even though the price list continued to appear faithfully every Tuesday and Friday. This state of anonymous publishing remained the case for seven years, until the end of 1786, when a new notice appeared:

Published Tuesdays and Fridays, by EDWARD WETENHALL, Stock-Broker appointed by the unanimous Vote of the Gentlemen of the Stock-Exchange, October 30, 1786. [3 November 1786]

From that date on, the *Course of the Exchange* took on an increasingly official character. With the first issue of 1811, the character of the price list changed dramatically, even though it continued to appear only on Tuesdays and Fridays and to bear the name of Wetenhall as publisher until the end of the nineteenth century. The list was more than doubled in size. In addition to the quotations of British funds and other securities, only 20 in number, there were added American securities, canals, docks, insurance, and waterworks.

One motive for this detailed history of the continuity of Castaing's *Course of the Exchange* over the period 1698–1810 is the stunning neglect to date of this invaluable source of data by economic and financial historians. McCusker stated that he knew of only four uses of it before the publication in 1978 of his handbook on exchange rates.[37] Each, including his own use, had been limited to a very small range of the data available. Since McCusker's statement, others have used this source, but they still have been limited in number and in the extent to which the data have been utilized. Part of the explanation for this unseemly neglect by scholars is the overwhelming amount of data available and the difficulty facing a single researcher attempting to transcribe it to computer-readable form. It is possible that individual scholars who encountered it while researching the eighteenth century felt overwhelmed and simply passed it by.

But for scholars with a desire to study issues requiring the use of quan-

---

[37] John J. McCusker, *Money and Exchange in Europe and America 1600–1775: A Handbook* (Chapel Hill: University of North Carolina Press, 1978), pp. 30–31.

titative materials, the more likely reason for the neglect was the extraordinary difficulty of finding full runs of the periodical. The *British Union-Catalogue of Periodicals* lists only a few locations, and each has only a very limited run.[38] Contemporary users probably saw no reason to preserve, much less bind, copies of this data source for the use of later generations, whether in Britain or abroad. However, the copies once in the library of the London Stock Exchange, now in the Guildhall Library, are bound in leather for each year, and the numeration begins anew with each year, rather than with each publisher as was the case with *Lloyd's List* during the early years of the eighteenth century.[39] So bound annual volumes may have been provided for reference, advertisement, or limited markets overseas.

The reliability of the *Course of the Exchange* and the *Amsterdamsche Courant*

In 1934, the Dutch economic historian J. G. van Dillen published a table of stock prices on the Amsterdam Beurs from 1723 to 1794, extracted from the *Amsterdamsche Courant*. He included prices for all the securities mentioned, as well as the rate of agio on bank money at the Wisselbank, but he limited his observations to, on average, every two weeks.[40] At the time van Dillen wrote, he was aware of other long runs of the Dutch share prices that had been published, but none were for as long a period, and each was limited to high and low prices for the year rather than the biweekly quotations he published.[41] For the English prices, van Dillen was aware of limited runs of English stock price currents that had been used by Rogers and Scott.[42] Although those gave more frequent quotes, they were for very short periods of time. Van Dillen was unaware of Castaing's *Course of the*

---

[38] James D. Steward, ed., *British Union-Catalogue of Periodicals*, Vol. 1 (London: Butterworth, 1955), p. 668, and *Supplement to 1960* (London: Butterworth, 1962), p. 237.

[39] The Guildhall Library has the *Course of the Exchange* for the years 1698–1720, 1727, 1732, 1734, 1736–9, 1742–1810, 1819, 1821, and 1837–89.

[40] J. G. van Dillen, "Effectenkoersen."

[41] J. G. van Dillen referred to a series of the Dutch prices for the period 1723–63 in the 10th edition of Le Moine de l'Espine's *De Koophandel van Amsterdam*, 10th ed. (Amsterdam: J. de Groot, 1801–2).

[42] Rogers had used Houghton, and Scott had used Freke, a short-lived competitor of Castaing's publication from 1714 to 1722: James E. T. Rogers, *The First Nine Years of the Bank of England* (Oxford University Press, 1887); William R. Scott, *The Constitution and Finance of English, Scottish and Irish Joint-Stock Companies to 1720*, 3 vols. (Cambridge University Press, 1910).

Exchange. Nevertheless, his recapitulation of 1,676 observations on as many as nine variables over two-thirds of the eighteenth century represents a major and lasting accomplishment.

The value of newspaper accounts, especially in Dutch newspapers, as opposed to institutional and archival sources, has been reasserted recently by Michel Morineaux.[43] Morineaux has been able to improve both the quality and frequency of Earl Hamilton's figures for silver imports to Seville by using contemporary newspaper reports. Indeed, he has found that for the entire seventeenth century and most of the eighteenth century (until 1778) it was the Dutch newspapers, rather than French, Italian, or Spanish, that contained the greatest detail and most accurate accounts of the annual or biannual treasure fleets arriving in Spain from Mexico or South America.[44]

The data from Castaing's *Course of the Exchange* can be used to check and compare the prices reported in the *Amsterdamsche Courant*. This provides an interesting check on the reliability of this newspaper source for other data. Not only has it been used by Morineaux for imports of silver and gold into Spain, and by van Dillen for Amsterdam share prices, but in addition the Paris dispatches usually included prices for Compagnie des Indes shares, and the Amsterdam column concentrated on ship movements and cargo contents of the East India fleet when it returned. Further, the operation of the Amsterdam stock market compared with the London market can now be analyzed not only in terms of the differences in trading practices,[45] but also in terms of the information flow coming to Amsterdam from London, because each issue had not only the Amsterdam prices from the previous day but also the London prices from three to six days earlier.

Two conclusions emerge from an analysis of the thousands of observations recorded to date from the *Amsterdamsche Courant* for the 15-year period 1720–35. First, printed stock exchange currents began to be enclosed with the twice-weekly dispatches from London to Amsterdam at the time of the end of the South Sea Bubble, and these led to a remarkable improvement in the accuracy of reporting of the prices of major securities on the London Stock Exchange in the *Amsterdamsche Courant*. Second,

[43] Michel Morineaux, *Ces Incroyables Gazettes et Fabuleux Metaux* (Cambridge University Press, 1985).

[44] Ibid., p. 55.

[45] Amsterdam prices were time prices, whereas London prices were spot prices, and at the semiannual dividend payment times the London prices were ex dividend, but Amsterdam prices were consistently with dividend. See Chapter 7.

the price movements of these securities on the Amsterdam Beurs closely followed those on the London Stock Exchange, with a lag of three days or less. It is likely that this lag was constant for the remainder of the eighteenth century. The implications of this for our understanding of the capital markets of the time will be pursued in later chapters. But the implications for economic historians in their quest for more and more data from an age in which government statistical "services" had not yet begun to make a contribution are immediately obvious and very heartening: Essentially private sources (usually, but not always, under municipal license) provided a continuing flood of frequent and reliable data.[46]

Throughout the century, one or two issues each week of the *Amsterdamsche Courant* also had a separate paragraph from London giving the prices of the main English funds as quoted on the London Stock Exchange three to six working days previously. The London data were always for a preceding Tuesday or Friday. For example, the lead paragraph for the Thursday, 19 November 1733, issue was dated "London den 13 November," that is, six days earlier in the New Style calendar, and ended with a listing of share prices for the Bank of England, the East India Company, the South Sea Company, and the old and new annuities of the South Sea Company. That is to say, the London paragraph in van Dillen's newspaper source carried direct information from the London Stock Exchange that presumably was superior to his information on Amsterdam prices for his purposes!

The practice of listing share prices at the end of the London dispatch began earlier than the summer of 1723, when the *Amsterdamsche Courant* began listing the Amsterdam prices.[47] The practice may well have predated 1720, but there can be little doubt that 1720 was a critical year for raising the interest of the *Courant* in financial reporting. In those years the *Courant* not only reported the share prices regularly in the London paragraph but also devoted most of the dispatch to analysis of the stock market bubble taking place. The London paragraph of 22 February 1720 mentioned that the South Sea stock was currently trading at 161 and was expected to rise to

---

46 Contrast one gloomy assessment of the age that preceded government statistics: Phyllis Deane, "The Implications of Early National Income Estimates for the Measurement of Long-Term Economic Growth in the United Kingdom," *Economic Development and Cultural Change*, (3 January 1955), pp. 3–38.

47 Van Dillen gave the first quote as 14 July 1723 (p. 19). In fact, the first quote appeared for 7 July 1723 in the 8 July issue. Van Dillen asserted that the English security prices were not given in the Amsterdam paragraph until 9 August. However, they first appeared in the 31 July issue.

200 and stay up to encourage people to trade their annuities in for shares.[48] The next week, the paragraph from Paris reported that a crash was due in the price of the shares of John Law's company.[49] As we know, that was the time at which simultaneously the Mississippi Bubble ended and the South Sea Bubble began. In the issue for Saturday, 30 November 1720, the London dispatch ended with a description of a printed list of share prices that had been rushed over from London and showed the prices for Tuesday. Moreover, hearsay regarding the fall in South Sea stock on Wednesday was mentioned.[50]

Table 2.1 summarizes the comparison of prices for the stocks of the Bank of England, East India Company, and South Sea Company as reported in both Castaing's and Freke's *Course of the Exchange* in London and in the London paragraph of the *Amsterdamsche Courant* on the days such prices were reported in the *Courant*. Because of the large number of observations available for each year, only 1720, 1725, and 1730 are shown. By far the fewest observations are available for 1720, because the *Courant* did not include stock prices in each London paragraph until the time of the end of the bubble. Even in 1730 the number was only 86, because the London paragraph appeared only once or twice a week, and each had only one day's quote in it. The three sources are compared by calculating the average absolute difference in prices for a given stock[51] and

---

[48] ". . . en de liefhebbers geven voor dat ze wel tot 200 zullen reyzen; maer veele zyn van gedachten dat men ze so hoog dryft, om de menschen haere Annuiteyten in actien te doen veranderen." [". . . and the devotees give odds it could well rise to 200; yet many think that it has been heated up so high in order to get people to convert their Annuities into shares."]

[49] "Sommige zeggen dat de straer Quinquenpoix van Parys herwaerds is overgebragt; maer al dit werk wil aen de houders van de Obligationen, waer van gedurende zekere jaeren interesten moesten werden betaelt, echter geen genoegen geeven" (*Amsterdamsche Courant*, 27 February 1720). ["Some say that Quincampoix Street has been brought over here from Paris; but everyone says it works well on the Obligation holders, who want to be sure that several years' interest are paid, before they will give satisfaction."] The same sentence was repeated in the next issue.

[50] "Deezen day zyn hier expressens van Londen gearriveert, meede brengende her gedrukte Feuillet van de Pryzen der actien, so als die Dingsdag tot Londen waren . . . ook zegt men dat 'er reeds tyding van Woensday zoude zyn, dat de Zuydzee tot onder de 150, en d'andere fondsen na proportie waren gedaelt" (*Amsterdamsche Courant*, 30 November 1720). ["This day the express mail arrived from London, bringing with it a printed leaflet of share Prices, as they were in London on Tuesday . . . also one says that the news from Wednesday should be that South Sea stock was traded under 150 and the other funds in proportion."]

[51] Because the levels of prices for shares of the Bank of England, South Sea Company, and East India Company were quite different, percentage differences would vary by stock

TABLE 2.1
Summary comparison of prices reported in the *Course of the Exchange* and the
Amsterdamsche Courant for shares in the Bank of England, East India Company, and
South Sea Company, 1720, 1725, and 1730

A. 1720
Amsterdamsche Courant – Castaing's *Course of Exchange*

	B of E	EIC	SSC
30[1]			
	1.81[2]	3.61	7.57
	(2.89)[3]	(6.45)	(20.54)

Amsterdamsche Courant – Freke's *Course of Exchange*

	B of E	EIC	SSC
32			
	2.40	3.88	9.44
	(3.42)	(5.40)	(19.78)

Castaing – Freke's *Course of Exchange*

	B of E	EIC	SSC
30			
	1.33	3.06	9.46
	(2.37)	(4.77)	(22.17)

B. 1725
Amsterdamsche Courant – Castaing's *Course of Exchange*

	B of E	EIC	SSC
80			
	0.11	0.25	0.10
	(0.34)	(0.70)	(0.37)

C. 1730
Amsterdamsche Courant – Castaing's *Course of Exchange*

	B of E	EIC	SSC
86			
	0.10	0.29	0.08
	(0.30)	(1.00)	(0.24)

[1] Number of observations.
[2] Absolute mean.
[3] Standard deviation.

then the standard deviation of the actual price difference for each possible pair of sources. The smaller the average absolute difference or the standard deviation, the more likely it is they used the same source. Because the *Amsterdamsche Courant* price was from London, all three represented London sources, and the purpose of this exercise is to see if the *Courant's* source was the price list of Castaing, of Freke, or of yet another.

without telling us anything about market integration. Using absolute differences keeps negative differences from canceling out positive differences in calculating the average.

For 1720, all three comparisons are quite erratic. For all three stocks, the absolute means favor Castaing as the information source for Amsterdamers, but the standard deviations in two of three cases favor Freke. The comparison between Castaing and Freke shows that even close competitors varied considerably during the manic year of 1720. Examination of the raw data reveals that the largest divergences occurred during the bubble period, late February through August, and were most dramatic in South Sea stock. Brian Parsons found similar problems in comparing the daily prices reported in the London *Daily Courant* and John Freke's *Course of the Exchange*. Because the largest divergences occurred when price movements were most violent, he suggested that they could have arisen because the prices were reported for different times of the trading day.[52] It is also possible that different brokers could have advertised different prices during hectic trading, reflecting different expectations. It is striking that the days of the week for the reported prices in the *Courant* were always Tuesday or Friday, the same days that both Castaing's list and Freke's list were printed. The explanation for this coincidence is certainly that those were the days when the mail packet boats left London for Amsterdam.

Also striking is the nearly perfect coincidence of the prices after November 30, the date for which we first learn that a printed price list had been sent from London to Amsterdam. The comparisons of the *Courant* and Castaing for 1725 and 1730 show the remarkable convergence that is obtained. Examining the raw data in this case shows that small differences did appear and were maintained for two or more weeks at a time. These usually were the times when dividends were paid by the companies in question, and the difference usually was in favor of the report in the *Courant*. This indicates that the *Courant* chose to print the price with dividend, whereas Castaing chose to print the price without dividend. In short, it appears that the intense interest in Amsterdam regarding the speculation in London during the South Sea Bubble promoted the use of a consistent and authoritative source for London prices, although the price reported to Amsterdamers was adjusted for their practice of including the dividend in the sale price of any share.

Table 2.2 takes a systematic approach to the question that naturally follows: Did information flow to both stock markets at the same time, or did it systematically flow from one market to the other? The *Amsterdamsche Courant* data for the English stocks being traded in Amsterdam

TABLE 2.2

Prices in London of shares in Bank of England, East India Company, and South Sea Company compared to prices in Amsterdam, with no lag, lagged 3 days, and lagged 6 days, 1725, 1730, and 1735

	Lag (Days)	B of E (A − L)	EIC (A − L)	SSC (A − L)
A. 1725				
	0	0.71[1] (1.06)[2]	1.98 (2.74)	0.75 (1.13)
	3	0.64 (1.03)	1.73 (2.34)	0.72 (0.97)
	6	0.60 (0.94)	1.38 (2.37)	0.77 (0.98)
B. 1730				
	0	0.44 (0.72)	0.83 (1.28)	0.36 (0.60)
	3	0.44 (0.62)	0.72 (1.05)	0.27 (0.37)
	6	0.43 (0.79)	0.84 (1.15)	0.35 (0.49)
C. 1735				
	0	1.18 (1.44)	1.77 (2.34)	0.80 (1.16)
	3	1.00 (1.26)	1.86 (2.55)	0.73 (1.05)
	6	1.09 (1.26)	1.57 (2.07)	0.54 (0.70)

[1] Absolute mean.
[2] Standard deviation.

are adjusted for the difference in calendars at that time [the English were still on the Old Style (O.S.) or Julian calendar, but the Dutch were on the New Style (N.S.) or Gregorian calendar] by subtracting 11 days from the Amsterdam date. The Amsterdam data are then compared with the London data for those dates they had in common. A second comparison is shown for the Amsterdam data lagged three days, and a third for a lag of six days. The possibility of Amsterdam price movements leading London price movements certainly exists, but it has not been explored.

Typically, the two sets of prices are very close, regardless of the lag, and generally the difference is negative, indicating that Amsterdam prices were higher on average. This is because Amsterdam prices were time prices rather than spot prices and because the Amsterdam prices included dividends, whereas London prices did not, at dividend payment times (see Chapter 6). In general, it appears that the three-day lag yields the smallest average differences. For 1725, that is the case for Bank of England and South Sea stock, but the zero-lag condition yields the smallest average difference for East India stock. For 1730, the zero-lag differences are smallest for Bank of England and East India Company stock, whereas the three-day-lag difference is smallest for South Sea stock. For 1735, just to complete the array of possibilities, the three-day-lag differences are smallest for Bank of England and East India stock, whereas for South Sea stock the zero-lag difference is nearly zero, and the three-day-lag difference is positive rather than the expected negative figure. In no case is the six-day-lag difference smallest on average.

If we make allowances for differences in pricing practices in the two markets, it appears that the Amsterdam market was tracing much more closely the actual prices on the London market on the same trading day as in Amsterdam, rather than following with a lag of three days or more the prices reported from London. This is yet another piece of evidence to add to the growing evidence that those early capital markets were as efficient and effective in their use of information as are our modern capital markets. It is likely that those market relations were long-lived and relatively stable, because there were no major improvements in the speed of communication between London and Amsterdam in the eighteenth century.

3. The early capital markets of London and Amsterdam

The origins of the joint-stock companies that arose in the great long-distance trades of the seventeenth century in western Europe lie at least as far back as the medieval *societas maris* and *commenda*. These were forms of limited-liability partnerships used extensively in merchant shipping to reduce risks by making specific arrangements regarding the sharing of profit (or loss) for each voyage. Partners were divided into investors, who stayed on land, and travelers, who went with the ship. In the *commenda,* the voyager risked no capital, only his life, and received one-fourth of the profits, whereas in the *societas* the voyager put up one-third of the capital and shared equally in the profits.[1] The *commenda* is believed to have derived from the practices of Arab shipping fleets in the Mediterranean during the Islamic expansion of the eighth to fifteenth centuries. W. R. Scott, in his classic work *The Constitution and Finance of English, Scottish and Irish Joint-Stock Companies to 1720,* distinguished three processes that led to the joint-stock companies of seventeenth-century England. One was to divide up among member merchants the corporate purchases made by the early regulated companies used by the British to carry on foreign trade (i.e., to share in the overhead costs). Examples are the Merchant Adventurers (export of cloth), the Staple (export of wool), and the Levant Company. The second was to extend the *societas* used by the Italian financiers in England during the thirteenth and fourteenth centuries to divide up and pay out profits to partners on a regular basis (i.e., to monitor and manage the activities of far-flung partners). The third was to transplant a joint-stock constitution from the Continent. Although Scott argued that this was the least important of the three, he noted the existence, if not the significance, of foreign influence in a number of early English joint-stock companies.[2] For us, the significance of foreign influence in

---

[1] Raymond de Roover, "The Organization of Trade," in M. M. Postan, E. E. Rich, and Edward Miller, eds., *Cambridge Economic History of Europe,* Vol. 3 (Cambridge University Press, 1971), pp. 49–53.

[2] William R. Scott, *The Constitution and Finance of English, Scottish and Irish Joint-Stock Companies to 1720,* 3 vols. (Cambridge University Press, 1910), Vol. 1, pp. 13–14.

"points of detail" in the organization of these companies lies in whether or not they increased the scale and scope of the secondary market for trading shares in the companies. In this perspective, the key development was the concept that the capital paid in by the original subscribers was permanently ceded to the company, which had undertaken a continuing series of ventures and was not invested merely for the duration of one or more ventures (e.g., a voyage, in the case of merchant shipping and the early English East India Company). The Dutch East India Company, as early as 1609, decided that subscribers could not demand their capital back from the company itself, but they could retrieve their funds by selling their shares to third parties. By contrast, the English East India Company did not make its capital permanent until the reorganization under Cromwell in 1650. Prior to that, the English compensated in part for the reduced marketability of a short-term and risky equity by making shares smaller in denomination, by not fixing the total number of shares to be sold, and by selling shares to the assembled merchants during the semiannual auctions of East India goods in London.[3]

Each period of peace and prosperity that followed in the seventeenth century tended to promote the creation of new joint-stock enterprises and to provide incredibly large profits to those trading companies already in existence. Such periods, however, were few and short-lived during that turbulent century. The apparent explosion of economic activity, new enterprises, and stock market activity at the end of the century, however, was destined to survive the major wars that followed. That episode may have begun with the infusion of Huguenot capital from France after the revocation of the Edict of Nantes by Louis XIV in 1685. The wealth brought to London by these merchants and noble families is reputed to have been worth over £3 million, but the new trades and skills brought by the artisans and craftsmen were worth far more.[4] The importance of these merchant families, particularly in the international trade and finance network maturing in England, is indicated by the decision of the General Court of the East India Company to pay 5% on the funds deposited there by the Huguenots who had fled France until such time as they withdraw those funds to begin permanent capital investments.[5] The Dutch capital and skills brought in the train of William III were equally impressive and reinforced the importance

[3] Ibid., p. 161.
[4] Ibid., pp. 313–14.
[5] Lucy S. Sutherland, *The East India Company in Eighteenth-Century Politics* (Oxford: Clarendon Press, 1952), p. 11.

of the Huguenot connections. A stock market boom occurred in the years 1692–5, despite the increased financial pressures of the War of the League of Augsburg. We know that by the end of 1695, at least 150 joint-stock companies were in existence, with shares traded in the coffeehouses, especially Jonathan's and Garroway's, that lay in Exchange Alley. Scott grouped the listings by Houghton into categories of new and old types of enterprises. The new enterprises dealt with (1) new products, chiefly those brought by the Huguenot artisans, such as white paper and lustrings, (2) armaments, such as saltpeter, sword blades, and guns, and (3) banking and finance companies, such as the Bank of England, the Million Bank, and the Orphans' Bank. The old enterprises concentrated on mines, salvage of shipwrecks, fishing, waterworks, manufacturers of iron and metals, and assorted miscellaneous schemes destined to be short-lived under any form of financing.[6] Scott estimated a total of £4,250,083 of paid-up capital in all these, with three-fourths being concentrated in the chartered companies: the Bank of England, the Million Bank, the African Company, the East India Company, Hudson's Bay Company, and the New River Company.

A general crisis occurred in 1695 as the finances of the state and the reverses of war had their effect. The disarray of the financial markets was compounded by the uncertainty surrounding the recoinage of 1696. By the beginning of 1698, however, a period of relative peace and prosperity set in, lasting until the financial obligations incurred by the government in the War of the Spanish Succession (1702–13) finally caught up with the capital markets in the crisis of 1708. There followed reorganizations of the East India Company and the founding of the South Sea Company. This inaugurated a new period of relatively undisturbed stock market activity that lasted until the great trauma of the bubble year of 1720. The resulting disorder was finally cleared away by the reorganization of the South Sea Company and the engrafting of new stock onto the Bank of England. But the key innovation likely was the creation of a new form of easily transferred annuities by both the South Sea Company and the Bank of England in 1723.

These periods of relatively stable operation of the stock market (there was little regulation except to license stockbrokers) enable us to analyze this early stock market in three 11-year spans: 1698 through 1708, 1709 through 1719, and 1724 through 1734. For each period we have con-

---

[6] Scott, *The Constitution and Finance*, Vol. 1, pp. 330–3.

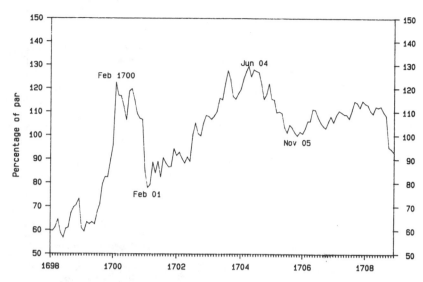

Figure 3.1. London stock price index, end-of-month prices, 1698–1708.

structed an index that traces the fluctuations of the entire market or, more precisely, the value of a balanced portfolio composed in exact proportion as the nominal capital of the constituent companies available for an investor in each interval. The monthly index is shown in Figures 3.1–3.3 for the successive stages. The missing period, 1720–3, was characterized by great disturbances in prices of all stocks, occasioned by the South Sea Bubble, and by wholesale reorganization of the structure of government debt. Detailed analysis of this period is deferred to Chapter 5.

Bank of England stock was the first stock to appear on a permanent basis and the one that has constituted our longest-lived security traded on the London Stock Exchange for two and a half centuries. According to Scott, "the ten years from July 1697 to July 1708 constitute a new epoch in the history of the Bank. . . . It was now to experience the benefits of peace and the mitigation of rivalry."[7] This period began with an engrafting of £1,001,171.5 onto the bank's original £1,200,000, the result of the bank funding for a limited period an equivalent amount of government debt. At intervals over the next 10 years, this engrafted stock was gradually paid off as the government repaid its debt to the bank. In March 1707, however, in

[7] Scott, *The Constitution and Finance*, Vol. 3, p. 213.

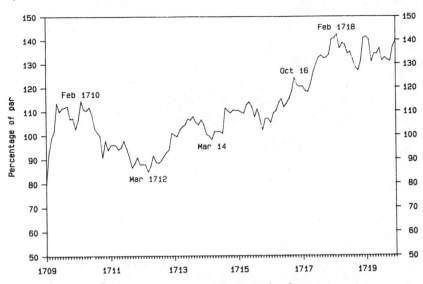

Figure 3.2. London stock price index, end-of-month prices, 1709–19.

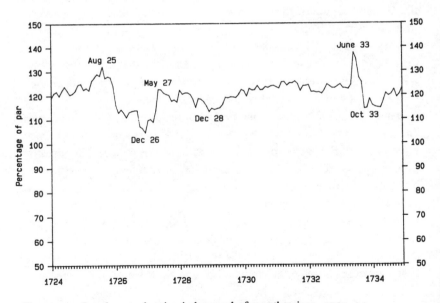

Figure 3.3. London stock price index, end-of-month prices, 1724–34.

order to meet fresh demands upon it by the government, the bank declared a 50% call on the original stock plus the engrafted stock, paid out nearly £100,000 to the existing stockholders, and ended up with a new permanent capital of, once again, £2,201,171.5. At the height of the pressures caused by the war in the years 1709–11, the bank successively doubled its stock, added 15%, and then added another 10%, so that it entered our next period of analysis with a capital stock of £5,559,995.75. In the aftermath of the South Sea Bubble, the bank, in order to purchase £4 million of South Sea stock, increased its own capital by another £3.4 million in 1722.[8] So in our third period of analysis, the bank's capital was £8,959,995.75, where it remained until 1742.

The companies trading in the East Indies were the next major sources of tradeable shares on the London Stock Exchange. The Old East India Company, also known as the London East India Company, began with a capital of £1,574,608.5, which it maintained during the entire first period, 1698–1708.[9] It was joined at the outset by the English East India Company, or New East India Company, which began in 1698 with a capital stock of £1,662,000, its share of a £2 million loan provided to the government. An additional stock of £581,700 was called up to provide working capital for carrying on the actual trade with the East Indies. These were traded and quoted separately on the London Stock Exchange. Both capital sums were reduced in July 1702 in the form of sales to the Old Company in order to equalize the roles of the two in carrying out the joint administration of trade to the East Indies until they were to be formally merged by 1709. So from July 1702 until the merger, the capital of the New Company was £988,500, and that of the "Additional Shares" was £332,400, both of which were traded actively on the exchange, along with shares of the Old Company.[10] Par value for the New Company shares was £100, whereas that for the

---

[8] There is some uncertainty over this figure, which is cited by both Scott and John Clapham [*The Bank of England: A History*, 2 vols. (Cambridge University Press, 1945)] via the authoritative "History of the Earlier Years of the Funded Debt, from 1694 to 1786." *British Parliamentary Papers*, Command Paper 9010 (1898), pp. 70–2. Fairman, however, gave a figure of £610,169.5 [William Fairman, *The Stocks Examined and Compared . . .* , 7th ed. (London: John Richardson, 1824), p. 52] and Adam Anderson asserted that in 1727 the bank's stock was reduced by £500,000 to £4,875,027 17s. 10$\frac{2}{9}$d. [*An Historical and Chronological Deduction of the Origin of Commerce, from the earliest accounts*, 4 vols. (London, 1764, continued to 1788 by William Combe and published for the last time in 1801; reprinted New York: Augustus M. Kelley, 1967), Vol. 3, p. 147]. We have chosen to stay with Scott and Clapham.
[9] Scott, *The Constitution and Finance*, Vol. 2, p. 177.
[10] Ibid., p. 188.

Additional Shares was £20. There is no record of dividends being paid on either set of shares, although £2 per share on the Additional Shares was returned annually in quarterly installments. But this was intended by the directors, and apparently treated as such by investors, as a reduction in the par value of the shares. By June 1707, £10 had been returned, and over the next year another £11 was returned, with some assets still to be realized, which amounted to a total of £66,005 4s. 1d.[11]

The Royal African Company suffered greatly from the misfortunes of war and the pressures on the London financial markets during the years 1693–7. A new issue of stock intended to double the existing nominal capital was authorized in October 1697, but by the time of its conclusion one year later, only £475,800 had been taken up, and that at a price of £12 per £100 of original capital. From October 1698 on, then, the nominal capital of the African Company was £1,101,050.[12] Various calls were made upon the stock, and bonds given in exchange. To encourage shareholders to pay up, very modest dividends were declared and paid over the years 1702 to 1707, but these were paid out of capital, as in all probability was the interest on the bonds. Scott concluded that "this mode of finance as well as the pressure of loans generally on the company at a critical period of its history was a more serious hindrance to its prosperity than the losses of the war or the competition of the separate traders."[13] The most recent analysis of the company's operations, however, concluded that the shareholders were largely well-informed merchants who were deliberately making a risky investment, but not investing very heavily in this particular venture. Although disappointed in the outcome, they likely were not surprised and certainly were not ruined.[14]

The Royal African Company's financial distress was not relieved even with the capital reorganization of 1712. Indeed, that was accomplished only after legal obstacles had prevented reorganizations proposed each year from 1709 until 1712.[15] At that time the existing nominal capital was written down to 10% of its face value, reflecting its market value, a call of £50 was made upon each share, and new stock was given in exchange for the old bonds, for a total of £451,350. Even that was gradually written

[11] Ibid., p. 187.
[12] Ibid., p. 27. Scott dates the new capital from October 1697, but this seems to be but another misprint.
[13] Ibid., p. 29.
[14] David W. Galenson, *Traders, Planters, and Slaves: Market Behavior in Early English America* (Cambridge University Press, 1986), p. 150.
[15] K. G. Davies, *The Royal African Company* (New York: Atheneum, 1970), pp. 92–5.

down over the next few years as shareholders failed to meet either the original call of £50 or the additional one of £25 in 1714. So one of the quoted stocks was a financial "basket case" throughout our initial two periods: 1698–1708 and 1709–19.[16] During the bubble year of 1720, the company made a fresh issue of engrafted stock that quickly rose in price and apparently encouraged the directors to revitalize the company's trade.[17] Anderson tells us that in 1727 the general court of the company "came to various resolutions for carrying on their trade, and for preventing the separate trades from interfering with them," among which was a proposal to reduce "their then nominal capital stock, so as every 800 pounds be reduced to one hundred pounds. . . . All which, however, came to nothing."[18] Despite Anderson's disavowal of the importance of these resolutions, the stock of the Royal African Company was quoted at 8 when the transfer books were closed in April, but traded at 67 when they reopened in May. So in our third period, the par value of a share is taken as £800 through April 1727, and £100 thereafter.

The Million Bank provides a counterpoint to the Bank of England and indeed to all the other stocks. Scott found it interesting for two reasons: First, it was the first example of a reverse-leveraged buy-out of government debt, that is, an operation in which underpriced government debt was directly exchanged at a favorable price for shares in a joint-stock company. (These kinds of debt-for-equity swaps are being used today by U.S. banks to reduce their loans to Latin America). The greatest, and last, example of this practice in the eighteenth century was to be the South Sea Company's scheme of 1720. Second, it was essentially a well-managed mutual fund in government annuities, and as such it gives us as accurate an account of the average rate of return on risk-free assets as we can find before the innovation of the South Sea annuities in 1723. According to Scott, the quotations on the stock of the Million Bank provide us "prices of a standard State security, which would occupy the same position in relation to the money-market then as Consols do at the present time."[19] We shall use its holding-period rate of return as our basic risk-free return.

Originally founded in 1695 to even out the risks and returns available to holders of lottery tickets on the Million Lottery Loan of 1694, the Million

---

[16] Davies (ibid., p. 80) noted that African stock fell almost continuously for 20 years after 1692.

[17] Ibid., pp. 344–5.

[18] Anderson, *Origin of Commerce*, Vol. 3, p. 144.

[19] Scott, *The Constitution and Finance*, Vol. 3, pp. 279–80.

Bank was intended to lapse in 1710, when the last payment was due on the lottery tickets. In fact, it lasted until 1796 because of a decision made in late 1699 by the directors to begin systematic purchase of reversions of single life annuities that had been issued in 1693 and 1694. These annuities could be extended from the term of the life of the single nominee to 95 years upon additional payment of four to five years' purchase, and this "reversion" could be purchased by new participants, such as the Million Bank. To generate income in the uncertain interval between purchase of the reversion and death of the nominee, the Million Bank also purchased life annuities directly. To carry out these purchases, new capital was issued, with the total nominal amount fixed at £500,000 at the end of 1700. The dividend was a uniform 5% in the period up to 1728, according to the final account rendered by the Million Bank to Parliament in 1796. However, we shall use Scott's surmise that the dividend was in fact 6% through 1716, 5% from 1717 through 1727, and 4% thereafter.[20]

The South Sea Company began its existence in May 1711 with a capital stock of £9,177,967 15s. 4d. created to buy up the existing short-term debt of the government, which had risen to enormous sums in the course of the War of the Spanish Succession. The stock was issued and trade begun in it in September 1711. At the end of 1715 its capital was raised to an even £10,000,000. The primary motivation for the company from the beginning was to fund a major part of the total national debt, accepting a lower interest rate on its share of the national debt than had been paid by the government previously. This interest received from the government, plus an annual management fee, provided the cash flow for dividend payments to shareholders, whose shares were more easily transferable than the short-term debt they had replaced. In addition, there was the prospect for lucrative trade with the Spanish Empire, now opened up by English naval successes in the West Indies. The charter of the South Sea Company granted it a monopoly of English trade from the Orinoco River on the east coast of South America on south to Tierra del Fuego and then north up the entire west coast. It was never made clear how this trade was to be carried on and what was to be traded. The Treaty of Utrecht assigned the *asiento* for carrying Negro slaves from Africa to Spanish America to the South Sea Company, but the fabled possibilities of this trade were quickly constrained by price and quantity restrictions imposed and strictly enforced against the company by the Spanish government. The remaining profits in the "black

[20] Ibid., p. 287, fn. 1.

market" that those restrictions created were exploited by outsiders, as had long been the case for the Royal African Company. So from the beginning, the South Sea Company was a financial giant hobbled within the restrictions of the *asiento* contract. In 1718, this trade was halted, a brief war with Spain was waged, and the company began to apply its resources to funding even more of the national debt. The culmination was its proposal, approved by the House of Commons in February 1720, to assume all the national debt not held by the Bank of England or the East India Company. That led to the South Sea Bubble, treated in detail in Chapter 5, during which the capital of the company was raised to the extraordinary figure of £38,564,180 (according to the company) or £37,802,203 (according to the government). Given the uncertainties over when the new stock would be transferable, however, combined with the daily volatility of all stock prices, any weighting scheme for that period would be arbitrary.

So the index is not calculated for years after 1719, until 1723, when the company was finally reorganized with a trading capital of £16,901,243 12s. 4d., with transferable shares, and a so-called joint stock of £16,901,240 1s. 4d. composed of transferable annuities. So even in disgrace, and broken in half, the South Sea Company was a financial goliath, outweighing by far any other organization in our stock index for the period 1723–33. In the years 1727, 1729, and 1732 the trading capital (and the annuity stock) was reduced, consummating in 1733, when the trading capital, down to £14,651,103 8s. 1d., was reduced to one-fourth that amount, and the remaining three-fourths was converted into the New South Sea Annuities bearing even lower interest.[21] It was clearly the prospect of receiving conversion rights into safe, if low-yielding, annuities that drove valuation of the South Sea stock in this latter period, rather than its dismal prospect for commercial successes, which at that time depended on whaling in the Greenland fishery.

The final company included in our index, appearing only in the last period, is the Royal Exchange Assurance Company. This was the larger (with £500,000 paid-up capital) of the two marine insurance companies chartered in the middle of the bubble year 1720. Both it and its companion, the London Assurance Company, received their charters in June 1720, and their stocks were quoted in the *Course of the Exchange* beginning July 1. The change in name on receipt of the charter did not alter at all the quoted price for either company from what it had been before. The Royal Ex-

---

[21] Fairman, *The Stocks Examined*, p. 97.

change Assurance was the continuation of the Assurance of Ships joint-stock corporation begun in 1718 as the Mines Royal company and enlarged under the vigorous leadership of Lord Onslow. This was called "Ships" by Castaing, but Scott asserted that it was called "Old Company" by Freke and was listed as "Onslow's Insurance" or "Onslow's Bubble" in the newspapers. The London Assurance Company was the chartered version of Lord Chetwynd's marine insurance company promoted by Stephen Ram and listed by Castaing as "New Company" and by Freke as "Ram and Colebrooke," but known in the newspapers as "Chetwynd's Insurance" or "Chetwynd's Bubble."[22] Both the London Assurance Company, capitalized at £258,314 to £414,315 in the period 1724–34, and the York Buildings Company, with a nominal capital of £1 million in 1724, which was steadily reduced in the manner of the African Company, have been omitted from the index. But whereas the York Buildings Company was subject to two great speculative surges in this decade, both marine assurance companies enjoyed steady growth in the price of their shares. That growth occurred in the context of regular dividend payments and a steady insurance business, although neither company's shares reached par in this period (£100 for the Royal Exchange Assurance and £12.5 for the London Assurance), and it appears the two together underwrote only about 10% of the marine insurance written in London. The rest was underwritten by the great mass of individual brokers and partnerships who increasingly came to be loosely affiliated as Lloyd's of London.

Figures 3.1–3.3 show the aggregate stock market index calculated on the equivalent of the "blue-chip" stocks of the London stock market in its early years. It began depressed at 60% of par value in 1698, but enjoyed a spectacular rally in 1699, followed by a relapse in 1700, and then sustained growth until the middle of 1704. This latter period was untroubled by the outbreak of the War of the Spanish Succession and was not seriously affected by the uncertainties of war finance until the change of ministries in 1708. The second period began with a rally as the East India Company resolved its internal problems, but quickly ran into the accumulated problems of war finance. The reorganization of the African Company and the founding of the South Sea Company helped to initiate a more or less steady advance of the market from March 1712 until the fresh outbreak of war with Spain in 1718. We pass over the interlude of the South Sea Bubble and its aftermath until Chapter 5. The period after the reorganization of 1723

---

[22] Scott, *The Constitution and Finance*, Vol. 3, p. 400.

was astonishingly dull by any standard, with only a mild disturbance in mid-1733 when the final reorganization of the South Sea Company was carried out in rather brutal form. The market, on average, remained above par, and the Walpole years were remarkable for the serenity indicated by the mild fluctuations from May 1727 until June 1733.

Overall, the index constructed here gives us a sensitive indicator of the reactions of the capital markets of Europe to the financial reorganizations, the new regulations, and the strains from military and naval demands in wartime experienced by England. Did the fledgling secondary, or resale, market for securities that had arisen in the London of William III as a private, entrepreneurial response to government innovations perform as we would expect a modern stock market to perform? To test this, we can inspect the market's performance in modern terms by calculating the monthly holding-period rates of return (HPR) for a balanced portfolio as well as the component stocks. The market index and the dividend paid out semiannually for each stock can be used to construct a monthly holding-period rate of return for the entire market. The holding-period rate of return is calculated by the formula

$$\text{HPR}_t = [(P_{t+1} - P_t) + D_{t+1}]/ P_t$$

where P is the price per average share as a percentage of par, and D is the dividend as a percentage of par.

This formula is also used to calculate the monthly HPR for each component stock. Figures 3.4–3.6 show the monthly HPRs for the market index. Although the graphs for the individual stocks are not presented here, they show substantial variance in the earliest years, 1698 through 1701, and then very mild fluctuations in the next two periods, as the graphs of the index indicate. The average rate of return remains positive, however, throughout. Table 3.1 summarizes the means, highs, lows, and standard deviations of the monthly holding-period rates of return in each period for each stock and for the market as a whole.

In the first decade, the market showed an average 0.9% monthly return (11.35% annual yield if compounded monthly). That was subject to wide swings, however, because the extremes observed in that period (from +0.33 to −0.20) were much greater than in the following two decades (from +0.18 to −0.077). It was the period 1709–19, however, from the reorganization of the East India Companies and the founding of the South Sea Company, that was truly spectacular and prosperous. The mean HPR was over 2% *monthly* (26.8% annual yield if compounded monthly), and

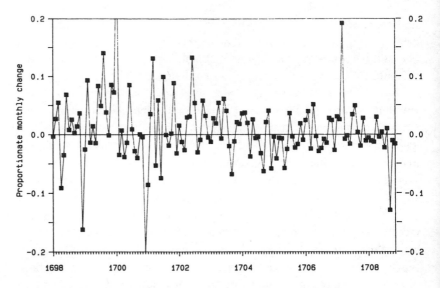

Figure 3.4. Holding-period returns for balanced portfolio, 1698–1708.

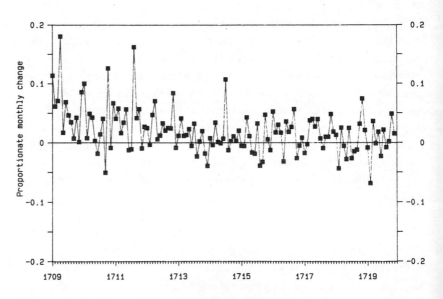

Figure 3.5. Holding-period returns for balanced portfolio, 1709–19.

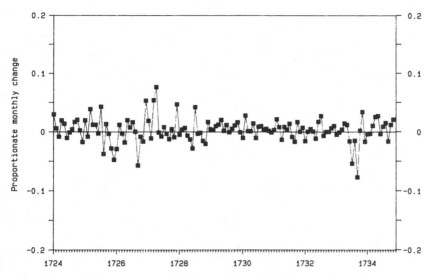

Figure 3.6. Holding-period returns for balanced portfolio, 1724–34.

the extremes were much reduced from the preceding period. The standard deviation was less than double the mean, compared with six times the mean in the first decade, and seven times in the third. It is small wonder that overconfidence in the strength and resilience of that market might have led to speculative mania. By the start of 1724 it was a much chastened market, very sedate in its performance, with an annualized holding rate of return of a bit over 3.5%. Despite its disappointing nature for speculative spirits, this was an appropriate environment in which to introduce the so-called Three Per Cent Annuities, to pay back more expensive government debt, and to encourage continued foreign investment in the public funds of Britain.

There is another way we can appraise the performance of the market in those early years, using modern techniques. It is customary for financial analysts today to regress monthly HPRs calculated over five-year intervals against the HPR for the stock market as a whole. The slope coefficient of such a regression is called the beta coefficient. Beta coefficients normally range from 0.5 to 1.5.[23] The lower values indicate that the stock has returns, on average, only half those of the market as a whole and must

[23] Eugene F. Brigham, *Financial Management,* 4th ed. (New York: Dryden Press, 1985), p. 222.

TABLE 3.1
Return and risk measures for London stocks
(monthly holding period rates of return)
1698-1708, 1709-19, 1724-34

	1698 - 1708	1709 - 19	1724 - 34
Bank of England			
Mean HPR (monthly)	0.009	0.008	0.004
High HPR	0.130	0.128	0.065
Low HPR	-0.122	-0.101	-0.075
Standard Deviation HPR	0.039	0.035	0.018
East India Company (Old)			
Mean HPR (monthly)	0.014		
High HPR	0.992		
Low HPR	-0.311		
Standard Deviation HPR	0.118		
East India Company (New)			
Mean HPR (monthly)	0.009		
High HPR	0.350		
Low HPR	-0.474		
Standard Deviation HPR	0.088		
Royal African Company			
Mean HPR (monthly)	0.001	0.007	-0.005
High HPR	0.639	0.704	1.443
Low HPR	-0.319	-0.345	-0.609
Standard Deviation HPR	0.109	0.163	0.175
Million Bank			
Mean HPR (monthly)	0.001	0.009	0.004
High HPR	0.270	0.110	0.050
Low HPR	-0.232	-0.049	-0.052
Standard Deviation HPR	0.049	0.029	0.013
East India Company (United)			
Mean HPR (monthly)		0.009	0.005
High HPR		0.149	0.123
Low HPR		-0.070	-0.095
Standard Deviation HPR		0.037	0.031
South Sea Company			
Mean HPR (monthly)		0.010	0.002
High HPR		0.138	0.089
Low HPR		-0.061	-0.178
Standard Deviation HPR		0.033	0.029
Ships Assurance Company			
Mean HPR (monthly)			0.012
High HPR			0.242
Low HPR			-0.103
Standard Deviation HPR			0.042
MARKET			
Mean HPR (monthly)	0.009	0.020	0.003
High HPR	0.330	0.181	0.077
Low HPR	-0.201	-0.068	-0.077
Standard Deviation HPR	0.059	0.038	0.020

therefore compensate by being a very secure investment, whereas the higher figures reflect a much better return than the market, but usually much more volatility as well. The stocks with low beta coefficients are favored by widows, orphans, and institutions with fiduciary responsibilities. The stocks with beta coefficients close to 1.5 are especially favored by speculators with good sources of information who are able to act very quickly to buy in or sell out. The calculations underlying this exercise are rather tedious, if simple conceptually, but they are important to carry out to see if the appurtenances of the London stock market at that early time, which we have described in very modern terms, really provided an efficient, operationally sound market for international capital. Table 3.2 summarizes these results.

As we would expect, the Bank of England's beta coefficient is well below 1, indeed below 0.5, for the first period. As a less volatile stock, its return can be expected to move less than proportionately with that of the market as a whole. This is consistently so for the Million Bank (Table 3.2). The beta is a very low 0.56 for the first period, during which it switches from being a closed-end to being an open-end mutual fund in government perpetual annuities. For the last two periods the beta sinks to 0.4, but from Table 3.1 we observe that its volatility is also substantially less than that for the market as a whole for those periods. The period 1698–1708 was dominated by the disputes between the two East India Companies. Their beta coefficients, by contrast to the two banks, are well above 1, as should be expected given the added risk each bore until they were consolidated in 1709. The so-called Additional Shares, issued as part of the transition to the final merger date, have lower beta coefficients than do the shares of either company. But one might expect this, because they are the outcomes of a negotiated settlement between the two companies and were systematically retired as the final merger date drew near in 1709. The beta coefficients for the Royal African Company in the first two periods seem too low. Subject to repeated attempts at bankruptcy settlements, which kept failing for want of clear legal precedence or act of Parliament, it should have had a beta coefficient higher than any other stock, instead of being close to 1. But the coefficient of determination (R^2) for the regressions in those periods is also very low; so not much confidence can be placed in the estimate. The beta coefficient of 1.51 for the last period, when it was in the process of being dissolved, seems more reasonable, but still it is unreliably estimated.

To summarize these indicators of market behavior, companies that were

TABLE 3.2
Estimated beta coefficients for London stocks,
1698-1708, 1709-19, 1724-34

	1698 - 1708	1709 - 19	1724 - 34
Bank of England			
R^2	0.499	0.645	0.747
No. of observations	131	131	131
Constant	0.005	-0.007	0.002
Beta coefficient	**0.47**	**0.73**	**0.74**
Standard error of beta	0.04	0.04	0.05
East India Company (Old)			
R^2	0.607		
No. of observations	131		
Constant	0.001		
Beta coefficient	**1.56**		
Standard error of beta	0.11		
East India Company (New)			
R^2	0.630		
No. of observations	123		
Constant	-0.001		
Beta coefficient	**1.17**		
Standard error of beta	0.08		
Royal African Company			
R^2	0.262	0.060	0.031
No. of observations	131	131	131
Constant	-0.008	-0.015	-0.009
Beta coefficient	**0.95**	**1.05**	**1.51**
Standard error of beta	0.14	0.37	0.75
Million Bank			
R^2	0.303	0.275	0.350
No. of observations	106	131	131
Constant	-0.000	0.001	0.002
Beta coefficient	**0.56**	**0.40**	**0.39**
Standard error of beta	0.08	0.06	0.05
East India Company (United)			
R^2		0.668	0.729
No. of observations		129	131
Constant		-0.006	0.000
Beta coefficient		**0.81**	**1.28**
Standard error of beta		0.05	0.07
Royal Exchange Assurance			
R^2			0.366
No. of observations			131
Constant			0.007
Beta coefficient			**1.26**
Standard error of beta			0.15

subject to nonmarket forces arising from negotiated settlements or protracted disputes, as would be expected, did not correlate well at all with the
market rate of return. But for companies that did correlate well, their beta
coefficients lie within a typical range and reflect a reasonable risk/return
trade-off – stocks that fluctuated more usually had higher rates of return
than those that fluctuated less. Moreover, these relationships held up consistently over the three decades of start-up, speculative boom, and reorganization.

4. The Banque Royale and the South Sea Company: how the bubbles began

> We are now to enter upon the year 1720; a year remarkable beyond any other which can be pitched upon by historians for extraordinary and romantic projects, proposals, and undertakings, both private and national; . . . and which, . . . ought to be had in perpetual remembrance, not only as being what never had its parallel, nor, it is to be hoped, ever will hereafter; but, likewise, as it may serve for a perpetual memento to the legislators and ministers . . . never to leave it in the power of any, hereafter, to hoodwink mankind into so shameful and baneful an imposition on the credulity of the people, thereby diverted from their lawful industry.
>
> Adam Anderson, *Origin of Commerce,* Vol. 3, pp. 91–2.

The Mississippi Bubble in France, the South Sea Bubble in England, and similar bubbles in Holland and Germany during the years 1719 and 1720 were parts of the first international stock market speculative boom and bust in capitalist Europe. The legacy of those episodes was substantial. The Bubble Act of 1720 in England limited the use of joint-stock corporations until well into the nineteenth century, and the French collective memory of John Law and his Banque Royale meant that "there was hesitation even in pronouncing the word 'bank' for 150 years thereafter,"[1] and, of course, they gave us the word "bubble" for describing purely speculative movements in asset prices. It is useful to present and analyze as clearly as possible these classic bubbles, useful not only for better understanding the economic history of the eighteenth century but also for grasping its significance for economic theory. It is intrinsically interesting for economic theory to observe the activities on capital markets when they were in a relatively pristine state.

The task of quantitative analysis and theoretical understanding is greatly aided by using the data set developed here for the London capital market. It is unfortunate that nothing comparable has yet been found for France or

---

[1] Charles P. Kindleberger, *A Financial History of Western Europe* (London: George Allen & Unwin, 1984), p. 98.

the Netherlands. Financial initiatives in both countries help explain the peculiar course of the South Sea Bubble in England throughout its duration. Moreover, the repercussions of the South Sea Bubble for those two countries were, if anything, more important for European economic history than were the bubble's effects within England. France had the largest domestic economy in Europe, and the Netherlands dominated the overseas enterprises of Europe. Despite the absence of a data source for either of these two mercantile and financial powers comparable to Castaing's *Course of the Exchange*, there do exist data resources for them that modern economic historians have just begun to exploit. Moreover, much more can be inferred about events in France and Holland from the data available in England.

The bubbles in France, in England, and then later in the Netherlands and Portugal that occurred in the years 1719–21 were part of the same historical process. The governments in all those cases were in the beginning stages of political modernization, with more limited monarchies and more powerful parliaments, but at the same time financially encumbered with antiquated tax systems and debt instruments. Political advantages were readily apparent to whichever party could tap directly into the financial markets and foreign trade opportunities emerging for northwestern Europe. The boldest initiatives were taken, as might be expected, by France, the most backward of the mercantile states. The greatest long-run success was enjoyed, as might also be expected, by England, the best endowed of the mercantile states in terms of both financial markets and foreign markets.

In this chapter, explicit linkages are drawn between the two major stock market crises of 1719–20 and the aftershocks in Amsterdam and Hamburg, using semiweekly exchange-rate data that were published regularly throughout that period. These have never been used before to analyze either the dynamics of the two major bubbles or the linkages between them. Though there has been extensive study of the two bubbles individually, there has been little investigation of the links between them, much less the links with the later bubbles in the Netherlands.[2] So the data

2 William R. Scott, *The Constitution and Finance of English, Scottish, and Irish Joint-Stock Companies to 1720*, 3 vols. (Cambridge University Press, 1910), Vol. 3, pp. 288–362, and John Carswell, *The South Sea Bubble* (London: Cresset Press, 1960), cited subjective statements about the movement of the speculation in Europe. Charles Kindleberger, *Manias, Panics and Crashes* (New York: Basic Books, 1978), mentioned briefly a transmission of the speculative mania. T. S. Ashton, *Economic Fluctuations in England, 1700–1800* (Oxford: Clarendon Press, 1959), took a short but close look at the transfer of capital between London and Paris and Amsterdam and the resulting effects on English exchange

we present in the various charts from both Paris and London provide a unique overview of each stock market bubble and the direct linkages between them.[3] The statistical analysis to be presented regarding the daily price data from the Mississippi and South Sea cases also represents the first empirical effort at characterizing the course of these bubbles in terms of the events in the foreign exchanges.[4]

Using quotations from the *Course of the Exchange* for information on exchange rates, gold and silver prices, and stock prices on the London market, we can chart the progress of this first pan-European stock mania. The stock prices are daily for the six trading days in London, whereas the exchange rates and gold and silver prices occur as twice-weekly quotes

rates. Adam Anderson, a clerk for the South Sea Company during the bubble, wrote his account much later in the century. He mentioned the presence of foreigners in both Paris and London during the height of each bubble, but he drew only parallels between the two, making no explicit links: Adam Anderson, *An Historical and Chronological Deduction of the Origin of Commerce, from the earliest accounts,* 4 vols. (London, 1764, continued to 1788 by William Combe and published for the last time in 1801; reprinted New York: Augustus M. Kelley, 1967), Vol. 3, pp. 79–126. John Law explicitly compared the two episodes in 1721, drawing conclusions very much to his favor, but he never addressed the issue of direct financial linkages between them: Paul Harsin, ed., *John Law: Oeuvres completes,* 3 vols. (Paris: Sirey, 1934), Vol. 3, pp. 198–235. Herbert Luethy, *La Haute Banque Protestante en France de la Révocation de l'Edit de Nantes à la Révolution. Vol. 2: De la Banque aux Finances,"* (Paris: SEVPEN, 1961), discussed the role of Geneva investors in both bubbles. Andre Sayous, "Les Répercusions de l'affaire de Law et du South Sea Bubble dans les Provinces Unies," *Bijdragen voor vaderlandsche Geschiednenis en Oudheidkunde,* 8:2(1940), pp. 57–86, described the role of Dutch investors in each and the effects of the bubbles on the Netherlands. F. P. Groeneveld, *Economische Crisis van het jaar 1720* (Gröningen: Noordhof, 1940), and Charles Wilson, *Anglo-Dutch Commerce and Finance in the Eighteenth Century* (Cambridge University Press, 1941) detailed the role of Dutch investors in English funds during this period and after. P. G. M. Dickson, *The Financial Revolution in England: A Study in the Development of Public Credit, 1688–1756* (London: Macmillan, 1967), did the most thorough job of making the links, but he relied on contemporary newspaper reports of bullion shipments and exchange-rate movements for his quantitative data. Though he reproduced fortnightly prices of stocks from Castaing (p. 139), the only exchange rate he gave was that on Amsterdam.

[3] This chapter is based on an unpublished paper by Larry Neal and Eric Schubert, "The First Rational Bubbles: A New Look at the Mississippi and South Sea Schemes," Urbana, IL, 1985. The exchange-rate movements during the Mississippi and South Sea bubbles were analyzed in detail by Eric Schubert: "The Ties That Bound: Eighteenth Century Market Behavior in Foreign Exchange, International Goods, and Financial Assets," unpublished Ph.D. dissertation, University of Illinois, Urbana-Champaign, 1986.

[4] Brian Parsons, "The Behavior of Prices on the London Stock Market in the Early Eighteenth Century," unpublished Ph.D. dissertation, University of Chicago, 1974, analyzed daily movements of stock prices on the London Stock Exchange in terms of weak tests of market efficiency during the South Sea Bubble, but ignored the foreign exchanges or questions of rational bubbles.

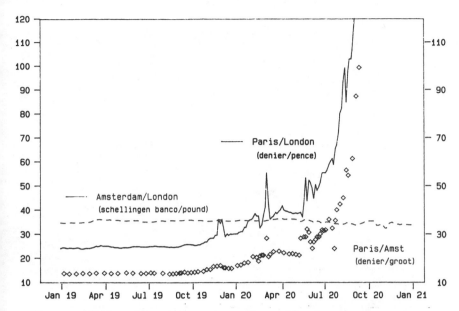

Figure 4.1. Paris exchange rates on Amsterdam and London, 1719–20.

(Tuesday and Friday) in the *Course of the Exchange*. We begin our coverage with January 1719, four months before the Mississippi Bubble started, and end it after December 1720, when the South Sea and Amsterdam bubbles had collapsed. Because the dates in the *Course of the Exchange* were quoted from the Old Style (O.S.) or Julian calendar, all dates listed in this book will be based on that calendar, even though both Amsterdam and Paris were using the New Style (N.S.) or Gregorian calendar.

Shown in Figures 4.1–4.3 are four exchange rates (three from London and one from Paris) and the price of gold. The exchange rates are as follows: the London-on-Paris exchange rate, which was given in pence sterling per French ecu or crown (equal to three livres tournois), but is converted here to be French deniers per English pence; the London-on-Amsterdam rate, in schellingen banco per pound sterling; the Paris-on-Amsterdam rate, measured in schellingen banco per French ecu; and the London-on-Hamburg rate, in schillingen banco per pound sterling. Unless otherwise stated, these are two-month usance rates. Although each exchange-rate series has its peculiarities, all show periods of sustained rises or falls, and all are marked by occasional "blips" (a sudden rise or fall followed quickly by a reversal). A sudden appreciation of a particular

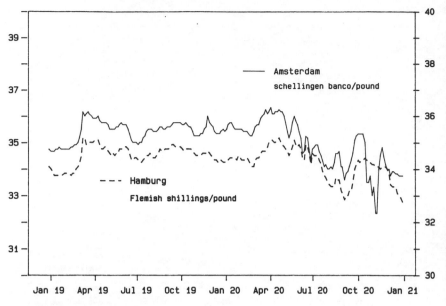

Figure 4.2. London exchange rates on Amsterdam and Hamburg, 1719–20.

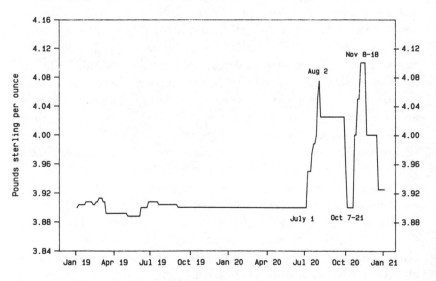

Figure 4.3. Price of gold in bars, London, 1719–20.

currency, followed by a full depreciation back to the normal exchange rate, usually signaled a scramble for liquidity in the country of that currency. Because short-term liquid assets were few, the scramble would focus on existing bills of exchange. That is to say, for any movement from one capital asset to another in any of the European countries at that time, bills of foreign exchange were the dominant devices used to make the transfer, rather than, say, specie, gems, or trade goods. As soon as letters from the country scrambling for liquidity had reached the merchant correspondents abroad and fresh bills had been authorized, the exchange rate would revert to its equilibrium level (which might, of course, not be the previous level, given the currency and credit manipulations of that period). Thanks to the sedate pace of business correspondence relative to the posting of exchange rates semiweekly at the Royal Exchange in London, the time series for each currency for that period show characteristic "signatures" when capital market disturbances occurred.

This may be called the "Ashton effect," because T. S. Ashton described it in detail as one of the statistical indicators of financial crises in the eighteenth century.[5] Whereas one sign of an impending crisis often was an adverse movement in the foreign exchanges, a sure sign of an actual scramble for liquidity was a sudden, short-lived appreciation in a country's currency. Ashton noted that the same thing occurred in the summer of 1914, when, briefly, there appeared to be a flight from the dollar to the pound, when in reality the outbreak of World War I had caused a sudden liquidity crisis in London. A depreciation in a currency's rate following the Ashton effect may overshoot the previous rate, in which case it indicates a capital outflow. The overshooting of the exchange rate may be called a "Kindleberger effect," because it indicates a transmission of the liquidity scramble in the first country to its closest trading partners. When the Kindleberger effect is confined to particular currencies, it enables us, in combination with the Ashton effect, to state where foreign capital flows are going and from whence they are coming at the end of any particular speculative episode. Kindleberger placed special emphasis on the destabilizing consequences of speculative capital movements from one financial center to another and illustrated his argument with historical episodes dating from the 1719–20 bubbles through the late 1970s.[6]

Examining the London–Paris series in Figure 4.1, we first note a small

5 Ashton, *Economic Fluctuations*, p. 113. Ashton gave credit, however, to Jacob Viner for the explanation of this nonintuitive result.
6 Kindleberger, *Manias*, gave the best exegesis of his argument in the historical perspective.

blip in the spring of 1719. This is easily overlooked, given the violent fluctuations to come, but it is interesting that this coincides with the start of Law's system in May 1719, with the formation of the Compagnie des Indes, the general trading monopoly company for France, on the basis of Law's existing Compagnie d'Occident. The historical literature suggests that money left London and Amsterdam for Paris in the late summer of 1719. Scott wrote that "Paris became the Mecca of speculators of Europe."[7] Carswell cited a report that 30,000 foreign speculators had entered Paris in the fall of 1719.[8] The graph of the London–Paris exchange rate shows a slight appreciation of the livre in mid-August, but the increase was small relative to the "background noise" of the previous two months. In September, at the height of the capital flow to Paris, the exchange rate actually depreciated!

The answer to the apparent paradox is that Law fostered the boom through a systematic money inflation (Table 4.1). The Paris exchange rate started to depreciate in late October 1719, and that continued to March 1720, when a brief period of stability began before the final burst of paper inflation. That depreciation was due to a slowing down and reversal of the capital inflow, along with the continued increase in the issue of bank notes and debasement of the livre by Law. In late November and early December 1719 the pound appreciated sharply with respect to the guilder and the livre. Because of the suddenness of the movements and the sharp drop in the price of French stock, we infer that a fair number of speculators took their profits and departed for England. Scott estimated that 500 million livres in bullion had been carried out in late 1719.[9] When the share quotations for the Compagnie des Indes had reached Law's target level of 10,000 livres (a 20-fold increase) in the middle of November (O.S.), the issuance during the next week of 30 million livres worth of new shares stabilized the price.[10] At the end of that week, stock market speculators left Paris for London.

[7] Scott, *The Constitution and Finance*, Vol. 1, p. 403.

[8] Carswell, *The South Sea Bubble*, p. 101.

[9] Scott, *The Constitution and Finance*, Vol. 1, p. 404.

[10] Edgar Faure, *Le Banqueroute de Law* (Paris: Gallimard, 1977), p. 269, said there were 30 million new shares (*titres*) issued, but that would imply nearly 300 billion livres worth. His source, Paul Harsin, ed., *Dutot: Réflexions politiques sur les finance et le commerce*, 2 vols. (Paris: Les Belles Lettres, 1935), Vol. 2, pp. 257–8, on the other hand, said only "30 millions," without specifying *titres* or livres. Dutot's summary of the total value of Compagnie des Indes stock at the end of November, however, was only 4.782 billion livres. The number of new shares issued in mid-November, therefore, must have been only 3,000, with approximate market value of 30 million livres.

TABLE 4.1
Issues of notes by Banque Royale from December 1718 to April 1720
(millions of livres)

Date of commission	Notes added	Total note issue
25 December 1718	18	18
31 January 1719	20	38
21 March 1719	21	59
11 April 1719	51	110
30 May 1719	50	160
14 July 1719	221	381
1 September 1719	120	501
13 October 1719	120	621
18 December 1719	360	981
26 January 1720	200	1,181
15 March 1720	300	1,481
25 March 1720	437	2,195
20 April 1720	362	2,557

Note: At the start of this period there was an estimated 1 billion livres in specie in the country, and 148 million livres in Banque Generale notes outstanding.

Source: Paul Harsin, *Doctrines Monétaires et Financières en France du XVIe au XVIIIe Siècle* (Paris: Libraire Felix Alcan, 1928).

Another exit of speculators' capital from Paris occurred in early February. On 12 February 1720, Law halted all dealings in France in stock, foreign exchange, and bank notes in an attempt to combat inflation and speculation. The price of Mississippi shares plummeted. At the same time, the English Parliament approved the South Sea Company's proposal for funding a large part of the national debt. So money left France and headed for England.

Popular pressure forced Law to reopen the Paris stock market on 23 February, with the purchase and sale of unlimited quantities of shares priced at 9,000 livres, and to reopen the offices where the paper currency, *billets de banque,* could be converted to silver. That restored the stock market boom, but speculation then took place in the billets de banque. The reaction of the Paris–London exchange rate at first was a case of the Ashton effect. Because speculators could not convert their shares of Mississippi stock directly into specie, but only into depreciating paper currency on the French market, the uncertainty of the situation led to an appreciation of the livre as holders of English bills of exchange on Paris sold their assets at a discount. Once the stock market in Paris reopened, the livre depreciated sharply, signaling the exodus of speculators.

The stock market gyrations continued in France with mostly domestic speculators until the middle of May 1720. On 10 May, in a fit of desperation, Law announced a deflationary decree, again in an attempt to save his system. Convertibility of bank notes to specie was to end. The official price of shares of the Compagnie des Indes was dropped to 8,000 livres, with a target price of 5,000 livres by 1 December. In response, the French exchange rate moved as it had in February, with an initial appreciation, followed by a sharp depreciation. However, the graph overstates the appreciation of the livre, because the quotes in London from 13 May through 20 May were "at sight" instead of the customary usance of two months. Therefore, they incorporated the sight premium as well as any appreciation during that week. Afterward, the quotes were again at usance, but the Kindleberger effect, or overshooting of the previous level for the exchange rate, shows up clearly nonetheless. Whether the remaining speculators, French and/or foreigners, took their money from France and put it in England for more profits or whether the French nobility took their specie to safer quarters, this depreciation signaled a capital outflow.

From the deflationary decree in May (which Law lifted a week later, again under public pressure) onward, currency debasements and increased bank-note issues resulted in a continued depreciation of the livre. The bankruptcy of 6 July (O.S.) of the Banque Royale shifted speculation in France from shares in the Compagnie des Indes to billets de banque, which declined in value until the exchange market in France closed in September 1720. The sharp appreciation of the livre in late September was the result of more traditional bankers regaining power and causing a repatriation of gold into France.

Turning to Figure 4.2 and the London–Hamburg and London–Amsterdam exchange rates, we can pick out the repercussions of the French speculative movements as the relative importance of London and Amsterdam shifted either as sources for capital inflows to France or as destinations for capital outflows from France. Carswell linked the speculative fever of the Mississippi and South Sea bubbles only in the late spring of 1720:

Buying orders for South Sea stock poured into London from Holland, 200,000 pistoles arriving in one consignment from Amsterdam towards the end of April.[11]

And to London that spring were coming a great many of those who, only a few months before, had been crowding the rue Quincampoix [French stock market].[12]

[11] Carswell, *The South Sea Bubble*, pp. 147–8.
[12] Ibid., p. 143.

Looking at the London–Amsterdam exchange rate (Figure 4.2) and the graph of South Sea stock prices (Figure 4.5), however, we can see an influx of foreign speculators into England in March. Both the price of South Sea shares and the English pound appreciated throughout the spring of 1720. By the first half of May, both South Sea stock and the London–Amsterdam and London–Hamburg exchange rates leveled off. That was the lull before the next storm, however. On 20 May the South Sea Company announced more conversions of the government debt, both long-term and short-term annuities, at £375, and granted loans to aid buyers of additional stock. The pound appreciated sharply as foreigners entered the market. After those large capital inflows in the spring of 1720, the pound began to depreciate in the summer. That signaled a reversal of the capital flow, first to Amsterdam, then to Hamburg. Carswell stated that "Amsterdam [in] June and July saw a crop of native promotions. . . . Others were on the way to Hamburg, where the Exchange was crowded from morning to night."[13]

One can explain the sharp fluctuations that highlight this June–July depreciation of the pound as temporary slowings in the capital outflow. Two events in the story of the South Sea Bubble seem to be responsible. The first sharp rise came as the result of another group of subscriptions of South Sea stock sold between 16 June and 22 June. The company offered £5 million in stock at £1,000 per £100 share. This issue pumped £4.75 million into the market, running the total to £11.4 million since April. The second rise, found for early July, was not associated with an issuance of stock, but may have been due to the French connection. The price of South Sea stock was hovering around £850 or more and had not yet begun its final plummet. Whereas the bankruptcy of the Banque Royale on 6 July (O.S.) in France caused both the pound and the guilder to appreciate relative to the livre, it appears that flight capital from France headed more toward London than toward Amsterdam.

The timing of the capital flows to Amsterdam and Hamburg are illustrated by the convergence of the London–Amsterdam and London–Hamburg rates for June. The pound depreciated relative to the Dutch schellingen banco, but the pound fluctuated around the pre-bubble level relative to the German schillingen banco. This implies a capital outflow directed toward Amsterdam. For July, the spread between the rates widened as the pound depreciated relative to the schillingen banco, signaling a capital flow increasingly headed toward Hamburg.

---

[13] Ibid., pp. 164–5.

The sharp rise and fall in Amsterdam and Hamburg rates in mid-August reflected the Ashton effect, signaling the financial panic that had begun. We shall take up in greater detail in Chapter 5 the exact circumstances that caused this panic that marked the end of the South Sea Bubble. Our interpretation differs from the traditional accounts only in terms of the underlying source of the panic, not in regard to its timing. The price of South Sea stock dropped sharply from the last half of August through the middle of October. On 24 September the Sword Blade Company (the bank for the South Sea Company) suspended payments, which intensified the scramble for cash in London's tight money market.

A brief respite came in mid-October as the pound appreciated sharply and gold prices plummeted. Those movements reflected the collapse of the Dutch boom in October and the arrival of 100,000 guineas in gold from Holland at that time.[14] That easing was short-lived. The English financial system faltered and remained precariously weak for the last three months of the year. As can be seen in the London–Amsterdam exchange rate (Figure 4.2) and the London gold price (Figure 4.3), a depreciated pound and high gold prices indicated sharp depreciations in bills of exchange and bank notes, respectively. A substantial widening between sight and usance exchange rates on Amsterdam, over 10 times higher in October 1720 than in 1723, indicated that interest rates in the international money market were very high. The major cause of this was the resumption of a gold standard in France after the fall and expulsion of John Law.

This brief history of the effects of the English South Sea Bubble on the London exchange rates shows clearly that the influence of Law's system in France was paramount at all stages – beginning, speculative boom, increasing liquidity crunch, and final collapse, as well as the protracted period required for recovery. The summary of the system that follows relies essentially on the data and analysis presented by Faure. Faure's study, in turn, drew heavily on the previous work by Harsin, but supplemented it with important new data on the share prices of the Compagnie des Indes, exchange rates in Paris on both Amsterdam and London, and the market values of bank notes issued by the Banque Royale.[15] These data are incorporated into Figure 4.4 and Table 4.1. Those studies, however, emphasized the singularity of the French experience, rather than its linkages to the

14 Scott, *The Constitution and Finance*, Vol. 3, p. 323.
15 Faure, *Le Banqueroute de Law*, added his own delightful appraisal of the high politics of the era, as acted out by principals possessing an amazing variety of sexual idiosyncrasies!

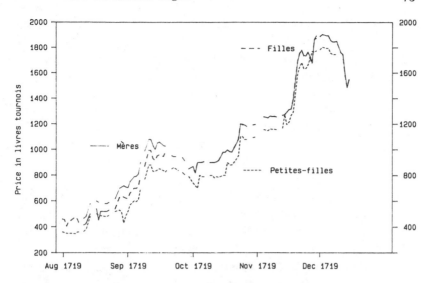

Figure 4.4. Mississippi Bubble, Compagnie des Indes shares.

British experience, which we emphasized earlier. The role of foreigners in their accounts was to come to Paris and marvel, rather than to transmit French economic disturbances elsewhere.

After a large-scale cancellation of government debt at the beginning of the regency of Louis XV, the crown still found it impossible to pay interest on the remaining debt, already discounted 75%. Desperate for solutions, the regent, the duke of Orléans, fell under the sway of the brilliant Scottish financier John Law. In May 1716, Law founded the Banque Generale, the success of which laid the basis for the greater enterprises to come. In August 1717, Law formed the Compagnie d'Occident, which, like the South Sea Company in its original charter of 1711, took over some of the national debt for special overseas trading privileges. Citizens and foreigners could exchange their holdings of government debt for stock in the company. The original nominal capital, par value 500 livres per share, was 100 million livres. The initial market value of the stock was below par at 300 livres. In December 1718, Law converted the Banque Generale into the Banque Royale, whose notes, denominated either in gold ecus or in silver livres, then became the medium for tax payments. In May, the louis d'or was devalued relative to the livre, so that the billets-livre became the preferred form of money for the public to hold. Also, in May 1719, the

Compagnie d'Occident was expanded to include the monopoly of trade with India and China and was renamed the Compagnie des Indes, with a new issue of 50,000 shares. In the summer of 1719, Law put the remaining elements of the system into place, acquiring the right for the company to mint coins and assuming the farming of the indirect taxes.

The decrees of 16–20 August 1719 (O.S.) completed the formation of the system with a bold step toward fiscal reform: the suppression and reimbursement of the rentes and many of the offices that had been sold in the previous two decades in order to raise money. The reimbursement took place in billets de banque at the offices of the company, which had to offer to the reimbursees as well as all other holders of existing government debt either bearer shares in the company with 4% annual dividends or *contrats de constitution de rente,* which carried a fixed return of 3%, the same reduced rate the government paid the company on the debt it held. Luethy considered that the fatal flaw in the system, because the reimbursements required large new issues of paper money.[16] Faure, on the other hand, believed that the reimbursees would have used their billets de banque to purchase one or the other of the company's obligations to avoid further depreciation of their assets. Based on the increased revenues projected from the tax farm on indirect taxes that had been given to the company for the next seven years, as well as revenues from the monopoly of the mint, these obligations, *actions rentières,* could have been very attractive, blue-chip investments. In effect, the elimination of direct taxes, offices, and the rentes could have been funded into the permanent capital stock of the company.[17] As it was, Law proceeded to his *plan fou* with three successive new issues of capital stock (the fourth, fifth, and six issues) in the company on 2, 17, and 21 September 1719 (O.S.).

These shares were issued at a face value of 5,000 livres each, with a promised dividend of 4%. Because the first three issues of shares had had face values of 500, 550, and 1,000 livres, the possessors of these *mères, filles,* and *petites-filles,* as they were popularly called, profited from enormous capital gains. Those who already held government debt, however, were not accorded any priority in purchasing these new shares, but were forced to buy them at existing market value. This meant that they had to hope for further capital gains on their shares in the company if they were to offset some of the losses they had already suffered on government debts.

16 Luethy, *La Haute Banque,* Vol. 2, p. 317.
17 Faure, *Le Banqueroute de Law,* pp. 225–8.

The third step in Law's plan was to raise the market value of the shares to 10,000 livres – this in order to reduce the effective rate of interest to 2%.[18]

To facilitate speculation, or, in his view, to mobilize the necessary capital, Law took the following steps:

1. He divided shares into fractions small enough so that modest investors would be able to purchase them.
2. He provided for installment payments, 10% per month, and further provided that the first two months could be deferred to the third. That meant that December and March were the months of reckoning.
3. He provided loans from the Banque Royale on the security of shares, even if only partially paid for.

To stabilize the price of Compagnie d'Occident stock after it had reached the desired level of 10,000 livres, Law took these additional steps:

4. Starting on 19 December (O.S.), he opened an office for the purchase and sale of shares in the company.
5. He later fixed the price of each share at 9,000 livres.[19]

All these steps can be seen as establishing the rules for a game whose object was to increase the price of shares of the Compagnie des Indes to 10,000 livres, later reduced in light of international pressures to 9,000 livres.

Law, in other words, manufactured the conditions necessary for a price bubble to occur in the stock of the Compagnie des Indes by encouraging foreign investors, mainly from England and Holland, as well as wealthy Frenchmen, to buy in while the price was being forced up. At the top of the bubble, when the price per share had reached his target level of 10,000 livres, the challenge to Law was to lock-in the foreigners or to offset their exit from the Paris market by bringing in a broader range of French participants. In other words, Law was creating the conditions necessary for a short-lived "rational bubble." This is defined in the current economics literature as a continuing rise in the price of an asset that is generated by market participants anticipating that rises in its price will continue to occur. By their actions, they make these anticipations self-fulfilling, at least for a limited period. The process must end, usually quickly, and when it does the price must return to the underlying fundamental level determined by long-run determinants of supply and demand. The challenge that Law posed for

[18] Ibid., pp. 232–3. Faure cited a number of Law's writings from 1715 to 1724 in which he repeated this sacrosanct number of 2%.
[19] Ibid., pp. 233–4.

himself, and for the French state, was to sustain the high price of Compagnie des Indes stock at the top of the bubble so that the French economy might benefit from a higher degree of monetization and a lower long-term rate of interest. He failed that challenge – a result considered inevitable by Richard Cantillon and his cosmopolitan clients.[20]

The appendix to this chapter provides some statistical tests to determine if the price of Mississippi stock in the fall of 1719 followed a pattern consistent with such a "rational bubble." The statistical results are mixed, one set indicating that Law had generated a complex form of such a rational bubble if only for the three months from mid-August to mid-November 1719, the other indicating that he was exercising the enormous power he possessed at that time (effectively controlling singlehandedly the fiscal, monetary, and exchange-rate policies of the largest economy in Europe) to shift market fundamentals in an unpredictable way.

These statistical results are not really surprising from a historical viewpoint. The system of John Law contained such a great mixture of elements and controlled directly so many of the conceivable policy variables that it has remained a fascinating question whether or not it could have worked, either in part or with some minor modification. Faure distinguished two parts to it – le plan sage and le plan fou – and argued that the "wise plan" could have worked very well if left on its own, but the "mad plan" that ensued prevented that. These two "plans" correspond, perhaps, to the "rational" and "irrational" bubbles discussed in finance literature today.

Irrational bubbles are those in which the relationship of an asset to its market fundamental simply breaks down because of overzealous trading or an unrealistic appraisal of the value of the stock. Kindleberger espouses this view of market bubbles. In this scenario, a shock to the economic system changes the perceived profitability of a particular enterprise. When that is coupled with easy credit, a boom ensues. Speculation spreads to sectors of society whose members normally avoid playing the market. These new entrants have little knowledge of the market and thus add an element of irrationality into it. Kindleberger's analysis suggests a mania that spreads from the market for the original asset to other assets – shares in all sorts of joint-stock companies, real estate, and a madcap variety of alternative assets. The South Sea Bubble fits his analysis as if tailor-made, especially if we rely solely on the analysis of Adam Anderson, who listed

---

[20] See Antoin E. Murphy, *Richard Cantillon, Entrepreneur and Economist* (Oxford: Clarendon Press, 1986), chap. 5–8.

all the frivolous schemes that arose during the height of the speculation on South Sea stock.

The motivation for the South Sea scheme was essentially the same as for the Mississippi Bubble: to refinance the immense debts accumulated by the government during the War of the Spanish Succession.[21] And the mechanics of the two schemes were very similar. In exchange for their annuities, holders of the existing government debt were offered new South Sea Company stock that promised capital gains. Two-thirds of the annuity owners made the exchange, in response to increasingly attractive terms offered by the directors of the South Sea Company. W. R. Scott, in his classic analysis, divided these directors into two groups: (1) an inner ring of prime movers privy to most of the details of each successive stage of the scheme and (2) the remainder of the directors, who probably were not. This creates the two classes of traders needed for a rational bubble to arise.

The operations consisted of four new issues of stock that were made on 14 April, 29 April, 17 June, and 24 August 1720 (O.S.). These could be purchased for one-fifth down (first and fourth issues) or one-tenth down (second and third issues), with the balance due in equal installments spread over 16 months (first issue), 32 months (second issue), 54 months (third issue), or 36 months (fourth issue). For the last two issues, loans could be obtained from the South Sea Company itself for the market value of the South Sea shares held by a purchaser.[22] According to Dickson, the rise in price of the shares occurred in three spurts: the second half of March, the second half of May, and during June. He argues that the first was due primarily to foreign speculation shifting from Paris to London, the second was due to increased participation by Dutch investors and the beginning of loans by directors of the company on security of South Sea stock, and the third was due to an immense increase in loans on stock, on subscription receipts, and even on subscriptions made verbally.[23]

The conclusion from our statistical tests, described fully in the appendix, is that a rational bubble in South Sea stock occurred, but only during the period 23 February through 15 June, precisely the period identified by Dickson as the interval when foreign participation was most active. In the periods before the entry of foreigners and after their exit, a rational bubble

[21] Dickson, *The Financial Revolution in England*, pp. 91–2. Cf. Earl J. Hamilton, "Origin and Growth of the National Debt in Western Europe," *American Economic Review*, 37(May 1947), pp. 118–30.

[22] Dickson, *The Financial Revolution in England*, pp. 123–5.

[23] Ibid., pp. 140–3.

does not appear, nor, using the same statistical techniques, do we find a rational bubble in the price of shares of either the Bank of England or the East India Company at any time, despite the sympathetic rise and fall in their prices during the South Sea Bubble.

In deciding which periods to examine for evidence of rational bubbles, we have used the movements in the foreign exchange rates when there were sudden rises and relapses to mark the entry and exit of outsiders – their exchange-rate signatures. Although the "outsider" category can be further distinguished between "speculators" and "suckers," implicitly we usually put foreign outsiders into the speculator group and domestic outsiders into the sucker group. In fact, of course, foreigners and natives could be either speculators or suckers, and as the earlier discussion of the Ashton effect demonstrated, both foreign and domestic speculators would have found it most convenient to enter and exit the capital markets of the eighteenth century through the medium of foreign bills of exchange.

The dominant foreigners mentioned at the time in both bubbles were the Dutch, and contemporary accounts credited them with being extraordinarily shrewd in picking their moments to enter and to leave. In fact, English and Irish investors played an important role in the Mississippi Bubble. Luethy mentioned the case of Jean Lambert, a director of the South Sea Company who came to Paris in August 1779 and who was expelled by Law in March 1720 under the charge that he had remitted £20 million to London in order to break the French exchange rate.[24] French investors were active in the South Sea episode. Luethy described the role of the Oglethorpe family, members of which moved freely between London and the New World and the Jacobite court in Paris.[25] Hamilton gave details of the most amazing example of all: John Law's short sale of £100,000 of East India stock in late summer 1719 at £180,000 for delivery in August 1720. That had to be covered in the summer of 1720 by buying East India stock at nearly double the agreed sale price. Law lost a fortune in doing that, and his London banker failed by the end of 1720. And all this arose, apparently, from a bet he made with Thomas Pitt in the summer of 1719 when he was initiating his system. The probable basis was to show his assurance that his Compagnie d'Occident would cause the fortunes of the British competitor to suffer.[26]

[24] Luethy, La Haute Banque, Vol. 2, p. 291.
[25] Ibid., pp. 294–5.
[26] Earl J. Hamilton, "John Law of Lauriston: Banker, Gamester, Merchant, Chief?" American Economic Review, 57(May 1967), pp. 275–6.

The depreciation of the exchange rate of the pound on Amsterdam and Hamburg in the summer of 1720 shows that speculators, whatever their nationality, first took their money to Amsterdam in June and increasingly headed toward Hamburg in July. Groeneveld dated the first joint-stock company proposal in the Netherlands as 10 June 1720 (30 May O.S.). Another scheme was presented in late July, and the remainder after 12 September (i.e., after the collapse of the South Sea Bubble). Although the Dutch schemes followed as hard upon the English bubble as the South Sea had followed the French, this does not mean that all the Dutch withdrew their funds from abroad and invested at home. Groeneveld gave many examples in the inventories of Amsterdam bankruptcies of holdings of South Sea as well as other English securities.[27] There are even orders dated 10 and 13 September 1720 (N.S.) from Portuguese Jews in Amsterdam, reputedly the shrewdest speculators of all, authorizing Joseph Henriques, Jr., in London to buy shares in the South Sea Company without limit.[28] Nevertheless, our evidence from the exchanges indicates that in September and October 1720, the speculators went home to Amsterdam and Paris. There was only one brief respite in the decline of the London exchange in mid-October, apparently in response to an effort by the Bank of England to draw on its debtors in Amsterdam.[29]

In sum, in all three episodes, French, English, and Dutch, our exchange-rate data have confirmed the importance of international movements of capital marked by Ashton-Kindleberger "signatures" in dating periods of price explosion, stagnation, and collapse. The suspicions of Dickson and Kindleberger that the bubbles were linked and that the stock mania was international in scope appear to be verified by quantitative techniques, although Kindleberger's argument that this was eventually irrational in the sense of becoming a general mania is not fully supported. The bubbles were serial, not compounding, as his argument would imply. A final note of caution must be sounded. Although the individual bubbles may have had significant periods of rationality, these did not coincide or even overlap. Given the disarray evident in the exchange rates for all three financial centers by the fall of 1720, it is clear that the immediate aftermath of the bubbles was disruptive to the international flow of capital among the European mercantile states, but it appears that the longer-run effects on their domestic economies were minimal and even beneficial, because all

[27] Groeneveld, *Economische Crisis*, pp. 79–80.
[28] Ibid., pp. 124–5.
[29] Dickson, *The Financial Revolution in England*, p. 151.

three countries enjoyed prosperity and expanding foreign trade for the next 15–20 years. More ironic is that the effects of these disruptions served to anchor firmly the financial links that had arisen between Amsterdam and London.

Appendix: Were the Mississippi and South Sea bubbles rational?

The statistical tests of the rational-bubble arguments in this chapter were performed using Faure's data for France and the *Course of the Exchange* data for England. In both cases, we ask if the prices of the shares of the Mississippi Company or the South Sea Company in fact followed a discounted martingale[30] during the period we believe outside speculators entered and left using foreign exchange as their intervention asset. The present value of the return above the market fundamental expected by speculators willing to bet that observed price increases will continue can be represented by the following difference equation:[31]

$$c_t = [(1 + r)q_t]c_{t-1} + z_t \quad \text{(with probability } q)$$
$$c_t = z_t \quad \text{(with probability } 1 - q)$$
$$E(z_t \mid I_{t-1}) = 0$$

where c is the return above the market fundamental, r is the period discount, z_t is the deviation of price from the market fundamental in the absence of market rigging, and I_t is the information available at time t.

This model defines a rational bubble. The participants will see a capital gain above the market fundamental in the next period if the bubble continues, or a return to zero expected speculative gain if the bubble bursts. If speculators are certain that the price will rise, we can see that an explosive process is under way. In each successive investment period, the price of the speculative object will rise even further, in a geometric growth process, above the fundamental price. But the longer the bubble lasts, the more probable it is that even the most avid speculators must realize that q, the probability of the bubble continuing, is falling. The speed with which q

---

30 A martingale is a repeated series of bets where the stakes are raised after each loss, so that with a positive probability of winning on each bet, the gambler may eventually win. The original term refers not to a bird, but to a piece of horse harness designed to keep the horse's head down while running or pulling a load.

31 Oliver J. Blanchard and Mark W. Watson, "Bubbles, Rational Expectations, and Financial Markets," in Paul Wachtel, ed., *Crises in the Economic and Financial Structure* (Lexington, MA: Lexington Books, 1982), pp. 297–8.

falls determines in the empirical analysis the duration of the bubble, and therefore its final height. So long as the parameter q does not fall too rapidly, a so-called rational bubble can occur in the price of the underlying asset. According to Tirole, a rational bubble with a finite horizon must meet two further stipulations. First, expectations must be myopic; sequential traders look only at the expected trading options in this period and the subsequent period, always believing they are not locked in for any longer time. Law initiated, and the South Sea directors imitated, the practice of paying for stock subscriptions in monthly installments, later changed to quarterly installments. That had the desired effect of creating precisely this kind of myopia by the first purchasers of the new stock issues. Second, there must be several "generations" of traders entering the market.[32] The device of issuing several subscriptions of additional stock was an essential element in the capital expansion of both the Compagnie des Indes and the South Sea Company. That also created, as we noted on the foreign exchange graphs, successive "generations" of outside speculators. From the theoretical viewpoint, then, sufficient conditions appear to have been in place to warrant asking whether or not each episode was a rational bubble.

For the Mississippi Bubble, the effective period during which we might find a rational bubble, or the "wise plan" in Faure's words, turns out to be from mid-July 1719 to the end of November (N.S.). However, Faure's daily price data do not begin until 1 August; so that determines the start of our test period for the French episode. Our empirical exercise is to take the first differences of the natural log transforms of the daily price quotes available from Faure and then to search for a detectable time-series pattern that is significantly different from "white noise" or a "random walk." This is equivalent to a weak test for market efficiency in the sense of Fama.[33] For purposes of claiming market efficiency, such searches for time-series patterns should yield (o, o) autoregressive, moving-average (ARMA) models (i.e., there is only white noise or random, unpredictable movements in the price changes). Formally,

$$d \ln P_t = o(d \ln P_{t-1}) + o(e_t) + u_t$$

so that each period's proportional change in price is just the random variable u_t with zero mean and a fixed variance and does not reflect the

[32] Jean Tirole, "On the Possibility of Speculation Under Rational Expectations," *Econometrica*, 50(September 1982), pp. 1170, 1175.
[33] Eugene Fama, "Efficient Capital Markets: A Review of Theory and Empirical Work," *Journal of Finance*, 25(May 1970), pp. 383–423.

previous period's proportional change in price, in which case it would be autoregressive, or the deviation from the mean proportional change in price (e_t), in which case it would be a moving average.

This is what we hope to find during periods before and after bubbles. During the bubbles, however, we should find a predictable movement, preferably described as an autoregressive movement with positive coefficients. Formally,

$$d \ln P_t = a_1(d \ln P_{t-1}) + 0(e_t) + u_t$$

This would be consistent with two or more classes of traders anticipating further price increases with some probability greater than zero. It may also be consistent with a steady growth process in market fundamentals, but changes in market fundamentals during the brief periods we are analyzing here are more likely to show up as moving-average processes. Formally,

$$d \ln P_t = 0(d \ln P_{t-1}) + b_1(e_{t-1}) + u_t$$

A predictable pattern that is best described as a moving-average process, then, may be consistent with a rational bubble, but it probably indicates instead an innovation in market fundamentals.[34]

Table 4A.1 summarizes the statistical results for the Mississippi Bubble. Taking the period from 1 August through 29 November 1719 (N.S.) for prices of the second subscription of shares of the Compagnie d'Occident (the so-called *filles*), we find that the best-fitting ARMA model is a (5, 0), meaning that the log of the change in price had a statistically significant dependence on the log of the change in price in each of the previous five periods. This is with daily data, but ignoring gaps that occurred frequently, not only regularly for each Sunday but also irregularly for religious and state holidays. If missing values for the holidays are filled in either by naive extrapolation from the last quoted price or by linear interpolation in the logarithms of the prices before and after the holidays, then a (0, 2) ARMA is selected. Checking for the best model on the run of prices from 20 November 1719 to 1 March 1720, we find it to be a (0, 0), or a random walk.

If we take the first results, ARMA (5, 0), they may indicate that a rational bubble with as many as five separate classes of traders was in progress during the period of the significant price rise in the shares of the Compagnie d'Occident and that an efficient market ruled until the system

---

[34] Moving-average processes are generally found, for example, when ARMAs are estimated on data series with missing entries, entry errors, or outliers.

TABLE 4A.1
Estimated ARMA models for Compagnie des Indes stock
during the Mississippi Bubble

Time period	Version 1[1] (n=78)	Version 2[2] (n=103)	Version 3[3] (n=103)
1 August to 29 November 1719	(5, 0)	(0, 2)	(0, 2)

[1]   All missing observations (each Sunday, plus all holidays) were omitted, giving a compressed time series. This may be a valid representation if traders simply halted their expectations or if no new information occurred on nontrading days.

[2]   The missing observations for holidays were interpolated naively by setting each equal to the last observation.

[3]   The missing observations for holidays were interpolated linearly in logs.

began its collapse in the spring of 1720. This would conform with Faure's judgment that "la folie de Law . . . est une folie raisonnée et raisonnante."[35] If we prefer to take the (0, 2) ARMAs, however, we find, when some allowance is made for the missing observations during holidays, that they indicate that Law's frequent interventions in the market to create the rise in prices acted as erratic shifts in market fundamentals to which participants reacted at different speeds. This interpretation conforms better to the more traditional analyses of Luethy and especially Levasseur.[36]

The same efficiency test used for the stock of Law's Compagnie d'Occident can be used for the major three English stocks – Bank of England, East India Company, and South Sea Company – using the daily price data from the *Course of the Exchange* (Figure 4.5). The results are listed in Table 4A.2. The best models are found for each stock in each of five separate subperiods that can be distinguished by exchange-rate movements. The first is the pre-bubble period for England, but the height of the Mississippi Bubble in France. Both the South Sea stock and the Bank of England stock show evidence of disturbances, but East India stock does not. The next period, 19 January to 5 April, continues to show nothing for

[35] "Law's madness was a reasoned and reasoning madness." Faure, *Le Banqueroute de Law*, p. 233.
[36] E. Levasseur, *Récherches Historiques sur le Système de Law* (Paris: Guillaumin et Cie, 1854); Luethy, *La Haute Banque*.

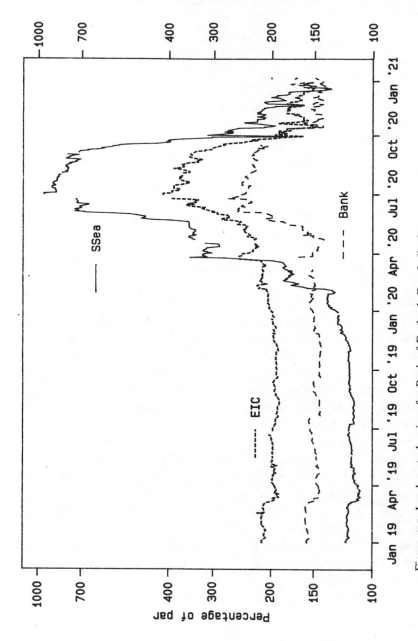

Figure 4.5. London stock prices for Bank of England, East India Company, and South Sea Company, 1719–20.

TABLE 4A.2
Estimated ARMA models for Bank of England, East India Company,
and South Sea Company during the South Sea Bubble[1]

Time Period	B of E[2]	EIC	SSC[3]
4 September - 18 November 1719 ($n = 65$)	(0, 3)	(0, 0)	(0, 1)
19 January - 5 April 1720 ($n = 67$)	(-, -)	(0, 0)	(2, 0)
20 April - 22 June 1720 ($n = 55$)	(0, 0)	(0, 0)	(1, 0)
29 June - 31 August 1720 ($n = 55$)	(0, 3)	(0, 2)	(0, 2)
4 September - 15 December 1720 ($n = 89$)	(-, -)	(0, 5)	(0, 0)

[1]   The program searched for the "best" autoregressive (AR) model up to 5 lags on first differences of the natural logarithms of the stock prices. Then the addition of moving-average models up to 5 terms for each AR model was compared. The one that minimized the expression

$$\log [\, \sigma^2_k + 2k/n \,]$$

where σ^2_k is the sum of squared residuals for the given model, k is the sum of terms in the AR and MA models, and n is the number of observations, was then selected as the best model. E. J. Hannan and J. Rissanen, "Recursive Estimation of Mixed Autoregressive-Moving Average Order," *Biometrika*, 69 (January 1982), pp. 81-94; "Correction," 70 (January 1983), p. 303.

[2]   One missing observation for 18 September 1719 was set equal to previous observation. At this point there is a one-time drop in price of Bank of England stock; without this, the estimated ARMA would be (0, 0). No ARMA was run for the period of the bubble, 19 January - 5 April 1720, or the post-bubble period, 4 September - 15 December 1720 because many observations are missing (5 - 23 March; 16 - 30 September) during those periods when the transfer books were closed for payment of dividends. There was a run on the bank in the period 29 June - 31 August 1720 [ARMA = (0, 3)].

[3]   The (2, 0) ARMA during the 5 January - 20 April phase had parameter values of 0.097 and 0.313. The (1, 0) ARMA during the 20 April - 22 June phase had a parameter value of 0.48.

East India stock, but a strong second-order autoregressive process occurs for South Sea stock. This implies that different groups of market participants were using the same information at different times – a bandwagon effect with different players for different sets. This conforms to the type of situation Tirole posits as necessary for a bubble period, as well as Scott's portrayal of the market rigging performed by the inner circle of South Sea

Company directors. (No model was picked for the Bank of England stock, because 2.5 weeks of observations were missing during the period they closed the transfer books to pay dividends.) In the following period, which is regarded as the height of the madness, according to the historical accounts, neither East India nor Bank of England stock shows anything but white noise, and though the South Sea stock continues to have a strong autoregressive movement in its growth rate, it is a first-order rather than second-order process. However, the fourth period, which is taken as the lull before the storm in the traditional accounts, shows marked disturbances for each stock. The post-bubble period shows continued disturbances for East India stock, perhaps because the directors of that company began to make loans on the security of East India shares, but none for the South Sea Company stock. During that period, everyone knew that a reorganization and settlement of accounts would take place for the company, but no one knew what it would be until 1721.

Table 4A.3 shows the best ARMA models for South Sea stock and their estimated coefficients during various subperiods of the bubble period when exchange-rate signatures occurred (sudden rises and relapses in the value of the pound sterling). The strongest bubble process appears to involve the period 23 February through 15 June, in the sense that the coefficients are highest in this period for both lagged terms. An anomaly does appear in the period 23 February to 16 May, when the best model is a (0, 2) or second-order moving-average process rather than an autoregressive process. The explanation technically is that the first-order term is very small in the AR process as well as in the MA process, and the selection technique takes the lowest-order AR model before it begins mixing in MA models. The explanation economically may be that in the early stages of the bubble, the second-generation investors were more important for getting the bubble under way. The "insiders" were clearly trying to get the "outsiders" into the game. Their maneuvers to accomplish this may be seen in theoretical terms as shifts in market fundamentals – and therefore are as likely to create an MA process as an AR process. It is interesting that the coefficient for the second-order term in the AR process estimated for the various subperiods is relatively constant, ranging from 0.28 to 0.31, whereas the first-order term is as low as 0.07 and as high as 0.21. This appears to be the statistical counterpart of the phenomenon reported by Dickson – that the bubble kept gathering its own momentum, so that the last two issues of stock were not at the initiative of the inner ring of the directors, but rather

TABLE 4A.3
Comparison of ARMA models for South Sea
stock price changes in different bubble periods

Time Period	Best Model	Estimated Coefficients[1]
19 January - 5 April 1720[2] (n = 67)	(2, 0)	[0.099, 0.31]
23 February - 16 May 1720[3] (n = 71)	(0, 2)	[0.095, 0.32]
23 February - 15 June 1720[4] (n = 97)	(2, 0)	[0.200, 0.31]
23 February - 22 June 1720[5] (n = 103)	(2, 0)	[0.210, 0.28]
5 July - 17 August 1720[6] (n = 37)	(0, 0)	

[1] The coefficients of the ARMAs were estimated with constant term suppressed. The exact-likelihood method of Ansley was used. Craig F. Ansley, "An Algorithm for the Exact Likelihood of a Mixed Autoregressive-Moving Average Process," *Biometrika*, 66 (1979), pp. 59-65.

[2] Bubble period between exchange-rate signatures, the sudden rises and relapses described earlier as the combined Ashton-Kindleberger effect.

[3] Bubble period between exchange-rate signatures. Linear interpolation of natural logs for missing data on 15, 18, and 19 April. When a (2, 0) ARMA process [a close second choice to the (0, 2)] was estimated for this episode, its parameters were [0.07, 0.29].

[4] Bubble period between exchange-rate signatures. Linear interpolation of natural logs for missing data on 15, 18, and 19 April.

[5] Bubble period from exchange-rate signature to data break. Linear interpolation of natural logs for missing data on 15, 18, and 19 April.

[6] Post-bubble period marked with exchange-rate signatures. When a (2, 0) ARMA process was estimated for this episode, its parameters were [-0.65, -0.32].

were their responses to the tremendous demand for new stock.[37] Our confidence in our finding that the South Sea Bubble was rational is strengthened by the fact that despite using the same procedures for identifying a rational bubble in Bank of England or East India Company stock, none was found for either in any of the five subperiods before, during, and after the South Sea Bubble. Although we have not examined prices of other assets, such as land or buildings, Dickson makes the interesting observa-

[37] Dickson, *The Financial Revolution in England*, pp. 126–8.

tion that greatly inflated prices sometimes quoted for real assets during the height of the bubble were generally for payment in South Sea stock, implying that the price would have been much less if payment had been made in cash or bank deposits.[38] If this is correct, then it is further evidence that the South Sea Bubble, meaning simply the accelerating rise in price of South Sea stock that occurred in the spring and summer of 1720 and nothing more, was a rational bubble. That is, it was not just a response to changes in market fundamentals, at least during the period that foreign money was entering the London market, nor was it irrational in the narrowest sense that our specific definition of "rational bubble" implies.

[38] Ibid., p. 147.

5. The Bank of England and the South Sea Company: how the bubbles ended

Adam Anderson's detailed description of the events of the South Sea Bubble has remained the authoritative source for all subsequent analysis of this fascinating episode at the dawn of financial capitalism.[1] Anderson's theme was simply that an inner ring of the South Sea directors had bribed the government into allowing them to hoodwink the holders of the existing government debt. That was the immediate, politically palatable, verdict reached as well by Robert Walpole. Because of his leadership in the financial reconstruction that followed the collapse of the bubble, Walpole became prime minister, and his term of office (1720–42) remains the longest in British history. All subsequent historians have echoed his verdict, with minor variations of emphasis on the political intrigues of the time, general corruption in the government and the society, the peculiar nature of the South Sea Company, or the infections from international speculative fevers.[2]

It is clear that the South Sea episode included a swindle by a subset of the directors of the company, as well as widespread bribes to high officials, court favorites, and members of Parliament that were in some cases quite large. It is not clear, however, that swindling and bribery were the primary elements in the situation. Although the directors of the company were fined severely, all of their estates being expropriated save for the £5,000 to £10,000 capital necessary for an eighteenth-century London gentleman,

---

[1] Adam Anderson, *An Historical and Chronological Deduction of the Origin of Commerce, from the earliest accounts*, 4 vols. (London, 1764, continued to 1788 by William Combe and published for the last time in 1801; reprinted New York: Augustus M. Kelley, 1967), Vol. 3, pp. 91–126.

[2] In addition to Adam Anderson, the standard accounts are John Carswell, *The South Sea Bubble* (London: Cresset Press, 1960), P. G. M. Dickson, *The Financial Revolution in England: A Study in the Development of Public Credit, 1688–1756* (London: Macmillan, 1967), Viscount Erleigh, *The South Sea Bubble* (New York: G. P. Putnam's Sons, 1933), William R. Scott, *The Constitution and Finance of English, Scottish and Irish Joint-Stock Companies to 1720*, 3 vols. (Cambridge University Press, 1910), and John G. Sperling, *The South Sea Company: An Historical Essay and Bibliographical Finding List* (Boston: Harvard Graduate School of Business Administration, 1962).

the company retained its charter, the government debt exchanged from South Sea stock remained converted, and foreign investors who had been attracted to the London stock market during the bubble continued to invest in English securities on a much larger scale after the end of the bubble. If the shrewd foreigners sold out before the bubble burst and took their gains with them abroad, as tradition has it, it is odd that investments by the Dutch and other foreigners in the English funds rose sharply in the next quarter century.

My interpretation, based on analysis of the daily stock prices, transfers and mortgages of Bank of England stock, and exchange rates, emphasizes, by contrast, the technical aspects of the bubble and the structural features of the securities and money markets of the time. In my interpretation, a good deal of the traditional evidence on the South Sea Bubble takes on a different meaning. It appears to be a tale less about the perpetual folly of mankind and more about the continual difficulties of the adjustments of financial markets to an array of innovations.

After the Glorious Revolution of 1688, British government finances were gradually reorganized during the next 25 years of wars on the Continent, and the London capital market responded to these changes. A new financial system based on large-scale use of foreign bills of exchange, easily transferable shares of joint-stock corporations, and securely serviced long-term government debt grew up to accommodate the government's financial needs. But its inadequacies and innovational vigor led directly to the South Sea Bubble. What this financial system required was another financial instrument to complete the existing structure. But such an instrument was created only in the aftermath of the bubble in the form of "South Sea Annuities." These were the first perpetual, as opposed to term or life, annuities issued to individuals as government debt.

Starting a bubble: the pipe, bowl, and soap

The motivation for the South Sea scheme in England was essentially the same as for the Mississippi Bubble in France that began in 1719: to refinance the immense debts accumulated by the governments during the War of the Spanish Succession (1702–13).[3] That war increased the British national debt from £16.4 million to £53.7 million.[4] For the British, the new

3 Dickson, *The Financial Revolution*, pp. 91–2. Cf. Earl F. Hamilton, "Origin and Growth of the National Debt in Western Europe," *American Economic Review*, 37(May 1947), pp. 118–30.
4 Hamilton, "Origin and Growth," p. 127.

long-term debts were accumulated largely as the £10 million capital of the South Sea Company, formed in 1711, and the £13.33 million of "long annuities."[5]

The South Sea Company was proposed in 1710 by George Caswall, a London merchant, financier, and stockbroker, and John Blunt, a London scrivener turned stockbroker. These two individuals remained the leading forces in the company until the collapse of the bubble in October 1720. In 1710 they proposed to the new government of Robert Harley that the £9.47 million of outstanding short-term war debts not secured by a specific tax be converted into equity in a new joint-stock company. This was the South Sea Company, which would enjoy the future profits anticipated from a monopoly on English trade to the Spanish Empire *and* the current cash flow on a perpetual annuity from the government paying £576,534 annually.[6] This was the same technique that underlay the founding of the Bank of England in 1694 and the New East India Company in 1698. The intention was to relieve the government's debt burden by substituting annual payments of 6% on long-term debt for redemption of an overwhelming amount of short-term debt. The new company could raise working capital on the security of its annuity from the government to exploit its monopoly privileges. The stockholders of the company thus exchanged their short-term government debentures, which were written in odd sums, deeply discounted, and difficult to transfer, for fungible and easily transferred shares in the company. These new shares were worth at least the annuity held by the company and promised further gains if the company made profits from its trade monopoly. The South Sea Company proved to be a success as a long-term funding operation of the government debt – 97% of the short-term debt was subscribed into its stock by the end of 1711. However, the government quickly fell into arrears on its payment of the annuity to the company, and so its stock did not reach par until October 1716.[7] It is clear that from the start the value of the stock was driven by the expected value of the annuity payments. These were simply 6% on the nominal capital of the company, which in turn paid a 6% dividend to its stockholders. But while the original short-term debt was selling at one-third discount, the shares of the South Sea Company gradually rose to a

[5] These required annual payments of £666,566 by the government until the end of the century. Evaluating the payments at 20 years' purchase gives the capital sum of £13.33 million.
[6] This annuity from the government yielded 6.09% to the company on its nominal capital of £9,471,324.
[7] Sperling, *The South Sea Company*, pp. 1–3, 25.

premium of one-third. The implied difference in yields to public holders of government debt, 9% on annuities versus 4.5% on South Sea shares, measures in large part the advantages of liquidity that the South Sea Company shares provided to the public holders of government debt.

By contrast, the company's trade with the Spanish Main was not successful, and the company failed to turn a profit on this monopoly. Trade did not begin until 1714 and was severely restricted in the years 1714–16 by Spanish officials in the New World. By mid-1716, negotiations with Spain directly had resolved most issues in favor of the company, but hostilities quickly arose between the English and Spanish governments. Although these culminated in a decisive English naval victory in the battle of Cape Passero in late 1718, some of the South Sea Company's ships and assets were seized by Spain.[8] The directors subsequently turned their attention fully to the further conversion of government debt, the one thing they could do well.

The second form of government debt incurred during the War of the Spanish Succession concerned annuities. These financial instruments had been introduced into British finance by William III in 1694. A stated amount of pounds sterling, which could be set at any level by the purchaser at the time of sale, was guaranteed to be paid to the registered owner of the annuity. These fixed payments were made so long as the nominee was alive, in the case of life annuities, or so long as the stated term of the annuity, in the case of term annuities. The owner of either was given a "Standing Order" to be presented at the Exchequer to claim the semiannual payments. In the case of life annuities, each time the owner, or the owner's agent, generally one of the London goldsmiths, collected the payment, evidence had to be presented that the nominee was alive. This usually was a note from the parish priest or local justice of the peace. All the life annuities created during the War of the Grand Alliance (1688–97) had a reversionary clause that enabled annuitants to convert to a fixed-term annuity on payment of an additional lump sum. Because the life annuities required semiannual notes that the nominee was alive, they were all voluntarily converted to long-term annuities within a few years. Only term annuities were offered to the public during the War of the Spanish Succession.

The Standing Orders for any annuity, life or term, at the Exchequer were assignable, but only in whole, not in part. That made them awkward to

---

8 Ibid., p. 24.

handle as legacies in cases involving more than one heir. It also meant that
they were not easily traded, a defect made worse by the variety of odd and
often large sums in which they were denominated. Moreover, the assignments or transfers of the Standing Orders were not recorded by the Exchequer. The Exchequer maintained only the initial subscription ledgers and
recorded the payments made against the Standing Orders presented at each
payment period. So while transfers were possible, they were very cumbersome, and it was expensive to prove title after a transfer or assignment had
been made. As a result, transfers of Exchequer annuities were few compared with transfers of shares in the joint-stock companies, occurring probably at one-tenth the rate.[9]

After the Treaty of Utrecht in 1713, a substantial boom occurred in the
London stock market that affected the shares of all the joint-stock corporations and raised the average price of a share from 100% to 120% of par by
early 1717.[10] Consequently, the government expected that it could reduce
its debt service by buying up high-interest, but difficult-to-trade, debt with
new issues of low-interest, readily marketable debt. It began that operation
with the Conversion Acts of 1717, initiated by Walpole, then chancellor of
the Exchequer. The final legislation enacted after he left office in 1717 permitted the conversion of several minor types of government obligations –
the "Lottery Loans" of 1711–12 and the "Banker's Annuities" of 1705 –
to redeemable annuities yielding 5%. These were managed by the Bank of
England instead of the Exchequer. That meant that transfers were recorded,
and the annuities could be assigned in part as well as in whole. Overall, the
floating debt of Exchequer bills was reduced substantially, a sinking fund
was established for reducing the national debt, and annual debt service was
reduced 13%.[11]

Walpole had originally proposed that the long annuities, with terms of 99
years, issued during the War of the Spanish Succession, also be converted
into the new redeemables, but that part of his proposal was dropped after
he was forced to resign from the government in April 1717.[12] The long
annuities could not be redeemed without the consent of the holders, and so

---

[9] Dickson, *The Financial Revolution*, pp. 457–67. Based on the only remaining transfer
   books from the Exchequer for that period, those of bankers' annuities created in 1705,
   only 4% of the nominal capital was transferred annually, compared with 44–50% of
   capital transferred for the Bank of England, the East India Company, or the government
   stock of 1717 administered by the bank in the same manner as its own stock.
[10] Dickson, *The Financial Revolution*, chap. 3.
[11] Ibid., p. 87.
[12] Ibid., p. 85.

they were known as the "irredeemables." Because these annuitants received nearly 7% yield on the original capital lent, they needed a guarantee
of substantial capital appreciation to compensate for the lower interest of
5% that the government was proposing to pay. But it still is not clear why
that part of Walpole's conversion proposal was dropped. Much has been
made of the high interest received by the annuitants, but more, it seems,
should be made of the annuitants' relative inability to cash in on the capital
gains that other asset holders were enjoying in the rising market of the
time. The new 5% redeemable annuities managed by the Bank of England
had risen 4% above par by the end of 1717, and their owners could readily
cash in, as contrasted with the difficulties faced by the holders of irredeemables. It may be that the London goldsmiths who held so many of the
Standing Orders saw conversion as a loss of the substantial fees they
charged to the owners and were able to muster enough political force to
block conversion. Or it may be that the supporters of the former Tory
government were especially concentrated among the annuitants and re-
sisted having parts of their portfolios administered by Whig institutions. At
any rate, the failure to convert the irredeemables was a major piece of
unfinished business that became more irksome as the stock market continued to advance (to between 130% and 140% of par by the end of 1719).
It even became a source of strategic weakness relative to France when the
success of John Law's "system" for converting France's debt became
apparent.

From its beginning, the South Sea Company was primarily an organization for the conversion of government debt. It resumed its activities in that
arena after Walpole was removed from office. In 1719, it carried out a
conversion of the Standing Orders from the 1710 Lottery Loan into new
stock issued by the company. That was a simpler version, indeed a trial
run, of the grandiose operations the company was to attempt the following
year. It is outlined in Table 5.1. In early 1719, the Treasury proposed to the
company that payments of £135,000 annually on the annuities created by
the Lottery Loan of 1710 should be capitalized at 11.5 years' purchase
(i.e., the various annuities, being in different sums, would all be priced at
11.5 times the annual sum they paid to their annuitants) and an equivalent
£1,552,250 of South Sea stock offered instead to the annuitants. The
annuitants would gain only a small percentage (3.48%) over their original
investment of £1.5 million. But that was a higher price than they could get
on the market for their annuities, because the annuity payments had fallen
into arrears. Moreover, they would gain a permanent asset in exchange for

TABLE 5.1
The South Sea conversion of Lottery Loan Annuities to company shares in 1719

Before		After
Public debtholders (actual conversion)		
Initial investment (1710)		
£1,048,111		£1,048,111
Annual receipts (for next 23 3/4 years)	(perpetual)	
£94,330		£54,221
Present value (1719)		
(@9%) £912,139		£1,236,666
(@5%) £1,294,447		(£94,330 x 11.5 x 1.14)
	Gain (@ 9%)	£324,527
	(@ 5.48%)	£-0-
Government (actual 69.85% conversion)		
Initial receipts (1710)	(1719)	
£1,048,111		£1,048,111
Annual payout (until 1742)	(perpetual)	
£94,330		£54,221
Present value (1719)		
(@9%) £912,139		£602,456
(@5%) £1,294,447		£1,084,420
	Gain (@ 9%)	£309,683
	(@ 5%)	£268,458
South Sea Company (actual 69.85% conversion)		
Initial capital (Jan. 1719)	(Dec. 1719)	
£10,000,000		£11,746,844
Annual receipts from government		
£508,000		£596,739
Present value		
(@9%) £5,644,444		£6,630,436
(@5%) £10,160,000		£11,934,784
	Capital increase (@9%)	£985,982
	(@5%)	£1,774,784
	Receipts	
	(sale of 95.56% of excess stock)	£592,800
	Less payments to Exchequer	£544,142
	Net	**£48,658**
	Value of 4.44% excess stock	£27,522
	Immediate gain	**£76,180**

one due to expire in 23.75 years, and they would be able to sell it more easily whenever it rose in value. In fact, South Sea stock was selling at 114% of par when the annuitants who converted received it in December 1719. Nearly 70% of the Lottery Loan was converted on those terms. By that voluntary conversion, the government reduced its annual payments of £94,330 on the Standing Orders to £54,240, and moreover it could then repurchase the debt it owed the South Sea Company whenever it chose. That gave the government the prospect of eventually retiring all its debt, which was seen as a great virtue at the time. But it also gave the government the power to undo the South Sea Company if its trade monopoly or financial influence was abused.

The South Sea Company benefited as well. It had contracted to increase its capital by £2.5 million if all the annuities were converted (by adding to the £1,552,500 of annuities converted a sum of £168,750 for arrears, and by a permanent loan to the government of £778,750). Because only 69% of the annuities were turned in, all these amounts were scaled down proportionately: The company's capital was increased by £1.75 million; £1.08 million went to the former annuitants, along with another £117,912 for arrears of interest; and the Treasury was paid £544,142. The latter sum was obtained by selling £520,000 of new stock at the current price of 114%, realizing £592,800. So the company was left with an immediate profit of £76,180.[13]

Everybody – proprietors, government, and the company – seems to have gained, and substantially, considering the modest amount of debt converted. If we compare the present value of the gains of all the participants using a 9% discount rate (Table 5.1), the proprietors gained £324,527 (the excess of the market value of their South Sea stock over the old value of their annuities), the government saved £309,683 (the difference in present values of their annual payments), and the company gained an increase in its minimum fundamental value (that derived solely from the annual payments received from the government) of £985,982, with an immediate gain of £76,180. No one was worse off, save perhaps the London goldsmiths, part of whose income had been derived from helping the former annuitants extract their annual payments from the intricacies of the Exchequer.

Part of the overall gain was due to a general rise in the securities market of the time, but it was achieved principally by substituting a more modern financial instrument – the perpetual, funded, and easily transferable share in a government chartered joint-stock company – for an instrument equally recent but encumbered by antiquated procedures for payment and transfer – the term annuity administered by the Exchequer. The improved liquidity of

---

[13] This is derived by subtracting the £544,142 paid to the Treasury from the £592,800 realized from the sale of the £520,000 stock (£48,658) and then adding the value of the remaining £24,142 stock at 114% of par (£27,522). Dickson (p. 89) gave a figure of £242,240 for profit on the whole operation, but he included £193,583 of claims the company had against the government that the company wrote off as part of its payment. That would be appropriate only if the company had already written off its claims previously and then had found a way to realize them.

government debt provided a gain that was shared by all parties. Nevertheless, that left the great bulk of the annuities outstanding. Therefore, much larger opportunities for financial improvement were still present, and the South Sea Company intended to exploit them in the plan it offered the government in late 1719.

Blowing up bubbles

The mechanics of the new scheme were very similar to the 1719 conversion, only on a much grander scale, with much greater possibilities of profit for the South Sea Company. All the government's remaining debt, except that owed to the Bank of England and to the East India Company, the other two chartered companies entrusted with administering the national debt, was to be subscribed into South Sea stock – provided the annuitants would accept the terms offered by the company. Holders of the £16,546,202 of redeemable government stock handled by the Bank of England would have no choice but to subscribe or else be bought out by the government on worse terms. The annuitants holding £15,034,688 worth of irredeemables would have to see the same attractions in the new South Sea Company stock they would receive as had the Lottery Loan annuitants in the new stock they received in 1719. The South Sea Company was authorized to issue new stock up to the nominal par value of the redeemable government debt they converted and whatever proportion of the long annuities (value nominally set at 20 years' purchase) and short annuities (value nominally set at 14 years' purchase) they induced to convert.[14]

---

[14] There is historiographic dispute on this point. My interpretation agrees with those of Scott (*The Constitution and Finance*, Vol. 3, p. 308) and Adam Anderson. Eli F. Heckscher, "A Note on South Sea Finance," *Journal of Economic and Business History*, 3(1931), pp. 321–4, however, asserted that Scott was mistaken and that the South Sea Company could have increased its capital stock without limit. Dickson (*The Financial Revolution*, p. 129, fn. 4) apparently agreed with Heckscher. Heckscher's argument was based on his reading of the authorizing statute: 6 George I, c. 4, section 48. That section allowed the company to raise "any Sums" it might need by calls on existing stockholders. That followed section 47, which stated the penalty to be paid by the company if it failed to take in long annuities and clearly referred to the recourse available to pay the penalty. That was not an issue of new capital stock but a call, or tax, to be levied on existing stock and was a feature also of the East India Company and the Bank of England. Section 30 of the act clearly set the limit on the new capital stock that could be issued. Section 58 went further and specified that the government could cancel the augmented capital from section 30 in whole or in part after 24 June 1727: *The Statutes at Large from the Fifth to the Ninth Year of King George I*, Vol. 14 (Cambridge: Joseph Bentham, 1765). It appears that Heckscher's English, though no doubt better than Scott's Swedish, was not as good as Scott's English.

TABLE 5.2
Key dates during the South Sea Bubble

1	1 February	Parliament passes the South Sea bill
2	14 April	First money subscription (£2,250,000)
3	28 April	Registration of two-thirds of irredeemable annuities
4	29 April	Second money subscription (£1,500,000)
5	19 May	Announcement of terms for registrants (£400 per share)
6	17 June	Third money subscription (£5,000,000)
7	22 June	Books closed for two months to pay £10 dividends per share
8	14 July	Registration of redeemable annuities (at Bank of England)
9	4 August	Registration of remainder of irredeemable and redeemable annuities (at Exchequer)
10	12 August	Announcement of terms for registrants of 14 July and 4 August
11	14 August	Fourth money subscription (£1,250,000 at £1,000 per £100 share)
12	15 & 17 October	Notification to South Sea directors of the amounts registered on 14 July and 4 August

The fatal attraction and duplicity of the scheme lay in the fact that the South Sea Company could set whatever conversion price it wished for the shares given to the debtholders in exchange for the old annuities. The higher the price the company could charge without discouraging the irredeemables from converting, the more of the new capital issue would be left to the directors to be used as they wished. If, for example, they set the conversion price of South Sea stock at the current market price of 135, £20 million of debt could be converted by issuing only £14,814,815 of new stock, leaving £5,185,185 for other uses. In the initial proposal presented 22 January 1720, they envisaged enough profit to warrant paying the government up to an additional £1,500,000 on the redeemables, and another £1,578,752 if all the irredeemables were turned in, for the privilege of carrying out the scheme. The Bank of England, on 27 January, countered with an even more generous proposal. The South Sea Company, in its response on 1 February, raised its ante to over £7,500,000.[15] The competition from the bank had forced the South Sea Company into committing well beyond its initial offer to a level that only its most optimistic calculations of what the market could bear could justify. The House of Commons accepted the South Sea Company's proposal, and it was enacted into law 7 April 1720.

The formal operation of the conversion operation began with the first subscription of stock on 14 April. That issue of new stock was intended to raise some working capital for the company, and so only money payments were accepted. None of the annuities were converted in this operation. The intended amount of new stock was £2 million, but it was quickly oversubscribed – the first quantitative sign of the extent of public enthusiasm for the scheme based on the proven advantages of increased liquidity and the prospect of monopoly profits. It was also the first indication of the inadequacy of the company's bookkeeping facilities for carrying out the conversion scheme. The amount of new stock issued was small relative to the total that was foreseen, but it was large enough to pay the bribes that had been promised to members of Parliament and officials in the government and to buy up enough redeemables to satisfy the government's requirement. Converting the redeemables purchased into new equity would increase the value of the company so long as the new shares commanded a premium. That could be maintained if the old shares maintained a premium over par, and that was likely, because the working capital obtained from the first subscription could be used to support the price of the existing stock. The new stock was not actually entered into the ledgers and available for transfer until December 1720; so only demand for the existing stock was increased, not the supply. The price rose correspondingly, from 288 on 13 April to 335 by 27 April.[16]

On 28 April the company held the first registration of the irredeemables. These were in two categories: the long annuities that had been issued for

---

[15] The clearest description of the proposals is given by Sperling, *The South Sea Company*, p. 28.

[16] These figures are in percentage of par value or, in the convention of the time, as the pounds sterling required to purchase £100 par value of stock. Stock could, however, be purchased in smaller units or even fractions, because all transfers were made simply by recording ledger entries under the accounts of both buyer and seller.

terms of 99 years and the short annuities issued for terms of 30 years. The government had agreed it would owe the company 20 years' purchase (20 times the annual annuity amount) on all the longs it converted and 14 years' purchase on the shorts. In its turn, the company offered the long annuitants 32 years' purchase, and the short annuitants 17 years' purchase, meaning that it offered both classes better terms than it was getting from the government, but with much better terms to the longs. However, it then took away that concession by charging both classes of annuitants £375 for each £100 of new South Sea stock subscribed. On that day, however, shares in the existing South Sea stock were selling between £335 and £343 for each £100;[17] so the price charged the annuitants for their new South Sea stock was reasonable if the current market price could be expected to rise further. So it is not surprising that £9,454,744 of the irredeemables, or 63%, were subscribed, nearly the same proportion as with the Lottery Loan conversion the year before. That was an overwhelming response, and the redeemables were still awaiting their deliverance!

A second "money subscription" was held the day after the first registration of annuities, 29 April, and it was quickly oversubscribed, even though the price per £100 share was raised to £400, whereas the current price of original stock was only £340. The announced issue was only £1 million, but the amount actually issued came to £1.5 million. The enthusiasm of investors (or speculators) for the South Sea conversion was mounting, and rightly so. The amount of new capital, at a minimum, would be the amount of redeemable debt outstanding plus the irredeemables subscribed, or £25 million. The first two money subscriptions were together only £3,750,000, well below the eventual total of new stock that would be created. The terms of purchase for the money subscriptions were very generous and amounted to buying on margin, albeit with fixed margin calls at regular intervals. Only one-tenth to one-fifth of the sale price was paid at the time of subscription, and the remaining payments were stretched up to three years. So these subscriptions would have been most attractive to speculators anticipating further rises in the price of South Sea stock and wanting to leverage their purchases as much as possible. But because the total sold on margin at that time amounted to only slightly over 10% of the total capital that would be in existence at the end of the debt conversion, it does not

17 Castaing, *The Course of the Exchange* (London: 1720), no. 36. Freke's competing price list, used by Scott in his classic history of the bubble, shows the range to be £332 to £344: *The Price Of the Several Stocks, Annuities, And other Publick Securities, Ec. with the Course of Exchange* (London), no. 89.

seem plausible that the money subscriptions were the primary contrivance used to blow up the bubble. They were the main device for speculators, but not the primary cause of the bubble itself.

Yet bubble there was. The price of South Sea stock continued to rise sharply, while the price of the underlying annuities remained stable. The bubble seems to have reached its peak just after the third money subscription on 17 June. The highest price, often quoted, was 1,050, found for 24 June in Freke's *Price of All Stocks,* but the more reliable source, Castaing's *Course of the Exchange,* gave a peak of 950 on 1 July. Freke's price included the dividend, which had been announced as 10% in stock,[18] whereas Castaing's price did not include it. But the jump was remarkable in both sources, and we can have no doubt that a new element was operating in the market. The new factor was that the transfer books for existing South Sea stock were closed on 23 June to prepare to pay the midsummer (29 June) dividend. So the price from 24 June until 22 August, when the transfer books were reopened, was not the spot price, as before, but rather the price "for the open[ing]" of the transfer books.

If we imagine that the spot price was unchanged throughout the summer, the difference between the time price (for delivery two months hence) and the spot price reflects the implicit interest rate or expected dividend rate. If the spot price was constant throughout, this gives a truly enormous forward premium by any standards, modern or historical, which cannot be accepted easily. But it seems not unreasonable that the spot price was constant, given that the next spot price on 23 August (740) was only slightly less than the last spot price on 22 June (765), and that the final sums to be converted were known within very narrow limits after the registration of irredeemables on 28 April.[19] Moreover, the prices of the underlying annuities began to sag at that time (Figure 5.1), and the prices of Bank of England and East India stock also began to fall (Figures 5.3 and 5.4). So it is likely that one of the most dramatic parts of the bubble, the final leap upward after 22 June, was in large part illusory and reflected not so much a buying mania as a desperate credit crunch in the London money market.

The foreign exchange rates of the period give us other evidence that a liquidity squeeze of unprecedented magnitude was pressing upon the bub-

---

[18] Anderson, *Origin of Commerce,* Vol. 3, pp. 95, 97.

[19] Whereas the first registration of the redeemables on 14 July brought in only £11,240,145 of them, or two-thirds of the total possible, the second registration of both the redeemables and the irredeemables on 4 August brought in together £5,371,071 of additional government debt, only slightly more than the £5,306,057 possible if all the remaining redeemables (mostly held at the Exchequer) had been forced to convert.

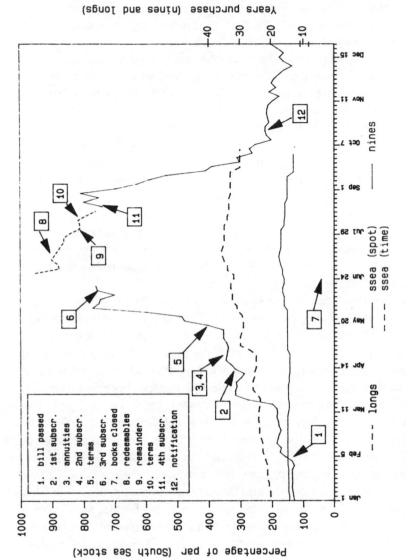

Figure 5.1. South Sea Annuities and stock.

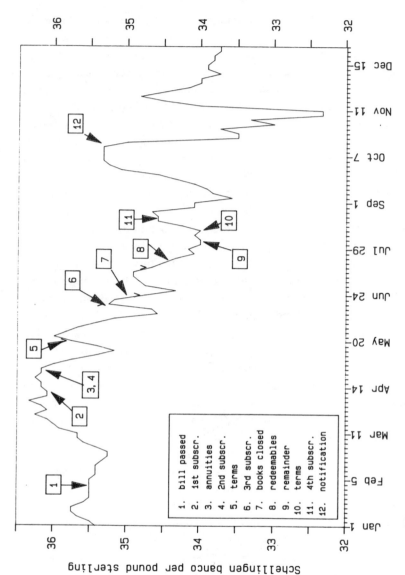

Figure 5.2. London–Amsterdam exchange rate.

ble in the price of South Sea Company stock. The rates of London on
Amsterdam plotted in Figure 5.2 indicate a credit crunch in London from
the time of the third money subscription on. Comparing the London–
Amsterdam exchange rate and the graph of South Sea stock prices, it
appears that there was an influx of foreign speculators to England in
March. Both the price of South Sea shares and the English pound appreciated throughout the spring of 1720. By the first half of May, both South
Sea stock and the London–Amsterdam exchange rates leveled off. There
then followed a marked decline in the pound sterling from 36s. 3d. on 22
April to 32s. 4d.[20] on 8 and 11 November, the lowest level of the century.
Note that the first major fall of the pound sterling occurred just before the
third money subscription, and the pound reached a very low level at that
time. This dates the beginning of the credit crunch in the London market.

The prolonged fall of the pound was interrupted by at least five sudden
appreciations of the pound, including one at the time of the third money
subscription. Those appreciations, however, were always followed by
equally sudden depreciations back to the original exchange rate or lower.
Such shocks in eighteenth-century exchange rates usually signaled a
scramble for liquidity in the country whose currency appreciated, discussed as the Ashton effect in Chapter 4. So the foreign exchanges provide
us strong evidence that credit became increasingly tight at the peak of the
South Sea Bubble. This supports our thesis that the sharp increase in the
forward price of South Sea stock on 24 June was due to an inward shift of
the supply of credit to the South Sea Company caused by external drains to
promotion schemes in the Low Countries and internal drains due not so
much to alternative promotions in the bubble companies, as the South Sea
directors suspected, as to the withdrawal of loans made on their stock by
the Bank of England, the East India Company, and the Million Bank.
Those reversals will be discussed in detail later. It was this inward supply
shift of credit that caused the forward premium on South Sea stock to rise
enormously at the end of June. An alternate explanation is that it was due
to continued outward demand shifts for South Sea stock. But that is incon-
sistent with the exchange-rate evidence, which shows scrambles for liquidity occurring at each call made on the subscribers to the first, second, and
third subscriptions.

---

[20] These are the amounts of Dutch bank money at two months usance that could be purchased
for £1 in London. See John J. McCusker, *Money and Exchange in Europe and America,
1600–1775: A Handbook* (Chapel Hill: University of North Carolina Press, 1978), pp. 42–
5, for a full discussion.

Before 23 June, however, there undoubtedly were demand shifts for South Sea stock, fueled, according to most accounts, by the increasing amounts the company loaned on its stock. It was that injection of fresh funds into the stock market that apparently caused the bubble in South Sea stock that occurred in the preceding month of May, before the transfer books were closed, and while prices were still based on spot transactions. The first lending on stock began 21 April, or as soon as cash became available from the first money subscription on 14 April. The terms were that for each £100 of stock deposited, £250 would be loaned, repayable in four months at 5% interest. A limit of £500,000 was set to be loaned, but the actual amount loaned was nearly £1 million.[21] That, according to Scott, had a double-barreled effect. It withdrew some £400,000 of stock from the supply available to the market, and it pumped another £1 million of purchasing power into the demand for South Sea stock.[22] Dickson emphasized the demand aspect more than the supply – the stock mortgaged clearly was unlikely to be sold in any event – but lacked specific evidence on stockjobbing by the South Sea directors or their agents. On 19 May the South Sea Company announced the next conversions of debt and the very favorable terms that were being given to the long-term and short-term irredeemables registered on 28 April. The company continued to grant more loans to aid buyers of additional stock. Those fresh loans were made at £400 for each £100 of shares. It was no doubt the demand for those loans that caused the third money subscription of 17 June to be taken. That was the bubble mania at its peak. Five millions of stock were subscribed (but, as in the first two subscriptions, not actually delivered) at 1,000%. Because 10% was required as down payment, the company took in exactly £5 million of cash. According to Anderson, of that sum, "the managers lent out in one day three millions, for supplying the stock market with cash."[23] By the end of June, another £1,750,000 was loaned out, and by 1 August the total that had been loaned by the South Sea Company on its stock *and on its subscription receipts* amounted to over £11,200,000.[24]

It is important to note here that the South Sea Company was forbidden by its charter from engaging in banking activities; so those loans had to be financed somehow by the South Sea Company. The Sword Blade Company

---

21 Scott, *The Constitution and Finance*, Vol. 3, p. 318. But Anderson puts the amount actually loaned at £900,000 (*Origin of Commerce*, Vol. 3, p. 95).
22 Scott, *The Constitution and Finance*, Vol. 3, p. 318.
23 Anderson, *Origin of Commerce*, Vol. 3, p. 97.
24 Sperling, *The South Sea Company*, p. 32.

had been taken over by Elias Turner, George Caswall, and Jacob Sawbridge in 1712. The latter two were directors of the South Sea Company during the bubble. Sword Blade became the major stockbrokerage firm of the period, issuing its own notes and bonds, which were accepted by the South Sea Company as cash payment. So the Sword Blade Company became the bank lending on demand to the South Sea Company to support its loans. But whereas the South Sea Company would accept Sword Blade promissory notes as cash payment, they were certainly not legal tender or bank notes. They should not be considered money, either, because they had little use as means of payment outside Exchange Alley.[25] When the Sword Blade Company failed on 24 September under the pressure of the Bank of England demanding redemption of its notes in specie or Bank of England notes, the South Sea scheme came to an end. It is doubtful that the bank ended the scheme deliberately in that way, because it had received the Sword Blade's notes as payment for new shares the bank intended to issue to take on part of the debt that the South Sea Company had converted. But it was that action that revealed to all participants that credit was indeed very tight.

To recap, the bubble blowing to 23 June was driven primarily by the lending of money on the mortgage of existing stock, and partly by the third money subscription. We can see the effects of these devices in Figures 5.3 and 5.4, which compare the prices of South Sea shares with those for East India Company and Bank of England shares. Each rose in three spurts: the second half of March, the second half of May, and during June. The first was due primarily to international speculators moving from Paris to London. The second was due to increased participation by Dutch investors and the beginning of loans by directors of the company on security of South Sea stock. The third arose from an immense increase in loans on stock, on subscription receipts, and on subscriptions made verbally.[26]

Bursting bubbles: an early scramble for liquidity

There are two things that bear emphasis from this account: (1) the importance of the market's expectation of the proportion of the irredeemables that would be converted and (2) the importance of knowing the premium over par that South Sea stock would command in the market. Also evident

[25] See the excellent discussion by Antoin E. Murphy, *Richard Cantillon: Entrepreneur and Economist* (Oxford: Clarendon Press, 1986), p. 168.
[26] Dickson, *The Financial Revolution*, pp. 140–3.

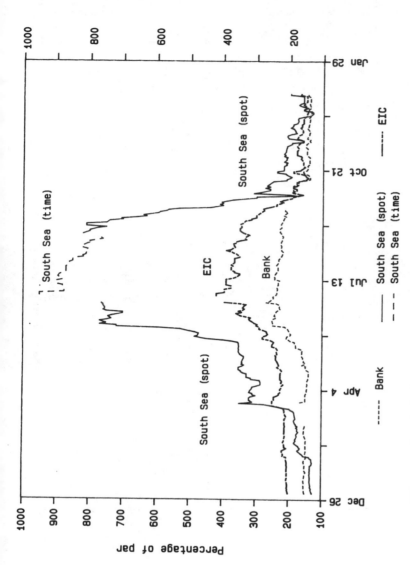

Figure 5.3: Castaing's share prices for Bank of England, East India Company, and South Sea Company.

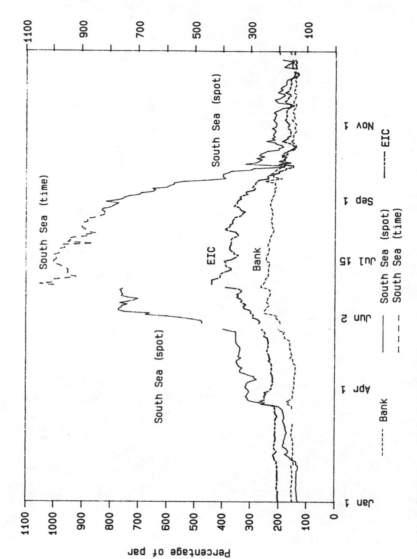

Figure 5.4. Freke's share prices for Bank of England, East India Company, and South Sea Company.

is the importance of timing, which all accounts have emphasized. My
reinterpretation comes from asserting that the very favorable proportion of
the irredeemables that were subscribed very early in the bubble and the
favorable terms given to those annuitants removed most of the uncertainty
about the market fundamental. Those terms were markedly more favorable
than had been foretold, and they created a mob-like impulse to participate
among a rapidly growing community of investors. The actions of the South
Sea directors from the third money subscription on can be interpreted as an
effort to limit participation. But it appears that in midsummer the General
Court of the South Sea Company reflected more the urges of the mob than
the machinations of Blunt, Caswall, and Sawbridge. The third money
subscription was a mistake, unlike the first and second subscriptions,
which were appropriate steps at the time and very conservative compared
with the third. And the third was a mistake primarily because the very high
price that was demanded for the stock, which may have been intended to
discourage the mob from further participation, backfired by draining £5
million from an already overextended money market. Even lending out as
soon as possible all the proceeds failed to offset the liquidity scramble that
had been caused. By that time, new investment opportunities had arisen in
competition with the South Sea Company: the so-called bubble companies
that began to be promoted in the London stock market. The most important
of these were two marine insurance companies that received their charters
in June and began to be traded on 1 July. And then payments on the first
and second subscriptions in South Sea stock – the equivalent of margin
calls – came due as well. My evidence on this point comes not only from
the high forward premium on South Sea stock from 23 June to 22 August
but also from the jolts experienced in the foreign exchanges.

The sharp rise and fall in Amsterdam rates in mid-August gave a clear
signal of the financial panic that had begun. It had been produced uninten-
tionally by the directors of the South Sea Company when they invoked a
writ of *scire facias* on 18 August against the York Buildings Company and
the New River Company. They were old chartered companies, like the
Sword Blade Company, that had changed activities from building waterworks to underwriting insurance. They had been attracting speculators
away from the South Sea Company, which then charged them with violat-
ing the Bubble Act enacted in June, which prohibited any chartered joint-
stock company from engaging in activities outside those authorized in its
original charter. That was ironic, because the charter of the Sword Blade
Company, which had long acted as banker for the South Sea Company,

authorized it only to make sword blades. So it, too, was technically operating in violation of the Bubble Act. The price of South Sea stock dropped sharply from the last half of August through the middle of October. On 24 September the Sword Blade Company bank suspended payments, intensifying the scramble for cash in a tight money market. That marked the final collapse of the South Sea Bubble.

The interpretation of the South Sea Bubble offered here tries to remove a good part of the irrationality of the participants, as characterized by most previous accounts, but it does not go so far as to argue that it was not a bubble at all, but just an example of a venal government manipulating market fundamentals. The argument that the bubble was really a reflection of shifts in market fundamentals supposes that the South Sea Company was being allowed by the English government to pursue by private funds the achievement of a general trade monopoly in England that the Compagnie d'Occident had been assigned by government decree in France. Antoin E. Murphy has justly noted that the excess capital stock the South Sea Company could offer to the public after the conversion of government debt into shares priced at 4 to 10 times par value did not constitute a current "profit" to the company, as argued by Scott and Dickson. Rather, it was a huge capital fund, a potential pool of credit amounting to £75 million, that would enable the company to exploit quickly any new profit opportunities that might arise in foreign trade or exploitation of marine resources – fishing, salvaging shipwrecks, insurance, and so on.[27] Its competitors nervously petitioned the House of Commons on 23 March 1720 to limit the future activities of the South Sea Company to the trading areas named in the act of 1 February so that it would not "oppress all private merchants in any branch of trade."[28] But the future fund of credit would have had to have been raised by selling the excess stock on the London stock market in competition with other uses of loanable funds. Without an enormous inflation in the economy, the South Sea Company's fund of credit could never have amounted to £75 million (derived by selling the stock at 10 times par). It seems even less likely that the general rise in stock prices of other companies and the proliferation of new bubble companies had been caused by the attempts of the South Sea Company to buy them out. A hostile takeover of the Bank of England and the East India Company by the South Sea Company could have been a possible future use of the fund of credit it

---

[27] Murphy, *Richard Cantillon*, pp. 161–2.
[28] Dickson, *The Financial Revolution*, p. 103.

was trying to create, but in mid-1720 it still was only a potential fund, not one currently disposable.

The question still may be asked whether or not we can measure to what degree the South Sea Bubble was a movement in fundamentals, a rational bubble, and an irrational surge. In fact, we cannot do that in the broadest sense implied by such a question: How many participants were gullible, how many shrewd investors, and how many sly manipulators, and what were the amounts invested by each? But we can refer back to Figure 5.1 and divide up the price movements into five phases. The first lasted from 1 February (131) through 19 May (355), or from the first acceptance by the House of Commons of the South Sea Company's proposal to its first announcement of terms for the debt conversion. The first phase was basically an upward shift in fundamentals caused by a proven financial innovation to be implemented on an unprecedented scale. The corresponding upward movement in the price of the long annuities, with a lag, helps confirm this assessment. The second phase, 19 May (365) to 22 June (765), was a rational bubble driven mainly by foreign investors providing an external infusion of credit to the London stock market and prompted precisely by the announcement of terms on 19 May that showed shrewd speculators what market rigging the South Sea directors were attempting. The third phase, 23 June (950) through 23 August (740), was the period when the South Sea Company's transfer books were closed and the prices were forward prices, or time prices, rather than the spot prices given before 23 June and after 23 August. The sudden jump from 765 to 950 was not part of the rational bubble, but rather a shift from spot to forward prices that revealed an enormous forward premium that reflected the pressures of the tightening credit market on the manipulators of the South Sea stock. The decline over the next two months merely reflected the convergence of the forward price to the spot price as the time of delivery shrank to zero. The fourth phase, 24 August (820) through 24 September (370), was the collapse of the bubble, caused by the unwinding of speculative positions taken during the run-up of prices under the pressure of very tight credit conditions. The final phase, 26 September (300) through the end of the year (200), reflected the uncertainties of the reorganization schemes being proposed for the company and what protection would be given various classes of subscribers and stockholders so that the price would sink below the fundamental level achieved in mid-May. Despite the collapse of the bubble and the volatility of the stock's price in the aftermath, however, it is useful to recall that the stock had begun the year at the level of 128. Any stockholders who had ignored the whole episode and simply held on to their original holdings would have realized a 56% annual yield if they had awakened 31 December 1720 and sold.

Cleaning up: the Bank of England's final victory

What role was played by the Bank of England in all this? Most accounts simply say that the bank was fortunate that its counterproposal to Parliament was not accepted on 1 February and that it withdrew in the nick of time from taking over a large part of the South Sea stock in mid-September. It was not until 1723 that the bank engrafted part of the South Sea stock into its own capital on much more favorable terms. But bank stock participated in the general stock market rise, even if the bubble in its price was very mild compared with that in South Sea stock (Figure 5.3). And on 10 May the bank allowed its stockholders to borrow on security of their shares. The terms were conservative, compared with those imposed by the South Sea Company, but were quickly liberalized, so that eventually a total of 962 mortgages were made, amounting to 29% of the bank's transferable stock.[29]

An analysis of the pattern of mortgaged stock indicates that the heaviest demanders of credit were stockbrokers. The leader far and away was Samuel Strode, with a total of £75,000 mortgaged. Another major borrower was Matthew Wymondesold, infamous as the broker for John Aislabie, chancellor of the Exchequer, who bought heavily into South Sea stock at the outset of the bubble and took £20,000 of South Sea stock as late as the third subscription.[30] The striking thing about the large sums borrowed by the brokers, however, is that they were all repaid promptly upon the calls made by the bank in late September (25%), despite evidence that a large number of borrowers failed to respond in a timely fashion and had 25% of their stock sold off from the end of October through the next April.[31]

Legend, incorporated into the standard accounts of the South Sea Bubble, has it that the knowledgeable and canny investors, meaning wealthy City of London men, represented by the Bank of England's directors and wealthy

---

[29] Computer analysis of Bank of England transfer books M and S, 2nd series, no. 35 and 41. For transferable capital, see William Fairman, *The Stocks Examined and Compared . . . ,* 7th ed. (London: John Richardson, 1824), p. 51.

[30] Dickson, *The Financial Revolution,* p. 96.

[31] Bank of England, General Court book H; entries for 29 September, 13 October, and 25 October 1720 and 6 April 1721.

Dutch merchants, sold their South Sea stock at high prices and invested their
speculative gains in safe, staid Bank of England stock.[32] The transfer
records of stock in the Bank of England, however, tell a different story. To
analyze how the South Sea Bubble was burst, it is most relevant to view the
trading activities of the directors of the bank and the 163 individuals who
gave addresses in the Netherlands. For these two groups, I have calculated
the number and value of their purchases and their sales on a daily basis. The
trading activities of the directors are summarized in Figure 5.5. The directors took longer positions in the stock of the bank immediately before the
closing of the transfer books on 8 March and up to 20 May, after the transfer
books were reopened on 8 April. After that, it appears that they reduced their
holdings, perhaps to increase their purchases of South Sea stock or annuities. After the end of August, they reduced their holdings considerably,
presumably to cover speculative losses in other assets. In sum, the directors
of the bank stayed with their investment in bank stock in the early stages of
the South Sea Bubble, abandoning it only in the most exciting period of the
bubble, and then were forced to liquidate increasingly after August as the
final collapse of South Sea prices and the other bubble companies occurred.

Legend also has it that the canny Dutch bought into South Sea stock at
later stages of the bubble and sold out at the peak. That is consistent with
their behavior on the bank stock, as they bought during the price rise, sold
during the price plateau of early summer, and then bought back heavily
during the low prices of the autumn. In fact, they ended up with cumulated
holdings exceeding those of the directors. Does this mean that as a group
they were even smarter than the bank's directors, or even the South Sea
directors, because they did not get fined for illegal participation in the
South Sea fraud or in any of the dubious bubble companies? Perhaps, but it
seems more likely that they found themselves as a group locked into
holding South Sea stock because of the paper losses they had sustained.
The sales of bank stock could have been to cover subscription calls on
South Sea stock. We saw earlier that fluctuations in the Amsterdam–
London exchange rate coincided with subscription payment dates on South
Sea stock, and the buildup of bank stock may have been in anticipation of
the engrafting of South Sea stock onto the bank's capital, a scheme suggested in September 1720 but not realized until 1723, and then on much

---

[32] Fairman, *The Stocks Examined*, p. 51: "Amidst the general speculation excited by the
subscription scheme, some of the more cautious persons sold out of South Sea Stock at
very high prices, and bought into Bank Stock; this naturally caused a considerable rise of
the latter, which got up to 260 per cent."

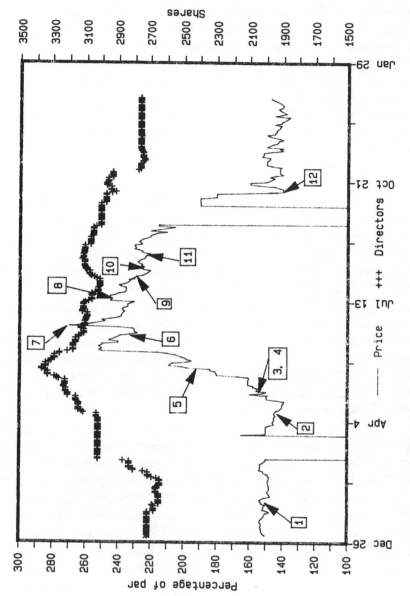

Figure 5.5. Bank directors' holdings of bank stock.

better terms for the bank than for the company. The bulk of the Amsterdamers' purchases were in units of £1,000, exactly that amount required to
vote in the semiannual General Court that would decide what role the bank
should play with respect to the South Sea Company and the remainder of
the government's debt conversion. By the end of November, the accumulated shares of the Dutch exceeded the total held by the bank's directors
(Figure 5.6). That pattern was less consistent with cautious or canny behavior on the stock market than with investors feeling that they were locked
into a dubious investment and resolving to influence the eventual outcome
by voting on decisions then being made by the strongest institution to
emerge from the collapse: the Bank of England.

The minutes of the directors' meeting in the General Court show that the
bank's relation with the South Sea Company was generally accommodating
before the bubble and most likely until the suspension of payments by the
Sword Blade Company bank on 24 September. There is no mention of
the South Sea Company as such in the year 1720 until the minutes of the
emergency meeting of 24 September. The bank was then taking in payments for subscribing £3,775,000 of new stock that would be used to buy
up part of the South Sea Company's stock valued at 400%. Notes taken in
payment drawn on Turner and Caswall and company, when presented to the
Sword Blade Company, were not accepted, and notice of that turn of events
was given to the General Court. A note was written in the margin of the
General Court's minutes: "Sword Blade Company don't pay"!

During the next week, the bank's directors took action on all fronts to
confront the obvious liquidity crisis caused by the failure of the South Sea
Company's banking affiliate, but they did so by accumulating their own
resources, and in the process made the crisis worse. By 10 November the
bank had gained strength, and the directors made a bold move. They
agreed to advance to the South Sea Company the deposit money remaining
from their mid-September subscription, but the bank governor, John Hang-
er, reported that he "did not think fit for the proposal to proceed further in
that manner." By 17 November a formal offer to the South Sea Company
was approved that insisted on much stiffer terms to the South Sea directors.
Part of the bank's aggressiveness appears to have stemmed from large
loans arranged in November through Andrew Pels & Sons in Amsterdam,
the leading Dutch merchant bankers. Dutch influence was being exerted
from the much larger presence of Dutch merchants or their attorneys in the
General Court at that time.

The next two years were given over to extended negotiations between

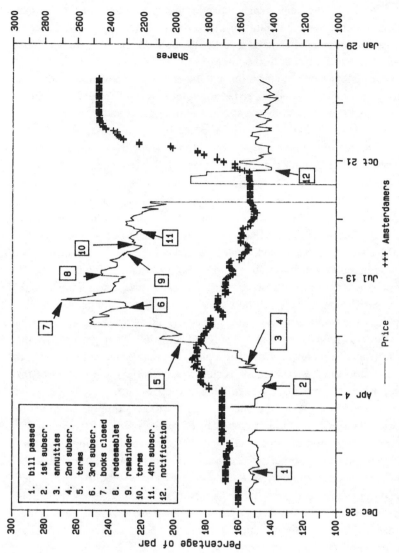

Figure 5.6. Amsterdamers' holdings of bank stock.

the bank and the South Sea Company. It was not until the end of 1722 that the new set of directors of the South Sea Company could bring themselves to acknowledge the control then being exercised by the bank. The bank's capital was increased by £3,409,000, and that of the South Sea Company was further reduced by £4 million. The final step in reconstruction was to split the £32 million of capital stock in half in midsummer 1723. One half remained the trading stock of the company, but the other half became fixed-interest stock, called the "South Sea Annuities." These were, in fact, perpetual annuities and were greatly favored by conservative Dutch investors over the next quarter century. That was the final financial innovation to emerge, and it completed a structure of financial instruments for the British government that proved its worth in each war for the next two centuries. Henceforth, the Exchequer and the army and navy could issue bills in times of emergency, and the bills could then be retired from the proceeds of selling new issues of perpetual annuities, which in turn could be retired at the government's discretion or left in circulation. The Bank of England created its first perpetual annuities in the Three Per Cents of 1726, but they were still irredeemable. The bank followed up with issues of redeemable, perpetual 3% annuities in 1727, 1731, 1742, 1743, 1744, 1745, 1750, and 1751. The latter issues were the basis for the most popular government security of the next 150 years when they were combined into the Three Per Cent Consol by the Consolidating Act of 1751.

6. The English and Dutch East India companies: how the East was won

The East India companies of the Dutch and of the English represented the most successful examples of merchant organization in the early modern era. Both exploited the possibilities of long-distance trade in highly valued exotic goods from the Orient to western Europe as well as seaborne traffic in the Asian trading world and, eventually, the potential for extracting taxes and tribute within Asia. Both confronted the problems of long voyages, delays in communications, political and commercial competitors in both Europe and Asia, and uncertain control over their agents. It was most likely the combination of the large scale of their operations, the long distances, and the lengthy transit times that led to the most important institutional innovation made by the two companies: the transformation of merchant trading or working capital committed initially to the duration of a particular voyage into fixed or permanent capital committed perpetually to the enterprise. The transformation was effected quickly by the Dutch company, apparently by 1612, whereas the English company had certainly made the transition by 1659.

After that transformation, both companies were joint-stock corporations whose shares were actively traded in surprisingly modern stock exchanges in both Amsterdam and London. The daily prices for the English company's shares are available from 1698 on, and the every-other-day prices for the Dutch shares are available for at least the period 1723–94. These are used later to weigh the relative importance of organizational, commercial, and political factors in determining the fortunes of each company over the course of the eighteenth century, when the English company overtook the Dutch. Consistent with Steensgaard's thesis, the conclusion emerges that the two companies shared in much the same way the profits arising from changing commercial possibilities and differed primarily in the way they confronted the problems of internalizing protection costs created by political conflicts. Because of differences in internal organization, the political events in Asia were more important for the Dutch, and those in Europe more important for the English.

118

The financial information discussed here has been used in summary form by modern historians, as well as by contemporary analysts in eighteenth-century Europe. Jean-Pierre Ricard, in the early eighteenth century, remarked on "the Dutch East India Company's average yearly divided distribution of 22.5 percent on the original subscribed capital," a dazzling figure that, according to the careful research of J. P. de Korte, had been reduced only to 18% by the end of the century, when the company had completed its life as a private enterprise.[1] Malachy Postlethwayt's entry on the Dutch East India Company in his 1751 *Universal Dictionary* explained that "one of the reasons why the Dutch East India company flourishes, and is become the richest and most powerful of all others we know of, is its being absolute, and invested with a kind of sovereignty and dominion, [it] makes peace and war at pleasure, and by its own authority; administers justice to all; settles colonies, builds fortifications, levies troops, maintains numerous armies and garrisons, fits out fleets, and coins money." On the English company, he remarked that "[it] is the most flourishing trading company in the kingdom, as likewise one of the greatest in Europe for wealth, power, and immunities; which appears by the ships they constantly employ, the beneficial settlements they have abroad, their large magazines and storehouses for merchandizes, and sales of goods at home, with the particular laws and statutes made in their favour."[2]

Thanks to Steensgaard's path-breaking study, we appreciate better the political significance of these new organizational forms of trade, as well as their economic significance. The studies of the Dutch East India Company (VOC) by Kristof Glamann, J. P. de Korte, and J. R. Bruijn and associates have added immensely to our knowledge of the economics of that great enterprise over the nearly two centuries of its existence as a private corporation. Likewise, the monumental efforts of K. N. Chaudhuri have made readily available a wealth of quantitative information on the trade and profits of the English East India Company (EIC), particularly in the hundred years 1659–1760, during which it displaced the VOC as the preeminent trading power between Asia and Europe.[3]

---

[1] Jean-Pierre Ricard, *La Négoce d'Amsterdam: contenant tout ce que doivent savoir les marchands et banquiers, etc.* (Rouen: J. B. Machuel, 1723), p. 400; J. P. de Korte, *De Jaarlijkse Financiele Verantwoording in de Verenigde Oostindische Compagnie* (The Hauge: Nijhoff, 1983), p. 93.

[2] Malachy Postlethwayt, *The Universal Dictionary of Trade and Commerce*, 4th ed., 2 vols. (London: 1774; reprinted New York: Augustus M. Kelley, 1971), s.v. "Dutch East India Company" and "East India Company."

[3] Niels Steensgaard, *The Asian Trade Revolution of the Seventeenth Century* (University of

120 The rise of financial capitalism

How can we organize the results of these impressive studies into a direct, quantitative comparison of the two companies? This would be useful so that we could determine the relative influences of each similarity and contrast on the progress of the two companies within the context of the northern European economy. Because of differences in internal organization, the bookkeeping practices of the two were sufficiently different that direct comparisons from the detailed records of their trading and financial activities are as difficult now as they were then. The answer, I argue here, is to be found in the quantitative price data left from the operations of highly integrated and reasonably efficient stock markets and foreign exchange markets in London and Amsterdam during the eighteenth century.

Prices from the stock markets

It was argued in Chapter 3 that the evaluations of the equity of each joint-stock company made by investors trading and speculating in their shares on the stock exchanges of London and Amsterdam were much the same as the evaluations of corporate enterprises that are seen in modern stock markets.[4] Modern finance theory suggests that modern stock markets are efficient in the sense that all information available each day to stock market traders is used fully in the determination of stock prices each day. Rumor and misinformation, as well as mistakes, will affect short-run price movements, but over the not so very long run the best information available on "fundamentals," the usual determinants of a company's profitability, will dominate the movements in share prices. If eighteenth-century stock markets were efficient in the same way, the information their price movements convey on market fundamentals will be very useful to modern historians.

Figure 6.1 shows the dramatic changes in the relative values of shares of the two trading companies as they were traded on the Amsterdam stock

Chicago Press, 1974); Kristof Glamann, *Dutch–Asiatic Trade, 1620–1740* (The Hague: Nijhoff, 1981); de Korte, *De Jaarlijkse Financiele Verantwoording;* J. R. Bruijn, F. S. Gaastra, and I. Schöffer, *Dutch–Asiatic Shipping in the 17th and 18th Centuries,* 3 vols., Grote Serie of *Rijks Geschiedkundige Publicatien,* Vols. 165–7 (The Hague: Nijhoff, 1979–87); K. N. Chaudhuri, *The Trading World of Asia and the English East India Company, 1660–1760* (Cambridge University Press, 1978); K. N. Chaudhuri, *Trade and Civilisation in the Indian Ocean* (Cambridge University Press, 1985).
4 Larry Neal, "Efficient Markets in the Eighteenth Century? The Amsterdam and London Stock Exchanges," *Business and Economic History,* 11(1982), pp. 81–100; Larry Neal, "Integration of International Capital Markets: Quantitative Evidence from the Eighteenth to Twentieth Centuries," *Journal of Economic History* 45 (June 1985), pp. 219–26.

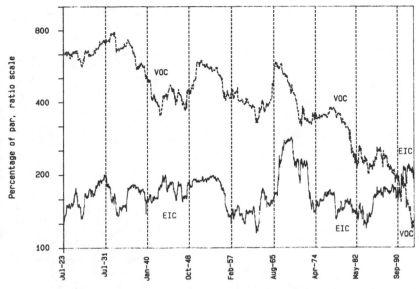

Figure 6.1. Share prices for English and Dutch East India companies, 1723–94.

market and reported irregularly in the *Amsterdamsche Courant*.[5] Although the EIC share prices varied a bit between the London and Amsterdam prices, the movements were very similar and the levels nearly identical.[6] Throughout the period 1723–94, the price of the VOC fell absolutely and relative to the price of the EIC. These are prices of individual shares. We must multiply these by the nominal capital stock in each year to get the total market evaluation of each company. The capital stock of the VOC remained constant at 6,440,220 florins throughout the period 1650–1790,[7] and the share capital of the English United East India Company remained at £3,194,080 from 1717 through 1785. In 1786, 1789, and again in 1793, its capital stock was raised in stages of £800,000, £1,000,000, and £1,000,000 to a total of £5,994,080. So the decline in share prices for the Dutch company shows precisely the relative decline in total market evalua-

5 J. G. van Dillen, "Effectenkoersen aan de Amsterdamsche Beurs, 1723–1794," *Econo-mische-Historische Jaarboek*, 17(1931), pp. 1–46.
6 See the analysis of the prices of EIC stock in the two markets in Larry Neal, "The Integration and Efficiency of the London and Amsterdam Stock Markets in the Eighteenth Century," *Journal of Economic History*, 47(March 1987), pp. 97–115.
7 de Korte, *De Jaarlijkse Financiele Verantwoording*, Bijlage 13. Divide the "Dividend bedrag" (total dividends paid) by "Dividend perc." (the dividend yield) to get the nominal capital stock.

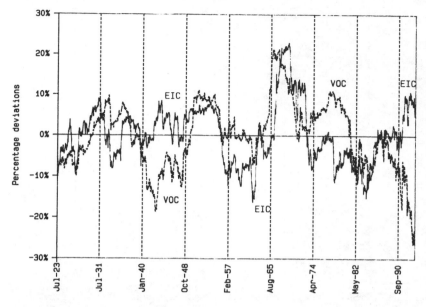

Figure 6.2. English and Dutch East India companies' deviations from trend, 1723–94.

tion. And the fluctuations in share prices for the English company show precisely the rise and fall in the market's evaluation of its total anticipated worth until 1786, when the recurring additions to capital meant that the share price understated the total equity by increasing amounts.[8]

In addition to this striking difference in trends, the noteworthy feature in the graph is the existence of long-period fluctuations in the price of each. To analyze the correlations of these between the two companies, Figure 6.2 shows the fluctuations as deviations from a simple linear, arithmetic trend for each series. This indicates that the fluctuations from the trend were roughly similar in timing, with the notable exception of the 1730s. It was in that period that the share prices of the VOC not only dropped most dramatically relative to those of the EIC but also moved inversely to, rather than directly with, those of the EIC. Figure 6.2 also shows that the volatilities in the price fluctuations of the two stocks were roughly the same.

[8] In addition to the usual cautionary statements about short-term fluctuations in "the market's" evaluation of a corporation, we should note that the price of VOC stock was really that of stock in the Amsterdam chamber, which represented only half the total enterprise. By the time our coverage begins, however, the variation of share values among the several chambers was likely unimportant.

Can these data be used to make stronger inferences about the historical forces that drove each company's profitability? Critics of modern efficient-market theory note that stock prices may reflect not only information about future profit possibilities but also information about current battles for control of company decisions that changes in ownership of stock may bring. Much the same arguments have been made about the behavior of stock prices in the eighteenth century.[9]

Josiah Child, for example, in his *Treatise Concerning the East-India Trade*, in 1681, observed that English investors were wary of buying into the EIC:

Because when we tell Gentlemen, or others, they may buy Stock, and come into the Company when they please: They presently reply, They know that, but then they must also pay 280 *l.* for 100 *l.* And when we say the intrinsic Value is worth so much; which is as true as 2 and 2 makes 4, yet it is not so soon Demonstrated to their apprehensions, notwithstanding it is no hard task to make out, that the quick stock of the English East India Company is at this time more than the Dutch quick stock, proportionable to their respective first subscriptions; and yet their Actions now are current at 440 *l.* or 450 *l.* per Cent.[10]

If Child was correct in thinking that stock in the EIC at that time was a better buy than stock in the VOC (and there is no reason to suppose he was correct), the difference in values reflected market imperfections. The exclusion of foreigners from purchase of English stock, even though the VOC gave foreigners the right to own stock from the beginning, may be an explanation. By the time the United East India Company merged the Old Company and the New Company in 1709, however, foreigners clearly were given the right to buy and hold stock in the English company. From that time, certainly, and probably from the time the New Company was chartered with permission for foreigners to hold its stock, the likelihood was small that such large differences in valuation could be maintained among the informed merchant community.

Although Child, in the seventeenth century, and all mercantilist writers in the eighteenth century (with the notable exception of Daniel Defoe) regarded the stock markets as reliable arbiters of the relative evaluations of the giant joint-stock companies of the time, modern scholars have expressed some doubts. The Mississippi and South Sea bubbles are under-

---

[9] For a critique of the efficiency of both eighteenth- and twentieth-century markets, see Philip Mirowski, "What Do Markets Do? Efficiency Tests of the Eighteenth Century London Stock Market," *Explorations in Economic History*, 24(April 1987), pp. 107–29.

[10] Josiah Child, *A Treatise Concerning the East-India Trade* (London: Robert Boulter, 1681). By "quick stock," Child presumably meant Asian goods in warehouses in Europe.

stood by modern scholars, as they were by contemporaries, as evidence of unbounded credulity by the investing classes and the ultimate irrationality of the primitive asset markets of the time.[11] Recent historians, however, have tended to upgrade their assessments of these early markets and to emphasize failures of government policy rather than institutional weaknesses in the markets.[12] I have gone so far as to argue that the South Sea Bubble was an original example of a rational bubble of the same nature as the rational bubbles occasionally observed in modern financial markets.[13]

For our purposes, this debate boils down to the question whether the course of stock market evaluations of the joint-stock companies represented merely irrational responses by a few large investors to rumors and suspicions, some ad hoc pricing rule adopted in the absence of reliable information, or some rational evaluation of the shares relative to other possible investments. The first position was stated most forcefully by Philip Mirowski, who found no evidence that share prices of the EIC were shaped by profit rates. That contrasted with his evidence that the profits of the London Assurance Company and the Million Bank determined in large part the market evaluation of their shares. It is anomalous that the London stock market could do a good job of evaluating the shares of two companies, but not of a third, larger company. Mirowski explained that anomaly by asserting that

both contemporaries and present-day historians identify East India shares as primarily a speculative purchase, due to their dependence upon such imponderables as the state of Indian politics and the relative strength of interlopers in the trade. The effect of the news must have been so extreme upon speculators in the India stock that it spoiled their ability to translate news into prospects of profitability.[14]

Mirowski used the contemporary account books of the three companies to determine their measures of profit rates, arguing that that was what the most rational investors would have had available to guide their investment decisions. In equation form,

[11] Burton Malkiel, *A Random Walk Down Wall Street* (New York: Norton, 1973); Charles P. Kindleberger, *Manias, Panics and Crashes* (New York: Basic Books, 1978).

[12] See Edgard Faure, *Le Banqueroute de Law* (Paris: Gallimard, 1977), on the Mississippi Bubble and P. G. M. Dickson, *The Financial Revolution in England: A Study in the Development of Public Credit, 1688–1756* (London: Macmillan, 1967), on the South Sea Bubble.

[13] Larry Neal and Eric Schubert, "The First Rational Bubbles: A New Look at the Mississippi and South Sea Schemes," unpublished paper, Urbana, IL, 1985.

[14] Philip Mirowski, "The Rise (and Retreat) of a Market: English Joint Stock Shares in the Eighteenth Century," *Journal of Economic History*, 41(September 1981), p. 575.

$$SP = f(PR_t, PR_{t-1})$$

where SP is the price per share, and PR is the rate of profit per share. Historians of both the Dutch and English companies, however, have been impressed by the extraordinary difficulties faced in calculating true profits, given the problems of goods in transit and of measuring working capital employed in the Asian trading world. If contemporaries were aware of these problems (and, of course, they were, because these were fundamental conditions of long-distance trade in the entire sailing era), they would have been more sensible to capitalize only the actual dividends paid out by the directors, and not take account of longer term capital gains that might be anticipated from believing dubious profit reports. Changes in a government's control over the finances of a company or in its control over trade routes and tax collections in Asia would, of course, change the assessments of the risks faced by the company.

I have performed my own tests on the performance of the markets by estimating a version of the standard capital-asset pricing model (CAPM) used in modern finance. In its simplest form, which is most likely applicable to the eighteenth century, the CAPM argues that the market value of a company's equity is the capitalized value of its annual payouts in the form of dividends. The discount rate used to capitalize the annual payouts can be adjusted to account for the risk factor that investors attach to the financial asset, as well as their expectations about future growth of dividends.[15] In equation form, this can be written

$$P_0 = D_1/(k_1 - g)$$

where P_0 is the price per share of the company's equity in time period 0, D_1 is the dividend paid out in the next time period (period 1), k_1 is the required rate of return investors demand on the stock in the next time period, and g is the expected rate of growth of dividends over time.

In the regression results presented in Table 6.1, I have calculated the expression on the right-hand side as the single independent variable, which has an expected coefficient of 1.0. In calculating this expression, I have consistently taken g, the expected growth rate of dividends, to be zero, because the period of analysis in each case is well past the initial rapid-growth phase of the company in question. The required rate of return investors demand on the stock, k, is a varying discount rate. In modern

[15] The model used is adapted from the discussion in the finance textbook by Eugene F. Brigham, *Financial Management*, 4th ed. (New York: Dryden Press, 1985), chap. 5–6.

TABLE 6.1
Regression results of the capital-asset-pricing model
for the Bank of England, the East India Company,
and the Dutch East India Company

Bank of England

Independent variable	Coefficient	Standard error	t value	Significance level
CAP(adj.)	0.999	0.015	67.72	0.0000

R^2(adj.) = 0.99; SE= 5.82; MAE= 4.1; DW= 1.77; rho = .667; 70 observations (1724-94)

English East India Company

Independent variable	Coefficient	Standard error	t value	Significance level
CAP(adj.)	0.925	0.045	20.67	0.0000

R^2 (adj.) = 0.86; SE = 17.39; MAE = 12.78; DW= 1.93; rho = .75; 70 observations fitted (1724-94)

Dutch East India Company

Independent variable	Coefficient	Standard error	t value	Significance level
CAP(adj.)	0.913	0.038	24.35	0.0000

R^2 (adj.) = 0.92; SE = 45.24; MAE= 32.813; DW=1.62; rho = .675; 54 observations fitted (1724-58)

English East India Company[1]

Independent variable	Coefficient	Standard error
CONSTANT	164.73	21.36
PR	0.190	0.37
PR-1	0.246	0.48
WAR3	425635.4	0.317

R^2 = 0.001; F = .20; 100 observations fitted (1710-1810)

Note: The dependent variable in each regression is the average annual share price; CAP(adj.) is the calculated average based on dividend rates, risk-free interest rates, and risk factors, as described in the text; SE = standard error of the regression; MAE = mean absolute error; DW is the Durbin-Watson statistic.

[1] Philip Mirowski, "The Rise (and Retreat) of a Market: English Joint Stock Shares in the Eighteenth Century," *Journal of Economic History*, 41 (September 1981), p. 575.

finance, it is a composite of the short-term return on a risk-free asset actively traded in the capital markets plus a risk factor based on the volatility of the capital markets plus a risk factor for the stock in question that takes into account its volatility relative to that of the entire market. I used the one-year holding return on Three Per Cent Consols in the London

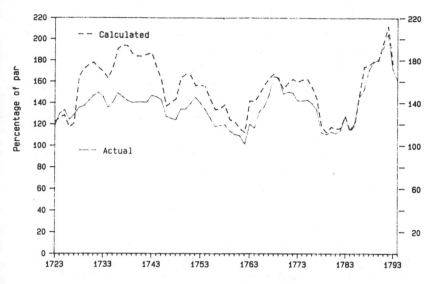

Figure 6.3. Bank of England shares, CAPM. The calculated price is annual dividends divided by the annual holding-period yield on consols. It has no risk adjustments.

market as my measure of the one-period return on a risk-free asset.[16] The data necessary to calculate the market's volatility as a whole are not available for periods after 1733 (see Chapter 3); so an arbitrary risk factor, the beta coefficient in the opaque terms of modern finance, was added into the calculation for each company's stock at certain periods. The graphs in Figures 6.3 through 6.5 plot the annual average share price against the CAPM-calculated share price without adding any risk factors. They show clearly which periods had greater risks for shareholders, because in those periods the actual share prices were consistently below the calculated share prices, even though the annual movements were very similar.

For the Bank of England's share prices (Figure 6.3), the model shows good tracking ability of the fluctuations throughout the 72-year period. In

[16] That required extrapolating the actual Three Per Cent Consol returns back from 1753, when they began to be quoted in the *Course of the Exchange*, to 1723, when the price quotes for the VOC began in the *Amsterdamsche Courant*. That was done by using the return on the Bank of England's Three Per Cent Annuity, the precursor of the famed Three Per Cent Consol, until 1726, when the bank issued its first annuity. For the remaining three years, the return on the South Sea Annuities issued in the aftermath of the bubble was used, because that was the largest single issue of security and was the most stable in price of any asset in that period.

the years 1728–45, however, there clearly was an additional risk factor
attached by investors to the bank's stock, a risk factor that was considerably reduced over the next period, 1746–76. Thereafter, bank stock appears to have been as risk-free as the Three Per Cent Consols. The first
period perhaps reflects the uncertainty attached to the bank's attempt to
take up the functions of the moribund South Sea Company as financier to
the government. Not only had the bank engrafted part of the stock of the
South Sea Company to its own in 1723, but from 1726 onward it also
issued annuities that turned out to be the precursors of the Three Per Cent
Consols. In 1742 its services to the government were rewarded by renewal
of its charter to 1764 and a strengthening of its monopoly position as the
nation's only joint-stock bank. The effect of that was delayed by the panic
caused in 1745 by the advance of the Stuart pretender to the throne to
within 127 miles of London. The bank's charter was renewed in 1764 and
again in 1782. It benefited in 1774 from the recoinage, which reduced the
price of gold from £4 1s. to £3 17s. 6d.[17] So the deviations of the CAPM-
calculated share prices from the actual share prices appear to be consistent
with the changed risks to shareholders as a result of the periodic changes in
the bank's relation to the government. In the regressions reported in Table
6.1, a risk adjustment factor of 1.3 was applied during the first period, and
1.1 during the third.

In the case of the EIC (Figure 6.4), a comparable risk factor evidently
was in play during the period 1723–56. During the first few years following the Seven Years' War, the model tracks very closely indeed and then
begins to diverge erratically from 1767 to 1772. Thereafter, although the
levels predicted by the model are close to those actually realized, the
annual movements are erratic. Fairman's account of the financial history of
the company explains convincingly the source of these deviations of the
model:

Early in 1764, the receipt of very unpleasant news from Bengal immediately caused
India stock to fall 14 per cent. The general administration of the Company's affairs,
both at home and abroad, became afterwards the subject of much discussion; and,
on the 29th August, 1766, the Court of Directors received a notice from the
Secretaries of State, that an investigation would take place in the next Session of
Parliament; in consequence of which the price of their stock fell from 230 . . . to
206, but . . . the dividend being increased to 10 per cent., it got up considerably,
the average price of the whole year being 254.[18]

[17] A. Andreades, *History of the Bank of England, 1640–1903*, 4th ed. (New York: Augustus
M. Kelley, 1966), pp. 143–59.
[18] William Fairman, *The Stocks Examined and Compared . . .* , 7th ed. (London: 1824), p.
125.

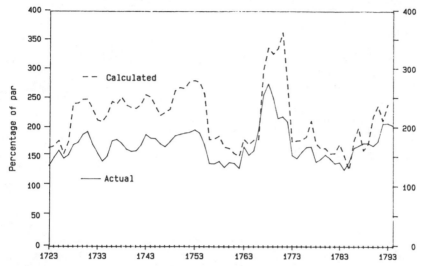

Figure 6.4. East India Company shares, CAPM. The calculated price is annual dividends divided by the annual holding-period yield on consols. It has no risk adjustments.

The Regulating Act of 1772 followed, which brought the company under the uncertain control of the government. The political uncertainties and financial consequences of that transition of the EIC – from a profit-making holding company operated for the benefit of participating merchants and shipowners to an instrument of the power of the British state in Asia – have been admirably discussed and analyzed by Lucy Sutherland.[19] The vicissitudes of the company's financial dealings with the state, which required annual payments of £400,000 by the company to the Treasury, while the Treasury guaranteed the assumption of Indian debts by the company, have been detailed by Fairman. These are clearly beyond the capacity of the model to capture. So the regression results reported for the EIC in Table 6.1, which include the observations for the entire period 1723–94, are less compelling than the results for the other companies.

The data for the VOC (Figure 6.5) show marked divergence from the model at the outset in the mid-1720s and then track fairly well until a risk factor appears to be at work from 1743 until 1757. It was in that period that the state was paid yearly an amount equal to 3% of the annual dividend as the price for extending the charter of the VOC from 1740 to 1756. Thereafter, the data track well until 1776. In the period 1755–74 the VOC was

[19] Lucy S. Sutherland, *The East India Company in Eighteenth-Century Politics* (Oxford: Clarendon Press, 1952).

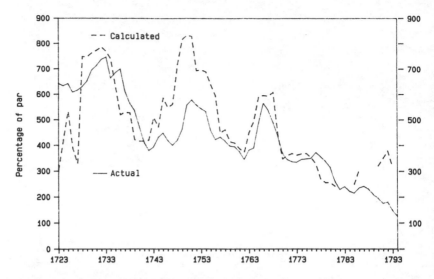

Figure 6.5. Dutch East India Company shares, CAPM. The calculated price is annual dividends divided by the annual holding-period yield on consols. It has no risk adjustments.

able to settle its pledge of 1,200,000 florins to the government by delivering saltpeter.[20] After that, chaos sets in for the model, but as in the case of the English company just discussed, this reflects the growing financial difficulties of both the company and the government, which led to formal control of the company by the state in 1785, after several years of skipped dividends. As with the Bank of England and the EIC, the deviations of the CAPM-calculated stock value from the actual prices of the VOC stock appear quite explainable in terms of the changes in the financial constraints placed on the company by the Dutch government. The first five years and the period after 1782 are omitted in the regression results reported in Table 6.1, and a risk factor of 1.3 is applied during the interval 1745–56.

The regression results are very encouraging to proponents of the idea that participants in the stock markets of the Age of Reason were rational in their economic behavior. The independent variable in each regression is the calculated value of the share price, assuming that the markets were efficient and that our measures of the risk factors are correct.[21] The coefficient

---

[20] Bruijn, Gaastra, and Schöffer, *Dutch–Asiatic Shipping*, Vol. 1, pp. 7–8.
[21] The regression estimates were done using generalized least squares, and the rho values shown for first-order autocorrelation were used to correct for serial correlation. The coefficient of determination was adjusted for first-order serial correlation in the residuals.

on the CAPM independent variable is statistically significant in each case and is very close to the theoretical value of 1.0 for the Bank of England and the two East India companies. The total variance explained by the simple regressions is quite high. For the EIC shares, the CAPM results provide a market contrast to the dismal results found by Mirowski. But they are all the more convincing because the CAPM also does well for the VOC and gives nearly perfect results for the Bank of England.

For our present purpose, relating merchant activity to the course of empire, these results imply that the financial markets of the time gave us important, and reliable, information. The stock prices for each company reflected regularly not only the economic calculations of European merchants but also their assessments of the political role played by the management of each company. We have a good retrospective understanding of the profits of each company (even if we are not sure how well the directors of each company understood these at the time) and a good comprehension of the political pressures placed on each company, both in Europe and in Asia. The course of stock prices for each company over time tells us how these economic and political events were comprehended by the stockholders of each company. This allows us, in principle, to determine which events were most important in determining the ultimate replacement of the VOC by the EIC as the preeminent trading entity between Asia and Europe.

The summary picture we can draw here is that during the eighteenth century the initial preeminence of the Dutch in the trading nexus between Asia and Europe was being eroded, primarily by the English, but no doubt also by others. The French company continued to do a large business in Asia until the defeats of the Seven Years' War. The Spanish strengthened their role in the Philippines, and the Portuguese continued to play an important entrepôt role in the Asian trading world. Meanwhile, the Austrian, Danish, and Swedish companies made inroads in the Baltic–Asian trade previously monopolized by the Dutch. That may be the inevitable lot of the pioneer profiteer, but the decline took a long time and had an interesting history during its course. When the stock prices of the two companies moved in similar patterns relative to the trend, we may infer that both were experiencing the effects of changed marketing conditions in either Europe or Asia. That clearly was the case during most of the century.

However, there were several intervals when the two price series moved inversely, indicating that one company was gaining on the other, at least relative to the trend. For example, the EIC lost relative to the VOC from mid-1731 to 1733, and then from 1736 until 1743 it gained sharply, with only a brief setback in 1739. From 1750 through the end of the Seven Years' War in 1763, the VOC gained relative to the EIC, especially during the war years. After the disturbances at the end of the war, the EIC did marginally better than its Dutch competitor until the Regulating Act of 1772. Thereafter, the VOC again gained relative to the EIC until it began its final collapse, leading to takeover by the Dutch government in 1787. The inverse episodes before the battle of Plassey deserve special attention, especially those in the early and late 1730s and early 1740s, a period of peace in Europe and internal stability in each company's organization.

Exchange rates

Figures 6.6 and 6.7 plot the fluctuations in the exchange rate between London and Amsterdam for the periods 1698–1722 and 1723–50. The rate is the two-month usance rate in London or Amsterdam. In that period, exchange rates were always quoted the same way in each city for ease of calculation; so the Amsterdam rates would also be somewhere near 35.5 schellingen banco per pound sterling, which was approximately 1 Flemish shilling below the mint par ratio.[22] Because these are usance rates, they include an implicit interest rate that covered the cost of waiting two months for payment in the foreign city after the bill of exchange was bought in the city of origin. The implicit interest rate meant that the quoted exchange rate would be slightly lower in Amsterdam, say 35s., and slightly higher in London, say 36s. That is to say, the guilder was worth more in Amsterdam than in London, because the guilders were paid currently, whereas the pounds were received only two months later. Likewise, the pound was worth more in London than in Amsterdam, because the pounds were paid currently, whereas the guilders were to be received two months later. Sight rates, which began in Amsterdam on London around 1706 and in London on Amsterdam at the end of 1720, included a premium paid at the city of origin for the right to obtain the foreign currency at the city of destination more promptly. So sight rates in Amsterdam typically were 2 grooten

---

[22] The mint par ratio between London and Amsterdam for that period was 36.59 Flemish shillings (Fl. s.) (Postlethwayt, *Universal Dictionary*, s.v. "Coin," 4th page of entry). That appears to have been in terms of bank money as opposed to current money (the exchange rates given in the exchange currents were for bills of exchange in bank money payable at the Bank of Amsterdam), but even so the rate appears too high for most of our period. But the actual rates observed in Figures 6.3 and 6.4 were seldom below 34.76 Fl. s., which would be approximately the specie export point in peacetime. The rate could obviously fall lower in wartime, as it did during the War of the Spanish Succession.

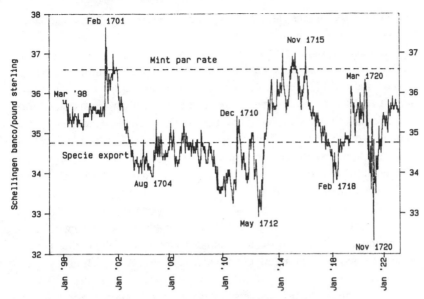

Figure 6.6. Exchange rate of London on Amsterdam, 1698–1722.

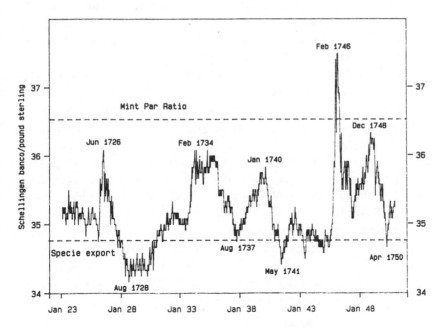

Figure 6.7. London exchange rates on Amsterdam, two months' usance, 1723–50.

higher than the usance rate, and sight rates in London were a standard 2 grooten lower than the usance rate, save during liquidity crises.

The rates seem to center about the 35s. level, but show prolonged swings between the mint par ratio of 36.59 Flemish shillings and the approximate specie point for export from London, 34.76 shillings. In the period 1698–1722, the pound fell relative to the guilder during the War of the Spanish Succession, and the fluctuations reflected accurately and promptly the exigencies of war finance. Note the especially low levels of the British pound during the crisis years of 1709–10. The South Sea Bubble shows up as a period of sharp fluctuations reflecting first capital inflows and then capital flight. In the next period, 1723–50, the fluctuations were much smaller, especially in the 1720s and 1730s. The War of the Austrian Succession had a similar but less pronounced depressing effect on the pound as had the War of the Spanish Succession in the earlier period. That reflected well the relatively smaller scale of the British effort in the latter war.

The foreign exchange markets operated on a larger scale and with a broader range of more experienced participants than did the stock markets of either Amsterdam or London; so the reliability of their market prices is much greater. However, they reflected different and broader economic forces. Obviously, the balance of total trade between the two countries could affect the relative demand for their currencies in the foreign exchange markets. But, more generally, it would be changes in the *relative* trade balances of the two countries with the rest of the world, not just with each other, that would alter the exchange rate of their currencies.

Particularly interesting for the 1720s and 1730s is the possibility of capital movements affecting the exchange rates. The price differences for EIC stock between the Amsterdam and London markets over the entire period 1723–94 are analyzed in the following chapter. There it is found that only in the period 1723–38 was a higher price in Amsterdam than in London strongly associated with a higher value of the pound sterling in terms of Dutch currency.[23] In the rest of the periods, higher prices in Amsterdam were strongly associated with a higher value of the Dutch currency. This suggested that in 1723–38, Dutch demand for English securities drove up the value of the English currency, whereas in succeeding periods a rise in the English exchange rate would drive up the value of English securities held in the Netherlands. It is interesting that it was

23 Neal, "Integration and Efficiency," p. 112.

precisely that period that P. G. M. Dickson identified as the most important period for foreign investment, especially Dutch, in the English public securities, including stock of the EIC.[24]

I have formalized and tested these ideas elsewhere.[25] Unfortunately, the econometric results were disappointing for the thesis that capital movements accounted for much of the exchange-rate fluctuations in that period. Nevertheless, it remains the case that the Amsterdam–London exchange-rate data show an unusual relationship to the mint par ratio for the 1730s, just as the price deviations from the trend of the English and Dutch companies show an unusual divergence from each other for the 1730s. What could have caused this disturbance in the foreign exchange markets and the offsetting price movements in the shares of the two companies, given the absence of war or major economic policy change?

Treasure and tea

The explanation for the dramatic rise in the fortunes of the English company and the equally dramatic decline in the anticipated fortunes of the Dutch in the 1720s and 1730s lies, according to both Glamann and Chaudhuri, in the way the two companies handled the tea trade with China. Glamann noted that the Dutch had the favored position until 1718, based on selling in European markets the tea brought to Batavia by Chinese junks. In that year, the VOC's governor general and council in Batavia decided to offer the Chinese fixed prices much lower than previously. That appears to have been a response by Batavia to orders from the Netherlands to charge higher prices to the Chinese for pepper (so that they would not be able to resell at a profit to European competitors of the Dutch). The Chinese were outraged and refused to come to Batavia at all for the next five years. The net result was that the European competitors of the Dutch began to buy tea directly from the Chinese instead of black pepper. Moreover, they found an exploding market in Europe for the better varieties of tea that were available to them in Canton. By the time the junks finally resumed voyages to Batavia in 1723, the market for their traditional green teas had been surpassed in Europe by the demand for black teas.[26] The EIC began importing tea directly from Canton on a regular basis in 1717, and each

---

[24] Dickson, *The Financial Revolution*, pp. 312, 321.
[25] Larry Neal, "The Dutch and English East India Companies Compared: Evidence from the Stock and Foreign Exchange Markets," in Tracy, ed., *The Rise of Merchant Empires*.
[26] Glamann, *Dutch–Asiatic Trade*, pp. 216–43.

succeeding decade until 1760 saw an accelerating rate of growth in the volume of its imports.[27] The Dutch eventually adjusted to the new marketing situation generated by European demand and different conditions of supply from China, but at a position distinctly inferior to that of the English.[28]

Tangible evidence of the relative failure of the Dutch in the new tea trade was the rise in bullion shipments relative to total exports that occurred in the 1720s and 1730s. Glamann did not give annual figures for shipments from the Netherlands to Batavia in the way that Chaudhuri did for the English company, because by that time an increasing amount of bullion could come on private account with passengers. That was especially so in the period 1724–35, when the turnover of ducatons (the Dutch-minted silver trading coin) in the general-commerce ledgers of the VOC in Batavia showed a remarkable increase from 948,739 florins in 1724–5 to over 7 million in 1733–4. Much of that arose from ducatons being shipped on private account by Dutch money dealers to Batavia and then turned in to the VOC to purchase bills of exhange payable in bank money in Amsterdam. Because the VOC in Batavia was paying a premium for ducatons in order to ship them to Canton or Bengal, speculators in the Netherlands could realize a profit of over 20% plus a 4% premium that the VOC regularly gave on bills of exchange for the interest lost during the time of transfer from Indonesia to Europe.[29] In sum, the VOC began in the eighteenth century to ship much larger sums of silver and (to a lesser extent) gold to Asia, both directly on its own account and indirectly by encouraging its passengers to smuggle silver coins to Batavia. Nevertheless, it appears from the analysis of Gaastra that it was not so much the increase in demand for silver by tea merchants in Canton that accounted for this rise, but rather the drying up of Asian sources of bullion that the Dutch had been able to tap in the seventeenth century. Preeminent was the loss of Japanese silver, but Spanish silver was no longer available to the Dutch from Manila, being used directly in Chinese trade, and even the northwestern Indian and Persian supplies were lost in the eighteenth century.[30]

[27] Chaudhuri, *Trading World of Asia*, p. 388.

[28] An excellent summary of the successful rise of the English tea trade and the failure by the Dutch is given by Holden Furber, *Rival Empires of Trade in the Orient, 1600–1800* (Minneapolis: University of Minnesota Press, 1976), pp. 129–35, 140–4.

[29] Glamann, *Dutch–Asiatic Trade*, p. 72.

[30] F. S. Gaastra, "The Exports of Precious Metal from Europe to Asia by the Dutch East India Company, 1602–1795," in J. F. Richards, ed., *Precious Metals in the Later Medieval and Early Modern Worlds* (Durham: Carolina Academic Press, 1983), pp. 447–76.

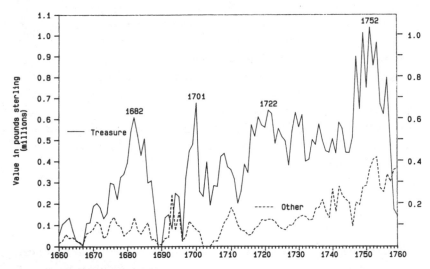

Figure 6.8. English East India Company exports of treasure and goods, 1660–1760.

By contrast, the EIC was shipping ever smaller amounts of bullion, both in absolute quantities and relative to commodity exports, during the 1730s (Figure 6.8). The apparent reason for the success of the English company relative to the Dutch was the salability of Indian goods transported by the English (mainly cotton textiles, but apparently also some opium, even at that early date) in the Chinese market. By contrast, the Dutch no longer had the textiles of the Coromandel coast of southeast India to ship to China, because of the increasing success of the French East India Company in that region. The encroachment of the English and others in the Spice Islands trade meant that fine spices could be provided in China by Amsterdam's competitors. In sum, it was not so much the loss of the tea trade in the early 1720s that damaged the Dutch relative to the English. The Dutch recovered from that setback rather quickly. But it was significant in foretelling the greater difficulty that would be faced by the VOC compared with the EIC in adjusting to competition from new companies, particularly the French.[31]

Our stock prices, it should be recalled, are from the Amsterdam market

[31] See the discussion of the growing success of the French company in the 1730s and 1740s by Paul Butel in James Tracy, ed., *The Rise of Merchant Empires*, Vol. 1 (Cambridge University Press, 1990), chap. 4.

for both the VOC and the EIC; so they show that the Dutch merchant community was well aware of the implications of these movements of bullion by each company from Europe to Asia and of the sale of each company's goods in China. The exchange-rate movements between London and Amsterdam indicated a strengthening of the pound due to the favorable effects on English trade balances of English success in the China–Europe tea trade and the India–China textile trade. That movement of the pound encouraged and abetted financial adjustments that led to a sharp fall in VOC equity valuation and a corresponding rise in the valuation of the EIC in the early 1730s and again in the early 1740s.

Conclusion

This exercise in statistical analysis of the financial data left in the historical record of northwest Europe in the eighteenth century should increase our appreciation, first, of the modernity of the financial markets of that time, second, of the rationality of the merchant community, which for the first time was trading and investing on a pan-European scale and responding to global economic developments, and, third, of the possibilities of using this overwhelming data legacy to illuminate other episodes in the course of trade and empire during that pivotal epoch.

For example, each company relied primarily on the shipment of bullion and specie, especially silver specie, to the Far East in order to effect payment for the Asian products it brought back to Europe. It appears from our stock market data that whichever company had the best access to sources of silver specie in a particular period also enjoyed at that time the greatest returns on its investments in Europe. The disturbances to trading opportunities and profits of each caused by the repeated outbreaks of war in Europe and Asia seemed to affect each company's profitability much the same way. The major exceptions were the early years of the War of the Austrian Succession and the French revolutionary wars at the end of the century. Both the Dutch and the English profited from the defeat of the French in the Seven Years' War.

The institutional structure that linked the home merchants in control of the finances of the overall enterprise with the merchants stationed in the East who had control over the trading activities of the company varied greatly between the two companies. These structural differences reflected the distinctive strategies of each company in dealing with "country," or intra-Asian, trade.[32] The Dutch controlled these activities strictly from the headquarters in Batavia, whereas the English were much looser. The Dutch company was rigidly divided into six chambers, with Amsterdam providing half the capital, but only 8 of the 17 Heeren (directors) who directed the overall affairs of the united company. The remaining Heeren were divided as follows: four from Zeeland, one each from Delft, Rotterdam, Hoorn, and Enkhuisen, and the final member rotated among the last four chambers. The charter of the English company, by contrast, was up for renewal at relatively short intervals, although those became increasingly longer as time went on. Even when the charter was not in question, stockholder revolts could easily occur, as in 1732 and again in 1763.[33] Because stockholders in the VOC delegated their powers to the Heeren XVII, their only effective means of influence was exit, rather than voice. The charter of the VOC did come up for renewal at intervals of 20 to 40 years, and at those times powerful stockholders could assert more influence. But during the Nine Years' War (War of the League of Augsburg, 1689–97) the charter due to expire in 1700 was extended to 1740 in return for a one-time payment of 3 million guilders.[34] For that critical period during which the value of the VOC declined markedly relative to the EIC, there was no threat of stockholder revolt or state control. It was perhaps that protection from internal innovation that made the VOC more vulnerable than the EIC to the external encroachment of competing European enterprises in Asia.

The greater rigidity of the VOC, and hence greater vulnerability to competitive pressures, also held true in the way it organized shipping between Europe and Asia. The Dutch ships were built and owned by the respective chambers. The EIC, by contrast, hired its ships each year until the large buildup of its own fleet during the Seven Years' War, when the Royal Navy was occupied in the Atlantic and Mediterranean war of blockade with the French navy. J. R. Bruijn argued that one cannot tell which of the two systems was more expensive. The English system appeared more flexible in form, but in fact "hereditary bottoms" appeared that were owned by a self-perpetuating shippers' group. That group exercised monopoly power over ships suitable for the East India trade and enforced it by

[32] The inference of corporate strategies from their organizational structures is now standard procedure in business history, but it was pioneered by Alfred D. Chandler, *Strategy and Structure: Chapters in the History of Industrial Enterprise* (Cambridge, MA: Harvard University Press, 1962).

[33] For 1732, see Chaudhuri, *Trading World of Asia*, p. 448. For 1763, see Sutherland, *East India Company in Politics*, pp. 141–91.

[34] Bruijn, Gaastra, and Schöffer, *Dutch–Asiatic Shipping*, Vol. 1, p. 7.

using their large holdings of EIC stock to elect a significant number of directors. The modal number of voyages for the English ships was four; for the Dutch it was six to seven.[35] Nevertheless, it is clear that the English led in innovations in navigation and construction (especially copper sheathing), resulting in shorter trips and fewer losses en route. The Dutch chambers, by contrast, were prevented from adopting foreign innovations because of the requirement for shallow-draft ships to gain access to their increasingly silted ports.[36] So although shipping prime costs per voyage may well have been less for the Dutch because of tight internal controls, it appears that the English likely enjoyed superior profits per voyage, especially after the middle of the eighteenth century, when the pace of shipping innovations began to quicken.

The marketing areas of the VOC were always continental Europe, whereas the EIC concentrated on its growing home market, and reexports of its imports were directed increasingly to the growing Atlantic empire of the British. Country trade within Asia was undoubtedly more important in quantity and value for each company than was the intercontinental trade, however. The Dutch dominated the southern Asian seas and the trade in exotic spices, whereas the English developed trade at the very edge of the Muslim world, where religious wars were always a possibility even in the absence of Christians. Finally, it is interesting to note the rallying of the VOC relative to the EIC in the peacetime period (in Europe) of the early 1770s. That clearly was due to the increasing control over the English company by its home government and its continued obligation to remit large sums as tax revenues.

The greater success of the English company in meeting the economic competition of the French, Austrians, and Scandinavians during the 1730s and 1740s enabled it eventually to achieve military victories over the French in India as well as in the Atlantic during the course of the Seven Years' War. It is ironic, but in accord with Steensgaard's thesis, that it was precisely the military success of Clive that in the next 20 years enabled the Dutch company to become a free rider on the naval security provided by the EIC. Until the fourth Anglo-Dutch war in the 1780s, the Dutch enjoyed the protection of the English from the competition of the French and other upstarts without paying nearly as much as the English were paying to maintain their military gains. And the stock and foreign exchange markets of the time reflected that turnabout.

[35] Ibid., pp. 94–5.
[36] Ibid., pp. 105–6.

7. The integration of the English and Dutch capital markets in peace and war

The preceding chapters have described a special form of economic integration that occurred in the first quarter of the eighteenth century between Europe's two leading mercantile cities: Amsterdam and London. An international capital market developed that led to increasingly wider-ranging capital markets for each center over the succeeding centuries. It also would have facilitated the progress of economic integration for northwestern Europe in terms of markets in goods and labor, had it not been for its use in the service of the rising nation-states and their exercise of national power. That early international capital market, however, seems to have been treated by historians mainly as an economic curiosity, largely because its operations have been viewed from the perspective of a particular center or nation, never as a whole. This chapter lays the basis for a greater appreciation of the international dimensions of financial capital in the eighteenth century by examining the operations of the London and Amsterdam stock markets in theoretical terms and analyzing the results in quantitative terms.

Shares of the great chartered joint-stock corporations in England were traded simultaneously on the stock exchanges of London and Amsterdam at least by the summer of 1723. We know this from the *Amsterdamsche Courant,* which began giving prices of English shares on the Amsterdam Beurs in its issue of 9 August 1723. However, we know also that trade in the shares of the Dutch East and West India companies was active from their foundation in the seventeenth century, but the *Courant* began reporting the prices only in its issue of 14 July 1723. So trade in English shares on the Amsterdam exchange probably occurred earlier as well. Amsterdam continued to trade English shares through peace, war, and revolution continuously into the twentieth century. A great quantity of evidence remains of this activity, including the daily prices of the shares in London, the prices of the same shares in Amsterdam (up to thrice weekly), the nearly daily transfers of those shares in the ledger books maintained in London, and the twice-weekly rates on foreign bills of exchange. Using modern theory and quantitative techniques, a great deal that is of interest can be inferred from the price data alone.

A crucial element in the set of financial practices brought to England by William III and his retinue was the resale of shares in joint-stock corporations, in other words, the modern stock exchanges. Although chartered joint-stock companies existed in England prior to the arrival of William, it appears that trade in their shares increased considerably in the early 1690s, and certainly the number of companies increased markedly in that decade. That growth of activity followed a very active period of stock trading in the Amsterdam Beurs in the 1680s.[1] To aid him in raising money for his participation in the War of the League of Augsburg against Catholic France, William brought with him numerous financial advisors and military contractors from Holland. Many were Jews and Huguenots who were eager to apply in a relatively backward England the financial techniques and institutions that had been developed over the preceding century in Amsterdam, as described in Chapter 1.[2]

Their activities in London came to concentrate on shares of the Bank of England (founded in 1694), the New East India Company (1698), the United East India Company (a consolidation of the Old and New East India companies that occurred in 1702), and the South Sea Company (1711). The early history of these companies was summarized in Chapter 3. The charter of each company permitted foreigners to own shares, and that right was

[1] On England, see K. G. Davies, "Joint Stock Investment in the Later Seventeenth Century," *Economic History Review*, 2nd series, 4:3(1952), pp. 283–301. On Holland, see the introduction by Hermann Kellenbenz, "Portions Descriptive of the Amsterdam Stock Exchange Selected and Translated by Professor Hermann Kellenbenz," in the Kress Library's edition of Joseph de la Vega, *Confusion de Confusiones* (Boston: Harvard Graduate School of Business Administration, 1957), p. xiii.

[2] Van Dillen gives a few of the more noteworthy examples of the Jewish financial investors. Moses Machado went with the king to England in 1688 and became his prime contractor for the campaign in Ireland; Joseph de Medina had a large contract as military supplier in 1713; Sir Solomon de Medina was the greatest army contractor of his day, financing in particular the campaigns of the duke of Marlborough. J. G. van Dillen, "De economische positie en beteknis der Joden in de Republiek en in de Nederlandse koloniale wereld," in H. Brugmans and A. Frank, eds., *Geschiednis der Joden in Nederland* (Amsterdam: Van Holkema & Warendorf, 1940), p. 584. Further, our earliest description of the operation of the Amsterdam stock exchange, Joseph de la Vega's *Confusion de Confusiones*, appears to be a highly florid elaboration of an earlier technical manual that he had prepared on the various techniques and regulations employed in the Effectenbeurs. The purpose of this manual most likely was to inform his countrymen who had gone to London and who wished to participate in the speculation that was beginning there. Hermann Kellenbenz, introduction to de la Vega, *Confusion de Confusiones*, p. xiv.

upheld by the crown and the companies despite occasional challenges from members of Parliament.[3] The shares of the three great companies were liquid assets for both English and foreign owners, because an active resale market existed for them in the London stock market and in the Amsterdam Beurs.

The early history of the information network connecting these two marketplaces was covered in Chapter 2. There the importance of the *Amsterdamsche Courant* as a source for the prices on the Amsterdam Beurs was discussed and its reliability analyzed. In the 1930s, the Dutch economic historian J. G. van Dillen recorded the prices given in the *Courant* every two weeks beginning 9 August 1723 (N.S.) and ending 19 December 1794. That effort resulted in 1,676 observations of Amsterdam prices for shares in each of the English companies over that period, the last three-quarters of the eighteenth century. For the same period there are over 30,000 observations from the London market; so van Dillen's reduced sample may be accepted with gratitude. For each date in van Dillen's Amsterdam series, I took the London quotation on the same trading day for each of the three stocks.[4] When I graphed the prices of each company in the two markets against each other, it was evident that the two markets were very closely correlated from the beginning of the period. This was clear from both the graphs of the price levels and the graphs of their first differences. Figures 7.1–7.3 show the differences between the Amsterdam and London prices for each stock on a magnified scale that exaggerates the apparent size and persistence of the actual differences, which were quite small. Table 7.1 indicates the nearly perfect congruence of the various price series. It shows the correlation coefficients between the levels (first line) and the first differences (second line) of the share prices in Amsterdam and London for the Bank of England, the East India Company, and the South Sea Company. The correlation coefficients are quite consistent for the levels across the four peacetime periods that occurred between 1723

---

[3] For details, see Larry Neal, "Efficient Markets in the Eighteenth Century? The Amsterdam and London Stock Exchanges," *Business and Economic History*, 11(1982), pp. 81–100.

[4] This exercise was complicated by two features: (1) The Dutch had been on the Gregorian calendar since the middle/end of December 1582, but the British did not shift until 2/13 September 1752. (2) The Amsterdam market traded Sunday through Friday, but the London market traded Monday through Saturday. To deal with the first feature, I counted back 11 days to find the corresponding London quotes before 13 September 1752; the second feature was dealt with by matching the Saturday quote in London to a Sunday quote in Amsterdam whenever one appeared.

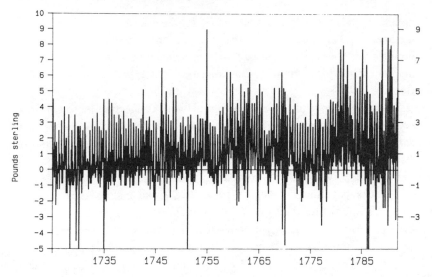

Figure 7.1. Bank of England share prices, Amsterdam–London, 1723–94.

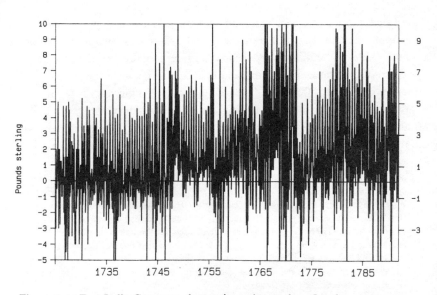

Figure 7.2. East India Company share prices, Amsterdam–London, 1723–94.

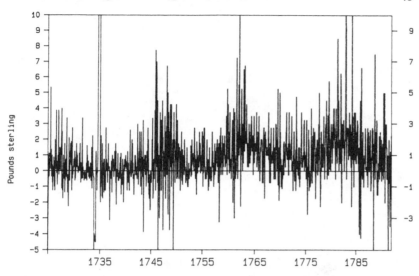

Figure 7.3. South Sea Company share prices, Amsterdam–London, 1723–94.

and 1794,[5] and they are consistently high for each of the three companies. The correlations for the first differences are naturally much lower, and they also show much more variation by company and by time period. Finding two such distinct price series for the same financial asset raises the question whether or not the two markets were closely integrated. If one looks only at the levels, the answer is a resounding yes. The first differences, however, raise more interesting questions about the sources of the varied patterns that occurred. The striking thing is the absence of any trend in any of the three stocks toward closer integration over the course of the century.

The apparently close and stable integration of the two capital markets will not surprise historians studying the eighteenth century, enamored as they are of the leisurely modernity of the Age of Enlightenment. Mail packet boats left London twice a week for Amsterdam, and four- to seven-day-old dispatches from London appeared each week in the Amsterdam and other Dutch newspapers. Dutch investors were represented among

---

[5] From Helen Keller's *The Dictionary of Dates* (New York: 1934) I chose 19 October 1739 as the start of the first war period (War of Jenkins' Ear) and October 1748 as the end (Treaty of Aix-la-Chapelle). The Seven Years' War began in August 1756, and for financial purposes in the capitals it ended with the Treaty of Paris signed 10 February 1763. I took 13 March 1778 as the effective date of hostilities in Europe arising from the American War for Independence, because that was when the treaty of alliance between France and the United States was communicated to England. The war ended with the Preliminary treaty signed in Paris on 30 November 1782.

TABLE 7.1
Correlation coefficients, London and Amsterdam stock prices

Period	Bank of England	East India Company	South Sea Company
Entire Period 1723-94			
Levels	0.994	0.993	0.989
Changes	**0.589**	**0.624**	**0.394**
Peace Periods			
8/09/23 - 10/19/39			
Levels	0.977	0.990	0.936
Changes	**0.416**	**0.550**	**0.069**
11/11/48 - 7/14/56			
Levels	0.983	0.988	0.983
Changes	**0.326**	**0.378**	**0.361**
2/18/63 - 3/04/78			
Levels	0.993	0.997	0.974
Changes	**0.649**	**0.711**	**0.337**
12/06/82 - 9/22/90			
Levels	0.996	0.987	0.969
Changes	**0.563**	**0.585**	**0.132**
War Periods			
10/21/39 - 10/23/48			
Levels	0.988	0.978	0.945
Changes	**0.534**	**0.604**	**0.168**
8/04/56 - 2/05/63			
Levels	0.976	0.963	0.979
Changes	**0.640**	**0.600**	**0.407**
3/02/78 - 11/20/82			
Levels	0.828	0.943	0.908
Changes	**0.465**	**0.536**	**-0.004**
10/08/90 - 12/19/94			
Levels	0.983	0.978	0.986
Changes	**0.769**	**0.580**	**0.686**

Note: This table presents levels (adjusted for differences in means) and first differences of actual prices.

Source: John Castaing, *The Course of the Exchange* (London: 1698-1795) and J. G. van Dillen, "Effectenkoersen aan de Amsterdamsche Beurs, 1723-1794," *Economische-Historische Jaarboek*, 17 (1931), pp. 1-34.

major holders of Bank of England stock from the beginning. Their holdings grew until 1751, with a "Dutch rush" occurring between 1721 and 1726. The Dutch continued to receive dividends and capital bonuses even when the Netherlands had become the Republic of Batavia in 1795 and then departments within the Napoleonic empire in the first decade of the nineteenth century.[6]

[6] John Clapham, *The Bank of England, A History. Vol. 1: 1694–1797* (Cambridge University Press, 1945), pp. 278–89.

How large were the Dutch investments in the English public debt? In the most recent summary of the available studies, Wilson relied on P. G. M. Dickson's benchmark figures for 1723–4 and 1750.[7] Dickson found that in 1723–4 the total foreign holdings of stock in the "big three" companies amounted to 9.3% of the total capital, but by 1750 the total foreign holdings in the same companies (by then, South Sea Annuities had replaced the original stock) amounted to 19.2%.[8] Looking more closely at the growth of foreign holdings in Bank of England stock, Dickson found that it was not until the time of the South Sea Bubble that foreigners, especially the Dutch, began to invest. He concluded that

as a result of the South Sea Bubble this trend was markedly accentuated [toward holdings of government and company stock]. By 1723–24 foreign holdings of English government securities had reached – for the first time – a really substantial size. They were to go on increasing in amount until the massive foreign disinvestment of the last twenty years of the eighteenth century.[9]

Even though modern scholarship has reduced the proportion of English funds held by foreigners from the heights of 40% or more estimated to Lord North in 1776,[10] the new lower percentages still exceed the proportions of foreign trade and foreign labor in the English economy of the eighteenth century.[11] The evidence is persuasive that economic integration between these two great mercantile powers occurred first through the movements of capital.

The more interesting question about Dutch investments in the English securities, whether they were destabilizing and speculative, as contemporary English opinion had it, or whether they were passive and on the whole stabilizing, remains unanswered. Evidence regarding these questions lies

---

[7] Charles Wilson, "Dutch Investment in Britain in the 17th–19th Centuries," in *Crédit Communal de Belgique, Collection Histoire Pro Civitate. No. 58: La Dette Publique aux XVIIIe et XIXe Siècles* (Brussels: 1980), p. 201.

[8] P. G. M. Dickson, *The Financial Revolution in England: A Study in the Development of Public Credit, 1688–1756* (London: Macmillan, 1967), pp. 312, 321.

[9] Ibid., pp. 311–12.

[10] Alice Clare Carter, "The Dutch and the English Public Debt in 1777," *Economica*, 20(May 1953), pp. 159–61.

[11] N. F. R. Crafts, "British Economic Growth, 1700–1813: A Review of the Evidence," *Economic History Review*, 36(May 1983), p. 197, puts exports as a proportion of national income for Great Britain between 8% and 12% during the eighteenth century and not over 15% until 1801. Neil Tranter, "The Labour Supply, 1780–1860," in R. Floud and D. N. McCloskey, eds., *The Economic History of Britain since 1700* (Cambridge University Press, 1981), Vol. 1, p. 211, puts the maximum share of foreign immigrants, mainly Irish, in the labor force at much lower levels.

primarily in the price data for the two markets.[12] These data can be used to see if either of the markets for English securities – the Amsterdam and the London stock exchanges – was less than efficient in setting prices.

Table 7.2 shows the initial results from time-series analysis of the four main time series of interest: the cash prices for Bank of England and East India Company stock quoted in London and the forward prices for the same two stocks quoted in Amsterdam. Basically, I test the proposition that the following equations accurately describe price movements in each case:

$$L_{it+1} - L_{it} = u_{t+1} \qquad (i = 1, 3; t = \text{time}) \qquad (7.1)$$

$$A_{it+1} - A_{it} = u_{t+1} \qquad (i = 1, 3; t = \text{time}) \qquad (7.2)$$

where L is the London price and A is the Amsterdam price.

The standard technique is to estimate autoregressive moving-average (ARMA) models for the changes in prices. If some combination of autoregressive and moving-average processes yields consistently good descriptions of price changes, then presumably interested speculators could have discovered these processes and used them to make profits in the markets. For efficient markets to have existed, the models should show (0, 0) – that is, that last period's price alone remains the best predictor of the current period's price. Table 7.2 shows the results from two different techniques for estimating ARMA models.[13]

---

[12] Quantity data are available as well because the Bank of England was responsible for recording transfers of ownership in "government stock," which included shares of the bank itself, as well as shares of the East India Company, annuities, and Consols. In principle, the records could be used to link foreign movements of capital to sustained rises or falls in the market price of British company shares, but the records are overwhelming in volume. To date, only Alice Carter has used the records, and that for only a three-month period at the beginning of 1755. Alice Clare Carter, "Transfer of Certain Public Debt Stocks in the London Money Market from 1 January to 31 March 1755," *Bulletin of the Institute of Historical Research,* 28(November 1955), pp. 202–12.

[13] This is a test of "weak-form" efficiency, as contrasted with "strong" or "semistrong" forms. The stronger forms require the market to respond or anticipate movements in fundamental determinants of the asset's price. Such tests were not performed, because data on fundamentals comparable to prices were not available. See, however, Philip Mirowski, "What Do Markets Do? Efficiency Tests of the Eighteenth Century London Stock Market," *Explorations in Economic History,* 24(April 1987), pp. 107–29. Both the "B-J" and "H-R" methods are strictly mechanical procedures that estimate the autocorrelation coefficients and the partial-correlation coefficients for up to 10 lags over the time series. The B-J, or standard Box-Jenkins, method determines which of these coefficients are statistically significantly different from zero, and then the investigator selects the most plausible model. G. E. P. Box and G. M. Jenkins, *Time Series Analysis: Forecasting and Control* (San Francisco: Holden-Day, 1970). The H-R Method is a recursive process in which each

TABLE 7.2
Estimated ARMA models, London and Amsterdam

Time Period	London		Amsterdam	
	H-R	B-J	H-R	B-J
Bank of England				
Entire period				
1723-94	0, 0	0, 0	0, 0	0, 0
Pre- and post-Barnard				
1723-37	0, 0	0, 0	0, 0	0, 0
1738-94	0, 0	0, 0	0, 0	0, 0
Peace periods				
1748-56	0, 5	0, 0	0, 1	0, 1
1763-78	2, 0	2, 0	0, 0	0, 0
1782-92	0, 0	0, 0	0, 0	0, 0
War periods				
1739-48	3, 0	3, 0	0, 0	0, 0
1756-63	0, 0	0, 0	0, 0	0, 0
1778-82	0, 0	0, 0	0, 1	1, 0
East India Company				
Entire period				
1723-94	0, 0	0, 0	0, 3	0, 3
Pre- and post-Barnard				
1723-37	0, 0	0, 0	2, 0	0, 0
1738-94	0, 0	0, 0	3, 0	3, 0
Peace periods				
1748-56	0, 0	0, 0	0, 0	0, 0
1763-78	0, 0	0, 0	0, 0	0, 0
1782-92	0, 0	0, 0	0, 0	0, 1
War periods				
1739-48	0, 0	0, 0	0, 3	0, 3
1756-63	0, 0	0, 0	0, 0	0, 0
1778-82	0, 0	0, 0	0, 1	0, 1

Source: Same as Table 7.1.

(note 13 continued)
autoregressive process up to order 10 is estimated, and then the residuals of each estimate are used to calculate variances. The process minimizes the expression

$$\sigma_k^2 + 2k/n$$

where k is the order of autoregressive process and n is the number of observations. Then, using ordinary least-squares regressions, ARMA models are estimated up to order $(p, 5)$,

For the period as a whole, the two methods are consistent in showing market efficiency in both markets for Bank of England stock and in the London market for East India Company stock. Both methods indicate that a (0, 3), in other words, a third-order moving-average process, existed in the Amsterdam prices of the East India Company. This appears to have been in place only after 1737, however. The remainder of the table shows the estimated results from the ARMA models for each period of war and peace after Barnard's Act (1734), which forbade any dealings in options or forward contracts by stockbrokers on the London Stock Exchange. Here the results are mixed, although most cases are clear random walks, that is, ARMA (0, 0). But it is only for the London market for East India stock that we find consistent evidence for an efficient market in each subperiod. In the two markets for Bank of England stock, we find subperiods when some kind of ARMA process seems to have been at work. It is interesting, however, that that never occurs in both markets for any given subperiod. The only subperiod when a (0, 3) ARMA appears for East India Company stock on the Amsterdam exchange was 1739–48, during the War of the Austrian Succession. For the same period, an anomalous (3, 0) ARMA is found for Bank of England stock on the London market. Because only the coefficient on the third term was significantly different from zero in each case, I suspected some data error. I found none, but did detect another possible cause of the anomaly.

Table 7.3 shows the average interval between Amsterdam quotes from the *Amsterdamsche Courant,* as well as the variance of the intervals and the number of observations in each wartime and peacetime period. The mean ranges from 15 to 16 days, as one expects for a fortnightly sample with occasional gaps for religious holidays. But the variance is especially high for the period of the War of the Austrian Succession and the peacetime between the Seven Years' War and the American War for Independence, when three of the six exceptions to random walks occur. This is reassuring for the validity of the remaining (0, 0) processes, because if a regular time-

(*note 13 continued*)
where p is the order of AR model selected earlier. Finally, the residuals of the estimated ARMA models are used to calculate sample variances, and (p, q) are selected to minimize

$$\log \sigma_{p,q}^2 + (\log n/n)(p + q)$$

where q is the order of MA process. E. J. Hannan and J. Rissanen, "Recursive Estimation of Mixed Autoregressive–Moving Average Order," *Biometrika,* 69(January 1982), pp. 81–94, and their "Correction," 70(January 1983), p. 303. The tests are repeated for the various peacetime and wartime periods.

TABLE 7.3
Regularity of observations,
Amsterdamsche Courant

Period	Mean	Variance	Number of observations
1723-39 (peace)	15.10	28.55	391
1739-48 (war)	16.01	43.87	207
1748-56 (peace)	15.35	19.05	185
1756-63 (war)	15.72	25.90	153
1763-78 (peace)	15.94	97.34	357
1778-82 (war)	14.98	10.16	115
1782-92 (peace)	15.17	21.94	189

Source: J. G. van Dillen, "Effectenkoersen aan de Amsterdamsche Beurs 1723-1794," *Economische-Historische Jaarboek*, 17 (1931), pp. 1-34.

series process exists, but is sampled at irregular intervals, the bias will produce a random-walk process. If a random walk exists in a series, on the other hand, but is sampled at irregular intervals, the possibility of finding a deterministic process arises.[14]

To reach a preliminary conclusion, efficient markets for the leading British financial securities appear to have been in place in both Amsterdam and London after the South Sea Bubble of 1720. Moreover, they apparently operated efficiently up to the outbreak of the French Revolutionary Wars near the end of the century. Various episodes of market inefficiencies leading to speculative profit possibilities probably did arise at times, but they appear to have been confined to the Amsterdam market. The anomalous periods merit closer examination, especially in terms of possible differences in the ways the two markets operated.

The key to understanding the (0, 1) and (1, 0) processes lies in the finding that the London prices were spot, or money, prices, whereas the

[14] Time-series purists will object that any irregularity in the timing of the observations violates the assumptions of the statistical technique, and so the irregular appearance of the *Courant* rules it out for time-series analysis. Given the frequency of religious holidays in the eighteenth century, even in Protestant Amsterdam and London, however, a case can be made that the irregularities in its appearance reflect precisely irregularities in trading activity on the Effectenbeurs. It is the market activity, after all, that is the underlying process, not the appearance of the newspaper.

Amsterdam prices were forward, or time, prices. The London practice likely arose as a matter of convenience, because no fixed settlement days among brokers existed originally, and time contracts could vary widely. But in 1734, Barnard's Act (7 Geo. II, cap. 8) forbade all dealings in options and future deliveries of stocks, with a fine of £500 to be levied on each person party to such a contract.[15]

According to one authority, Barnard's Act was persistently violated.[16] Dickson, on the other hand, believed that the act may have been effective in transferring options business to Amsterdam and encouraging London traders to deal on margins.[17] Castaing's price list was consistent in showing prices at money, although S. R. Cope speculated that the curious practice of printing the names of the Bank of England and the East India Company in capital letters may have developed to indicate securities in which dealings in time were possible.[18] Because the Bank of England came to handle the transfers of stocks for the chartered companies, purchases could in principle be made for a forward date at which the transfer would be made at the bank. Hence, the illegality of dealing in futures and options may not have eliminated the practice in the London market – indeed, the introduction of stiffer bills in the House of Commons in 1745, 1756, 1771, and 1773 suggests that futures trading continued – but it no doubt did eliminate the printed quotation of future prices for those contracts.

Amsterdam, by contrast, always dealt in time contracts, because legally binding possession of shares in the Dutch East India Company was not possible until the actual transfer of the share or shares was entered in the company's books. Entry, however, had to wait until the books were opened

---

[15] Malachy Postlethwayt, "Stock-Jobbing," in *The Universal Dictionary of Trade and Commerce,* 2 vols. (London: 1774; reprinted New York: Augustus M. Kelley, 1971).

[16] Thomas Mortimer, *Every Man His Own Broker: Or a Guide to Exchange Alley,* 3rd ed. (London: 1761).

[17] Dickson, *The Financial Revolution in England,* p. 508, quoted a letter by an Amsterdam broker to a Haarlem merchant in 1735 stating that ". . . in London only cash purchases and sales can be made."

[18] S. R. Cope, "The Stock Exchange Revisited: A New Look at the Market in Securities in London in the Eighteenth Century," *Economica,* 45(February 1978), p. 18. On this point it is interesting that Houghton followed the same practice in his early listings of stock, but clearly stated that the companies whose names were printed in "Great Letters" were those that had charters, whereas those that had asterisks in front of them were patent monopolies. John Houghton, *A Collection for Improvement of Husbandry and Trade,* 9 vols. (London: Randall Taylor et al., 1692–1703; republished Westmead, Farnborough, Hants.: Gregg, 1969). The list of stocks in No. 106 (Friday, 10 August 1694) has this note: "Great Letters by Charter, (*) by Patent."

for the payment of dividends. Joseph de la Vega's original description of
the Amsterdam Beurs, in fact, described "putts" and "refuses" in very
modern terms for options trading. The extensive trading of dealers with
one another on both hedging and speculative contracts in the same stock
required regular "rescounter" settlement dates to settle the net differences
and straighten out the accounts among the various brokers. Such settlements occurred quarterly, on the 15th of February, May, August, and
November.[19] The quarterly rescounters may have been for the English
funds only, because de la Vega reported monthly rescounters, on the 20th
of the month for real stock, with payment due the 25th, and on the first of
the month for "ducaton" shares.[20] (Ducaton shares were small fractions of
actual Dutch East India Company shares that were devised to enable smaller investors to trade; the cash value of each original share had increased to
very high levels indeed.)

Van Dillen noted the difficulties in deciding whether the figures in the
Amsterdamsche Courant were cash or time prices:

Until 1747 this is not mentioned, but in comparing them with those found in
brokers' notes preserved from 1725 to 1737 it appears that in that period the
quotations are cash prices. In the year 1737 both prices are sometimes mentioned.
After this year we find generally the forward rates. From 1759 onwards the quotations are often followed by the name of the next settlement month, e.g., "all of
February." The difference between the cash price and the next paying month is,
however, not more than a few percent.[21]

If the Amsterdam prices quoted on the English securities were for future
delivery, then in general they should lie above the London cash prices
quoted on the same day. Figure 7.4 illustrates why.[22] At regular intervals,
dividends are paid on each security. If nothing else happens to disturb the
price of the shares from time 0 to time A on the graph, the nominal value of
each share will be fixed at the level of the horizontal axis. When the
dividend is paid at time A, the value of the dividend is added to the nominal
value of the share. Cash transactions in the shares between time 0 and time
A will take into account the forthcoming dividend payment, which the
buyer of the share will receive. So the cash prices between time 0 and time
A will show a gradual upward trend along line $0B$. A contract made at time

[19] Isaac da Pinto, *Traité de la Circulation et du Crédit* (Amsterdam: 1771), p. 305.
[20] de la Vega, *Confusion*, introduction by H. Kellenbenz, p. xviii.
[21] J. G. van Dillen, "Effectenkoersen aan de Amsterdamsche Beurs, 1723–1794," *Economische-Historische Jaarboek,* 17(1931), p. 13.
[22] Louis le Bachelier, "Theory of Speculation," translated by Paul Cootner, ed., *The Random Character of Stock Market Prices* (Cambridge, MA: M.I.T. Press, 1964).

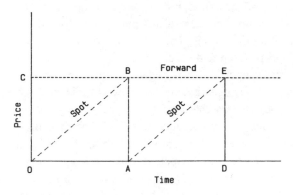

Figure 7.4. Effects of regular dividend payments on spot and forward prices (the Le Bachelier effect).

0 for future delivery of the share at time A, however, will require the buyer to pay a "contango" to the seller, equal, in the absence of disturbances, to the price of the share plus the dividend. The need for such a payment arises because the seller will hold the share until the delivery date, but will then yield possession of the stock, and its dividend, to the buyer, who only then will make full payment. This means that the forward price equivalent for the cash price that runs along line oB will be line CB, which always lies above the cash price, but gradually converges to it at the dividend payment date.

If the differences between Amsterdam and London prices arose because Amsterdam prices were always time, or forward, prices, whereas London prices were time prices until Barnard's Act in 1734 and spot prices thereafter, then the Amsterdam prices should have been the same as the London prices, with only small random disturbances, until 1734 or until 1737, when Barnard's Act was made a perpetual law. Tables 7.4 and 7.5 present results for linear regression of the difference between the Amsterdam price and London price at a given date on three variables: (1) DAYSDIVD, the number of days from the date of the observation to payment of the next dividend; (2) PAYTIME, a dummy variable set equal to unity during the times London prices were quoted ex dividend; (3) AMEXPREM, the number of penningen banco[23] the English pound sterling was worth less its mint

---

[23] The Amsterdam-on-London exchange rate was given in Dutch schellingen and penningen banco per English pound. Each Dutch schelling contained 12 penningen.

par ratio. Only the Bank of England and East India Company stocks are
analyzed, because the South Sea Company stock was essentially dormant
for most of the period after 1730.

The variable DAYSDIVD is intended to capture the declining difference
between future and spot prices as the dividend date approaches. Its coefficient should be positive, because the dependent variable is the Amsterdam
price minus the London price. On average, it should be equal to one-half
the annual dividend, because dividends were paid semiannually. For each
subperiod, its effect is estimated separately in the third equation. The
second equation in each panel adds the effect of AMEXPREM, whereas the
first equation has all three explanatory variables. Comparing the third
equation in each panel over the two tables, one notices that only for the
pre–Barnard Act period does the constant term in the regressions become
statistically different from zero, and it does so for both the Bank of England
and the East India Company. For the entire period from 1738 to 1794, and
for the three peacetime periods within, the constant terms are insignifi-
cantly different from zero. This implies that the contango rate was, on
average, the same as the dividend rate, which one should expect in the
absence of persistent expectations for things to improve or to deteriorate.
The finding also means that no serious barriers existed to equalizing the
rates of return on the same financial assets in the two different countries.

The presence of a constant term that is negative and significantly different from zero for the pre–Barnard Act period could imply either segmented
capital markets or exuberant speculators, if in fact the Amsterdam prices
were consistently future prices. Inspecting the pattern of residuals and
estimating the regression for subperiods within the period from 1723 to
1738 leads me to believe that speculators were generally bullish. On average, the Amsterdam price was higher than the London price even in the
period from 1723 to 1737, although the difference was much less than it
became after 1737. This holds for both stocks. If the Amsterdam prices in
this pre–Barnard Act period were spot prices like the London prices, then
the negative constant term in the regression implies optimistic expectations
by investors. The evidence of the exchange-rate variable further strengthens this presumption.

There remain differences between the regression estimates for the Bank
of England stock and the East India Company stock. On average, the price
difference was 1.6 points for bank stock and 2.5 points for East India
stock. The point difference reflects the generally higher dividend rates paid
by the East India Company stock. In sum, the regression results, combined

TABLE 7.4
Summary of regression results, Bank of England,
Amsterdam-London price difference[1]

DAYSDIVD[2]	AMEXPM[3]	PAYTIME[4]	Constant	R^2	DW Observations
1723-39[5]					
.005	.002	1.999	-.140	.30	1.78
(4.37)[6]	(0.24)	(8.84)	(-0.52)		387
.010	.003		-.397	.16	1.63
(8.77)	(0.31)		(-1.35)		388
.009			-.480	.16	1.63
(8.78)			(-4.01)		389
1739-48[5]					
.009	.056	1.141	1.284	.31	1.55
(5.34)	(4.95)	(3.55)	(4.02)		203
.012	.056		1.118	.28	1.40
(7.86)	(4.84)		(3.44)		204
.011			-.233	.20	1.25
(7.16)			(-1.32)		205
1748-56[5]					
.010	.003	.758	-.137	.34	1.51
(7.15)	(0.25)	(2.73)	(-0.47)		181
.012	.002		-.275	.32	1.32
(9.39)	(0.16)		(-0.94)		182
.012			-.316	.32	1.32
(9.42)			(-2.18)		183
1756-63[5]					
.011	-.014	.515	-.193	.19	1.40
(4.69)	(-1.08)	(1.14)	(-0.50)		149
.012	-.013		-.250	.19	1.38
(5.95)	(-1.02)		(-0.65)		150
.012			.071	.19	1.36
(5.99)			(0.32)		151
1763-78[5]					
.016	-.008	.243	-.537	.32	1.44
(10.95)	(-1.21)	(0.87)	(-2.30)		353
.017	-.009		-.577	.32	1.42
(13.04)	(-1.22)		(-2.52)		354
.017			-.353	.32	1.42
(13.07)			(-2.56)		355

TABLE 7.4 (*cont.*)

	DAYSDIVD[2]	AMEXPM[3]	PAYTIME[4]	Constant	R^2	DW Observations
1778-82[5]						
	.010	-.025	.567	-.14	.21	1.60
	(3.79)	(-2.68)	(1.10)	(-0.43)		111
	.011	-.025		-.223	.21	1.53
	(4.95)	(-2.67)		(-0.68)		112
	.011			.364	.16	1.42
	(4.82)			(1.44)		113
1782-90[5]						
	.017	-.033	.492	-.122	.35	1.72
	(7.56)	(-4.31)	(1.11)	(-0.52)		185
	.018	-.032		-.196	.35	1.70
	(9.08)	(-4.28)		(-0.87)		186
	.019			-.166	.29	1.55
	(8.90)			(-0.71)		187
1790-4[5]						
	.009	-.002	1.761	.568	.20	1.58
	(2.21)	(-0.18)	(2.46)	(1.14)		75
	.015	-.002		.253	.15	1.44
	(3.90)	(-0.17)		(0.51)		76
	.015			.207	.16	1.44
	(3.93)			(0.50)		77

Note: All regressions are ordinary least squares.
    [1] Outliers removed and set to regression plane.
    [2] DAYSDIVD = days to next dividend payment.
    [3] AMEXPM = changes in the exchange rate.
    [4] PAYTIME = whether the London price was with (0)
        or *ex* dividend (1).
    [5] Subperiods:
        1723-39 [Peace, pre-Barnard]
        1739-48 [War of Austrian Succession]
        1748-56 [Peace, no financial crises]
        1756-63 [Seven Years' War]
        1763-78 [Peace, panics of 1763 and 1772]
        1778-83 [War for American Independence]
        1783-90 [Peace]
        1790-94 [French Revolution, war]
    [6] *t*-statistics are in parentheses under respective coefficients.

Source: Same as Table 7.1.

TABLE 7.5
Regression results, East India Company,
Amsterdam-London price difference

DAYSDIVD[2]	AMEXPM[3]	PAYTIME[4]	Constant	R^2	DW Observations
1723-39[5]					
.006	-.001	2.884	-.477	.24	1.90
(3.21)[6]	(-0.11)	(7.93)	(-1.07)		387
.012	-.005		-1.00	.12	1.69
(7.28)	(-0.34)		(-2.10)		388
.012			-.851	.12	1.69
(7.29)			(-4.43)		389
1739-48[5]					
.015	.068	1.383	1.251	.29	1.54
(5.74)	(3.95)	(2.75)	(2.52)		203
.018	.069		1.072	.27	1.38
(7.93)	(3.95)		(2.14)		204
.018			-.633	.22	1.28
(7.61)			(-2.44)		205
1748-56[5]					
.016	.028	2.032	.427	.41	1.69
(7.05)	(1.40)	(4.51)	(0.93)		181
.016		2.024	-.137	.41	1.68
(7.07)		(4.48)	(-0.62)		182
.021			-.416	.35	1.40
(9.91)			(-1.85)		183
1756-63[5]					
.013	-.044	.872	-.800	.27	1.43
(5.15)	(-2.99)	(1.72)	(-1.78)		149
.015	-.046		-.959	.26	1.38
(6.69)	(-3.07)		(-2.16)		150
.015			.156	.22	1.29
(6.56)			(0.60)		151
1763-78[5]					
.021	-.063	.835	-1.42	.19	1.56
(6.57)	(-3.83)	(1.35)	(-2.75)		353
.023	-.063		-1.55	.19	1.55
(8.17)	(-3.84)		(-3.03)		354
.023			.016	.16	1.49
(8.15)			(0.05)		355

TABLE 7.5 (*cont.*)

	DAYSDIVD[2]	AMEXPM[3]	PAYTIME[4]	Constant	R^2	DW Observations
1778-83[5]						
	.028	-.036	.684	-1.40	.41	1.93
	(7.16)	(-2.71)	(0.91)	(-2.83)		111
	.029	-.036		-1.51	.41	1.91
	(8.64)	(-2.76)		(-3.18)		112
	.029			-.66	.38	1.77
	(8.38)			(-1.78)		113
1782-90[5]						
	.020	-.028	.839	.359	.33	1.79
	(7.33)	(-2.99)	(1.55)	(1.34)		185
	.022	-.028		.244	.32	1.73
	(9.15)	(-3.01)		(0.94)		186
	.022			.320	.29	1.65
	(8.90)			(1.22)		187
1790-4[5]						
	.016	-.010	1.776	.709	.19	1.69
	(2.82)	(-0.50)	(0.71)	(1.11)		75
	.021	-.012		.495	.17	1.66
	(4.24)	(-0.60)		(0.78)		76
	.021			.267	.18	1.65
	(4.27)			(0.53)		77

Note: All regressions are ordinary least squares.
  [1] Outliers removed and set to regression plane.
  [2] DAYSDIVD = days to next dividend payment.
  [3] AMEXPM = changes in the exchange rate.
  [4] PAYTIME = whether the London price was with (0)
    or *ex* dividend (1).
  [5] Subperiods:
    1723-39 [Peace, pre-Barnard]
    1739-48 [War of Austrian Succession]
    1748-56 [Peace, no financial crises]
    1756-63 [Seven Years' War]
    1763-78 [Peace, panics of 1763 and 1772]
    1778-83 [War for American Independence]
    1783-90 [Peace]
    1790-94 [French Revolution, war]
  [6] *t*-statistics are in parentheses under respective coefficients.

Source: Same as Table 7.1.

with the evidence of market integration presented earlier, demonstrate that the small but persistent differences in prices that remained between the Amsterdam and London markets for the British securities were due to the fact that the London prices were cash, or spot, prices, whereas the Amsterdam prices were forward prices.

When the semiannual dividend payment dates approached, the transfer books for the particular stock would be closed so that the sums due to each owner could be calculated and made ready. During that period, which usually lasted two weeks, the stock would be quoted ex dividend. Any deliveries of stock taking place during that period would not include the dividend about to be paid, because the clerks would be making the payment ready for the currently registered owner. So I calculated the variable DAYSDIVD as the number of days from the given date to the day the first ex dividend quote appeared in the *Course of the Exchange*. In Amsterdam, on the other hand, it appears that the quoted price always included the dividend. A printed form that Dickson cited for sales of stock made in Amsterdam for delivery (and payment) in London made explicit provision that if the receiver of the stock did not get the current dividend, then he deducted that dividend from the stated price he had agreed to pay. That arrangement was stated clearly in a contract dated 4 April 1730 between Jacob Reynst and David Leeuw, both of Amsterdam, which Dickson translated:

I the undersigned acknowledge to have Bought from *Heer David Leeuw One Thousand* Pounds Sterling Capital Share of the *Bank of England* at London, at a price of *a Hundred and Forty Five and a Quarter per Cent* remaining after the Dividend paid last October, for settlement on next *15 May*, the which £*1000* I oblige myself to receive in London at the stated Price. And in case in the interim any Dividend is paid, it shall be to my profit and to reduction of the above Price. Contrarywise all supplementations and Calls shall be at my expense, in the usual way. All done in good faith at Amsterdam the *Fourth April* Seventeen hundred and *thirty*.[24]

To capture the difference in quoting prices during the period dividends were being calculated, I set up a dummy variable, PAYTIME, which is set to unity for the first observation after the ex dividend quotes began in London. It proves to be positive, as expected, and usually significant, especially for the earlier years. It also has the felicitous effect of reducing substantially the serial correlation in the regressions.

Because transfers of stock had to take place in London, where the actual

---

[24] Dickson, *The Financial Revolution in England*, p. 335. This quotes a preprinted form, on which the items shown in italics were entered by hand.

stock had to be paid for in pounds sterling, one would expect some effect in the Amsterdam market from fluctuations in the exchange rate with London. Taking deviations in the observed sight rate from the mint par ratio as the measure of changes in the exchange rate (AMEXPREM), what effect should one expect on the Amsterdam price of an English stock (in English pounds sterling) of, say, an increase in the value of the English pound relative to the Dutch guilder? Recognizing that any effect would be merely transitory until prices were equalized on the basis of the new exchange rate, one might expect the demand for English stock in Amsterdam to be shifted downward (any given price in pounds sterling would then be felt to be more expensive by a Dutch purchaser), while the supply of the English stock in Amsterdam would be shifted outward (any given price in pounds sterling would then be more attractive to a Dutch supplier). This is illustrated in panel (a) of Figure 7.5. The joint effect of the shifts in demand and in supply would be to reduce the price of the English stock in Amsterdam relative to its price in London. Because the dependent variable in the regressions is the Amsterdam price minus the London price, while the independent variable for the effect of the exchange rate is the price of the pound sterling in terms of Dutch bank money less the mint par ratio, the expected sign on the exchange-rate variable is negative. That is, the higher the value of the pound on the foreign exchanges, the lower one expects the price of a British security to be in Amsterdam relative to London.

In fact, the estimated coefficient for the exchange-rate variable does not prove to be statistically different from zero in the earliest period, and when it does become significant, it has a positive sign! For periods after midcentury, however, it always has the expected sign and often is significantly different from zero as well, especially in the regressions from which outliers have been removed. The anomaly that needs to be explained, then, is the positive sign and significant effect before 1750, especially during the War of the Austrian Succession. The most likely explanation stems from the fact that 1723 to 1750 was precisely the period when the Dutch built up their holdings in the English joint-stock companies and long-term government debt most rapidly. Dickson found that Dutch holdings of Bank of England stock rose from 10.5% of the total capital in 1723–4 to 30.3% in 1750, while their share of East India Company stock rose from 13.4% to 21.4% over the same period.[25] It would appear, then, that before 1750 the

---

[25] Dickson, *The Financial Revolution in England*. Calculated from Tables 47 and 48, pp. 312–13, for 1723–4 and from Tables 50 and 51, p. 321 and p. 324, for 1750.

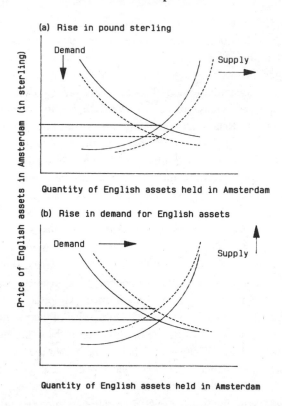

(a) Rise in pound sterling

Demand

Supply

Quantity of English assets held in Amsterdam

(b) Rise in demand for English assets

Demand

Supply

Quantity of English assets held in Amsterdam

Price of English assets in Amsterdam (in sterling)

Figure 7.5. Effects of a rise in the London rate of exchange on prices of English securities traded in Amsterdam.

massive inflows of Dutch capital to the English long-term securities market were sufficient to drive up the value of the English pound whenever surges of Dutch demand lifted the Amsterdam price above the level predicted by the purely technical factors embodied in the variables PAYTIME and DAYSDIVD. This phenomenon is illustrated in panel (b) of Figure 7.5.

My final step in the regression analysis was to remove outliers. The graphs of predicted versus actual values of the Amsterdam–London price differences reveal a very close clustering of the actual value to the regression plane, with a few (less than 2%) of the observations causing much of the unexplained variance. Setting the outliers equal to the predicted value (or the actual value in the few cases where it turned out that an error had been made in the data entry) greatly improved the goodness of fit, without altering the size or significance of the estimated coefficients. (An exception is the AMEXPREM variable, which did prove responsive in some time periods to the removal of outliers.) Some of the outliers may be due to errors of transcription in the original data source. Some of the numbers in van Dillen's table, for example, appear to be in error – two digits are reversed, or two columns are reversed. But most of the anomalies in the van Dillen table appear to occur in the *Amsterdamsche Courant* as well.[26]

It is essential to confront as well the second source of transcription error – that from the original source on the actual trading day in London or Amsterdam to the printed source now used by historians. How much error occurred must remain a matter of speculation, but extensive use of the *Course of the Exchange* during the preparation of this book revealed very few typographical errors – such as inconsistencies in the date headings (which had to be altered with each issue) or reversal of data entries. But such errors would, of course, have been easier for the original typesetters to locate.

Studying the pattern of residuals for the period from 1763 to 1778, for which the largest number of outliers occurs, suggests another explanation: that the outliers appeared as a result of very short term sharp movements on the London Stock Exchange. If one observes the London price for three days prior to the outlier, in most cases the difference from the Amsterdam quote largely disappears. If the next observation is also an outlier, it nearly always has the opposite sign. This suggests that information of great influence on the price of English stocks reached London before it reached Amsterdam. Because my observations are taken from the same day for both markets, ephemeral information of the kind associated with panics (the panics of 1763 and 1772 fell within the period) that reached one market before the other would not be reflected in the price difference. In anything other than panic situations, ephemeral fluctuations are not a problem, because the Amsterdam prices were taken only every two weeks, and most information would have reached both markets. It is not surprising, then, that the worst fits occur between 1763 and 1778 and again between 1790 and 1794.

The regression results strengthen the conclusion that the London and Amsterdam markets were efficient and well integrated from the second quarter of the eighteenth century onward. The spot prices quoted in the

---

[26] I checked the 10 most dubious numbers from van Dillen against photocopies of the *Amsterdamsche Courant* I obtained from the New York Public Library. Only three, those for East India stock on 16 November 1733 and 3 April 1789 and that for South Sea stock on 25 November 1793, proved to be van Dillen's mistake in transcribing.

London market followed a random-walk process consistent with efficient markets. The forward prices in the Amsterdam market were highly correlated with them. The semiannual dividend payments in London then produced regular patterns in the Amsterdam prices, both because of the le Bachelier effect and because of the practice in London of quoting prices ex dividend during the preparation of dividend payments, whereas Amsterdam quoted them with dividend. Those regular patterns, however, were sometimes masked by unusual expectations (during the War of the Austrian Succession, for instance), fluctuations in exchange rates, or panics. For those unusual periods, one finds random walks in general, although the time of the War of the Austrian Succession remains an anomaly.

Economists and historians will regard these findings differently. For historians, they will simply confirm in large part the authoritative work of Dickson on the operation of the London capital markets in that period and his perceptive comments on the Dutch influence. Dickson's work on the Dutch, in turn, relied heavily on the earlier work done by Carter, van Dillen, and Wilson.[27] All were agreed on the importance and effectiveness of the integration of the two capital markets at the dawn of modern capitalism. After all, even Karl Marx regarded the establishment of the national debt in England as the single most effective device in the "primitive accumulation of capital."[28]

For economists, the quantitative results should strengthen their confidence in doing analytical work on the financial relations between London and Amsterdam.[29] The pioneer work in this regard was done by Robert

[27] Alice Clare Carter, "Dutch Foreign Investment, 1738–1800," *Economica*, 20(November 1953), pp. 322–40; "Dutch Foreign Investment, 1738–1800, in the Light of the Amsterdam 'Collateral Succesion' Inventories," *Tijdschrift voor Geschiednis*, 66(1953), pp. 27–38; "The Huguenot Contribution to the Early Years of the Funded Debt, 1694–1714," *Proceedings of the Huguenot Society of London*, 19:3(1955), pp. 21–31; "Financial Activities of the Huguenots in London and Amsterdam in the mid-Eighteenth Century," *Proceedings of the Huguenot Society of London*, 19:6(1955), pp. 313–33. All these are reprinted and summarized in her book *Getting, Spending and Investing in Early Modern Times* (Assen: Van Gorcum, 1975). Cf. Charles Wilson, *Anglo–Dutch Commerce and Finance in the Eighteenth Century* (Cambridge University Press, 1941), and his "Dutch Investment in Eighteenth Century England," *Economic History Review*, 2nd series, 12(April 1960), pp. 434–9. Van Dillen's works were cited earlier.

[28] Karl Marx, *Capital* (London: Lawrence & Wishart, 1970), Vol. 1, pp. 754–6.

[29] Brian Parsons, "The Behavior of Prices on the London Stock Market in the Early Eighteenth Century," Ph.D. dissertation, University of Chicago, 1974, concentrated on the daily course of prices during the South Sea Bubble and found that the market operated efficiently, although he found unexplained differences in the price quotes from different sources. Philip Mirowski, "The Rise (and Retreat) of a Market: English Joint Stock Shares

Eagly and V. Kerry Smith, who used interest-rate and foreign-exchange-rate data in the framework of an interest-rate arbitrage model. They asserted that their results "support the general hypothesis of a trend towards increased integration among money markets during the course of the century, but at the same time they show that during individual subperiods there was considerable variation in this trend."[30] The results reported here show that as well, but their most interesting feature is the high level of integration that existed at the *beginning* of the second quarter of the eighteenth century and the *continuing* efficiency of both stock markets, rather than a trend toward improved integration.

True, the operations were disturbed by repeated wars (each marked by different financial techniques and consequences), by trade disturbances, and by occasional financial panics, much as operations on financial markets continue to be disturbed today. Nevertheless, the disturbances of the eighteenth century never changed the fundamental economic characteristics of the two markets in the way that modern policy measures of sovereign nation-states manage to do. Neither country attempted an independent national monetary policy between 1723 and 1794 – they did not control capital movements, withhold taxes on dividend or interest payments to foreigners (or even tax dividends and interest until Pitt's income tax of 1798), change monetary standards, manage exchange rates, or attempt to regulate the size of the money supply. There was an absence, therefore, of the modern impediments to efficient operation of multiple-listing markets. (Witness, by comparison, the current difficulties in expanding multiple listings of stocks among the members of the European Community.) In other words, two remarkably modern capital markets were permitted to interact in an unfettered (and hence unmodern) fashion. That may be why economic integration occurred between the two countries first in the capital markets, well before comparable degrees of integration could be achieved in good markets or labor markets.

in the Eighteenth Century," *Journal of Economic History,* 41(September 1981), pp. 559–77, compared internal accounts of profitability for several joint-stock companies with the pricing of their equity on the stock market. He found increasing discrepancies for the latter part of the century. But see my discussion of his results on the East India Company in Chapter 6.

[30] Robert Eagly and V. Kerry Smith, "Domestic and International Integration of the London Money Market, 1731–1789," *Journal of Economic History,* 36(March 1976), p. 210.

8. The English and Dutch capital markets in panics

Measuring the degree of integration in financial markets is difficult both theoretically and empirically. The theoretical difficulties are well illustrated in the literature dealing with U.S. capital markets in the late nineteenth century.[1] This literature takes advantage of the plentiful data that can be found for regional interest rates, but it confronts an inherent theoretical problem by trying to measure an economic phenomenon – integration of capital markets – with a variable measuring rod. The measuring rod, the short-term interest rates earned by banks on a broad class of loans, must vary as local regulations vary, as the riskiness and duration of the loans within the category vary, and as monopoly rents vary. All these variations must be allowed for if a consistent measuring instrument is to be obtained. If they are not, then the possibility always remains that divergences or convergences of interest rates between two capital markets may be due to factors other than integration or separation of the two markets. These difficulties of interpretation are inherent in the use of the interest-rate arbitrage model to derive a measuring standard.

In this chapter we can take advantage of the price series developed in the preceding chapter to measure the difference in the prices of a share of stock as quoted on the same day in the domestic exchange for the company and in a foreign exchange. Fritz Machlup referred to this as the simplest test of

[1] The literature begins with Lance Davis, "The Investment Market, 1870–1914: The Evolution of a National Market," *Journal of Economic History*, 25(September 1965), pp. 355–99 (commercial paper market), and continues with Richard Sylla, "Federal Policy, Banking Market Structure, and Capital Mobilization in the United States, 1863–1913," *Journal of Economic History*, 29(December 1969), pp. 657–86 (national banks), Larry Neal, "Trust Companies and Financial Innovation, 1897–1914," *Business History Review*, 45(Fall 1971), pp. 35–51 (trust companies), John James, "The Development of the National Money Market, 1893–1911," *Journal of Economic History*, 36(December 1976), pp. 878–97 (local monopoly), Richard Keehn, "Federal Bank Policy, Bank Market Structure, and Bank Performance: Wisconsin, 1863–1914," *Business History Review*, 48(Spring 1974), pp. 1–47 (local regulations), and Marie E. Sushka and W. B. Barrett, "Banking Structure and the National Capital Market, 1869–1914," *Journal of Economic History*, 44(June 1984), pp. 463–77 (risk premia).

all for market integration, because the product is standardized, identical in the two markets, and the cost of transport between the two markets is essentially zero.[2] Oskar Morgenstern went so far as to assert "on different national stock markets the prices of the same shares are as a rule not at variance, owing to perfect arbitrage."[3] Because the same shares have the same risk of default by definition, and the legal terms of the underlying contract are the same for all shareholders, we avoid all the problems mentioned earlier that are associated with using interest rates on short-term or long-term securities as measures of financial integration.

But even in regard to the price of a given stock, differences in the two markets still may arise from delays in information and from differences in investor preferences in response to the information, which will be reflected in price differences. These price differences provide a measure of the separation or lack of integration of the two markets. The absolute level of these price differences will depend only on the transactions costs between the two markets. (However, because the largest portion of transactions costs turns out to be brokers' fees, and these are charged as percentages of the sale value in each market examined in this chapter, it is the ratio of the price differences to the average values of the shares in the two markets that is the best measure of transactions costs.) The duration of a given price discrepancy between the two markets will depend on the length of time required for the transmission of information between the two markets. The average difference in price between the two markets will normally depend on differences in quoting prices (e.g., money prices usually are lower than term or on-account prices) and differences in transactions costs of all kinds (taxes on transfers, brokers' fees, implicit interest rates for trading on account times the normal length of settlement) between the two markets, as well as on the typical premium or discount ruling in the exchange rate for the two currencies involved. But these kinds of transactions costs are trivial compared with the problems of risk and legal enforcement that plague measures of interest rates across national boundaries. Moreover, they also exist and must be taken into account for interest-bearing securities.

How can we best use these stock price series to measure the integration of financial markets? If perfect arbitrage, in the words of Morgenstern, occurs within the constraints of transactions costs, information delays, and

[2] Fritz Machlup, *A History of Thought on Economic Integration* (New York: Columbia University Press, 1977), p. 26.

[3] Oskar Morgenstern, *International Financial Transactions and Business Cycles* (Princeton University Press, 1959), p. 508.

price movements in the intervening foreign exchange market, there should exist no detectable time-series pattern in the price differences between the two markets. That is, the random-walk behavior of efficient markets (in the weak sense of Fama) should be observed not only for the price movements in each market but also for the differences in prices between the two markets. If something other than a random walk is observed, then unexploited arbitrage opportunities remain between the two markets, and they cannot be considered fully integrated. In other words, using prices of mutually traded securities in two markets, we expect the usual tests of financial integration – high correlations in price levels or price movements (as found in the preceding chapter), or low coefficients of variation (standard deviations divided by the mean) – to be passed with flying colors. We need a more sensitive test that can indicate differences in the timing and impact of a given information set on traders operating in the two markets. The test proposed and implemented here is to see if we can find ARMA (0, 0) models, not in the price levels observed on each market, as is usually done in studies of individual markets, but in the *price differences between the two markets*.

In the preceding chapter we analyzed data on the prices of shares of the major British joint-stock companies as traded on both the London and the Amsterdam exchanges, starting in the second quarter of the eighteenth century. For the period beginning at the end of the nineteenth century, we have daily data on the prices of American railroad shares as traded in each of the major European stock exchanges. At that time, each market was informed within hours of prices in the other markets via multiple submarine cables. Moreover, forward orders were regularly placed by London traders for particular securities and foreign exchange in the New York market to take effect after the London market closed. There still were no formal taxes, regulations, or controls on capital movements. Further, each country was formally on a full gold standard; so there were no uncertainties associated with the acceptability of a means of payment across national boundaries. In short, all the conditions for the perfect arbitrage of Morgenstern were in place and working.

We have, then, in these historical data on share prices across two or more national markets, the possibility of measuring the integration of European capital markets against the standards set just before World War I and involving nearly two centuries of experience, the very centuries that witnessed the budding and full flowering of the world capitalist economy. Did integration proceed at a steady pace, or in fits and starts? How did it respond to political divisions, wars, changes in trade policies, changes in monetary standards, and periods of inflation and depression? These are some of the questions that in principle can be tackled using these data, but in this exploratory effort they will have to be ignored. First must come the work of developing this alternative standard of measurement.

The interest-rate arbitrage model, used in previous studies, has proved difficult to specify correctly in theoretical terms and more difficult, even treacherous, to implement empirically. Morgenstern found it to work as expected during the late nineteenth and early twentieth centuries only during periods of financial crisis. Those were periods when interest rates changed sharply in the financial market that originated the crisis, creating large interest-rate differentials internationally. Only for those periods could Morgenstern find the sequence he expected in the interest-rate arbitrage model: gold flowing into the market with higher interest rates, its exchange rate rising, and then its prices rising. By contrast, the asset-pricing model described earlier might be expected to work least well during such episodes. A liquidity scramble in one center should drive down prices of all financial assets, and if the crisis had not yet appeared in the other market where the security was traded, we would expect a gap larger than normal to emerge between the prices in the two markets. (This would be the corollary of an unusual widening of the interest-rate differential in the interest-rate arbitrage model.) For our present purposes, we may as well measure capital market integration with the asset-pricing model during successive financial crises that were propagated from one of the financial centers to the other (i.e., in the "worst-case scenario"). The crises have been selected on the grounds of their availability of data and their characteristics as truly international crises that affected both markets, but with differences in intensity and timing. The crises that met these joint criteria were the crises of 1745, 1763, 1772, and 1793 for the capital markets of London and Amsterdam, the crises of 1825, 1873, and 1907 for the London and Paris markets, the crises of 1873 and 1907 for the New York and London markets in American railroad stocks, and the crisis of 1907 for the Amsterdam market once again.

The panic of 1745

According to T. S. Ashton,[4] this crisis was confined to London, and its interest really lay only in the sharp fall of British government security prices with the brief but surprising success of the Jacobite rebellion in

---

[4] T. S. Ashton, *An Economic History of England: The Eighteenth Century* (London: Methuen, 1966).

Scotland from September 1745 to April 1746. Both East India Company stock and Bank of England stock were in the category of government securities, however. Because the War of the Austrian Succession (1740–8) included England in the 1745 period, it is interesting that Ashton found no particular influence from the financial requirements of the larger war on the English capital markets. That war, however, was a major source of financial disturbances for the Amsterdam market. James Riley dated the start of Dutch interest in lending to foreign governments as beginning with the activities of Dutch investors on the London market in that period.[5] The Dutch Republic became a belligerent at the end of that war, during 1747 and 1748.[6] Finally, Austrian obligations to Dutch investors had been based on revenues from Silesia. When that province was lost to Prussia early in the war, the Austrians stopped paying interest to their Dutch creditors on the Silesian bonds, and the Prussians saw no point to assuming them. That was a continuing source of financial pressure on the Dutch markets, therefore.[7]

The panic of 1763

A panic confined to the London market had occurred in 1761. In mid-1763, however, a crisis began in Amsterdam with the failure of the financial house of De Neuvilles. As a scramble for liquidity began in both Amsterdam and Hamburg, bankruptcies occurred in other northern European cities. Prices of British securities fell as the foreign holders cashed them in, and the pound sterling fell as bullion was shipped out. Ashton claimed the crisis was most severe in Amsterdam in August and September and worst in London in October of 1763.[8] To capture both panics, I have taken the quotations from June 1761 to June 1764 for analysis.

The panic of 1772–3

In June 1772, a panic occurred in Scotland when Alexander Fordyce, a partner in the London house of Neale, James, Fordyce, and Down, who had been speculating on East India stock, absconded to France.[9] From

---

[5] James C. Riley, *International Government Finance and the Amsterdam Capital Market, 1740–1815* (Cambridge University Press, 1980), p. 14.
[6] Ibid., p. 78.
[7] Ibid., pp. 88–9.
[8] T. S. Ashton, *Economic Fluctuations in England, 1700–1800* (Oxford: Clarendon Press, 1959), pp. 126–7.
[9] Ibid., p. 128.

Scotland, the liquidity scramble spread to London and then to Amsterdam by October, when a Dutch firm, Clifford & Sons, went bankrupt. According to Riley, international support was mobilized quickly on behalf of other firms in Amsterdam, but the longer-term consequences were the formation of a cooperative fund organized among the firms in Amsterdam to dome to the aid of firms that were solvent but illiquid, and a substantial contraction of the acceptance credit business in Amsterdam. Complaints of a shortage of coin in Amsterdam continued through 1773; so I have taken the period January 1772 to January 1775 for analysis. Kindleberger saw this as a classic example of a crisis spreading from one center to another, but prevented from becoming more general and severe by the ad hoc formation of a lender of last resort.[10]

The panic of 1791–4

The War for American Independence and the French Revolution each caused disturbances on the London Stock Exchange and in the foreign exchange markets for sterling. But in each case the disturbance was limited either in duration or to the British market alone. Far more serious were the disturbances that led up to the formal declaration of war between Britain and France in February 1793 and the military successes of the French armies that led eventually to the occupation of Amsterdam in 1795. The establishment of the Batavian Republic in 1795 under revolutionary rules of the game also led to the publication of an official price list for the Amsterdam Effectenbeurs that began in 1795.[11] According to Ashton, the war crisis in the exchanges preceded the actual war, as was usually the case, and by summer 1793 the financial crisis was over.[12] I have taken the period December 1791 to December 1794 for analysis of this episode, which really began in France, was transmitted equally to Amsterdam and London, and finally was terminated in Amsterdam by French occupation.

This completes the list of panics for the eighteenth century for which we have data only on the Amsterdam and London exchanges. It is interesting to see how they compare with the various panics of the nineteenth century, which were truly international, because that is when integration of capital markets is traditionally supposed to have begun, and to have continued

[10] Charles Kindleberger, *Manias, Panics and Crashes* (New York: Basic Books, 1978), pp. 48, 123.
[11] Johann de Vries, *Een Eeuw vol Effecten, Historische schets van de Vereniging voor de Effectenhandel en de Amsterdamse Effectenbeurs, 1876–1976* (Amsterdam: Vereniging voor de Effectenhandel, 1976), p. 20.
[12] Ashton, *Economic Fluctuations*, pp. 133–4.

until World War I. In the nineteenth century, the variety of securities that were quoted on separate national stock markets increased, the number of stock markets that participated in cross-national listings increased, and enormous improvements in communication among the various markets occurred.

The panic of 1825

According to William Smart, the panic of 1825 was a sharp, unexpected reversal of the boom of 1824. The root cause, in Smart's analysis, was the anticipatory export of goods to South America by British merchants counting on payment eventually from the great loans that were made in 1824 to Latin American countries. When the Latin American ventures proved to be little more than empty mine shafts (literally the case in some of the major investments), a readjustment was in order.[13] Because the Latin American stocks and bonds were issued in London and the recipient countries had no developed stock exchanges at that time, the best security for examination is the French rente. The chief security traded in the London Stock Exchange was the French 5% rente of 1817. A conversion scheme, however, was enacted in the course of 1825 to replace these with new 3% rentes. (The *Times* carried a report of the debate in the Chamber of Deputies over the conversion plan in May 1825.[14]) The *Times* could not make up its mind which security, or both or neither, to report in its daily listings of the prices on the exchange. At one point during the panic of December, the two rentes were quoted with different exchange rates for the franc! The importance of the British holdings of the French rente for the British capital market, as well as for the French government, can be gauged from the following report in the *Times* on 3 January 1826: "An express from Paris, which arrived yesterday morning, with information of a rise of 1 per cent in the French 3 per Cent Stock, contributed to give a tone of cheerfulness to the money transactions of the Exchange." The data for the London market were collected from the London *Times,* and the data for the Paris market were taken from *Le Moniteur Universal.*

The panic of 1873

The panic of 1873 was perhaps the most uniform and widespread financial panic of the nineteenth century. Its origins in the United States have been

[13] William Smart, *Economic Annals of the Nineteenth Century, 1801–1820* (New York: Augustus M. Kelley, 1964), Vol. 1, p. 295.
[14] London *Times,* 13 May 1825.

traced to gold-corner attempts by Jay Gould or to stock manipulation in the Northern Pacific Railway by James J. Hill, and in Europe to excessive German speculation in railroad issues during the boom set off by the receipt of French reparations after the Franco-Prussian War of 1870. It initiated a long period of falling prices in all the major countries, and security prices in all financial centers were sharply affected.

Complicating our measurement of stock prices in separate national markets for this crisis is the fact that it occurred during the "greenback" period for the United States, when paper money issued by the U.S. Treasury was legal tender. However, gold currency was also legal tender; so the two circulated together, with, typically, a premium paid for the gold dollar in terms of the greenback dollar. That varied daily. A further complication was that the gold dollar also fluctuated daily in relation to the British pound sterling. It turns out that American securities were quoted on the London market in terms of the gold dollar, but they were quoted on the New York market in terms of the greenback dollar.[15]

Offsetting the multiplicative uncertainties of a fluctuating foreign exchange rate and a fluctuating internal conversion rate of two legal currencies was the development of transatlantic telegraphic cables that permitted the daily exchange of information between the New York and European markets. This episode helps distinguish the effects of speedier communications from those of increased uncertainties in monetary regimes on the integration of capital markets.

To establish this, I have examined the London and Paris markets again in terms of the French 3% and 5% rentes and added a comparison of the London and New York markets in terms of two well-known but separately managed railroads – the infamous Erie, whose mismanagement by Gould was becoming evident at that time, and the Illinois Central, which was actively traded in the London market, but not in New York.

The panic of 1907

The panic of 1907 has its main interest now as the milder earthquake that preceded the crash of 1929. It was not equally felt everywhere in the capitalist world economy. London had experienced its financial stringency in 1906, and a few, but very few, observers linked that to the subsequent problems in New York. In the London market, however, events in New

[15] Lawrence H. Officer, "The Floating Dollar in the Greenback Period: A Test of Theories of Exchange-Rate Determination," *Journal of Economic History*, 41(September 1981), p. 633.

York during the panic of October 1907 were followed closely, and it is clear that efforts to stabilize prices in New York were persistently undermined by sell orders from London and Amsterdam. Paris was affected only briefly and with a delay, but Germany participated fully. Italy, it turns out, experienced much the same kind of investment boom, monetary growth, and stock market speculation before the 1907 panic as the United States, because its monetary base was enlarged by emigrants' remittances from the United States.[16]

The cross-tides of information among the capital markets over the submarine cables had developed by that time to the extent that each day the London *Times* carried a list of the previous day's prices on the New York Stock Exchange of some 50 American securities, including not only the opening, closing, and previous day's closing prices but also the London price of the security as stated in New York. Then, of course, these same American securities as traded on the London Stock Exchange were listed with their spot and term prices. Finally, shorter lists of securities traded on the "Continental Bourses" were printed, including Paris, Berlin, Vienna, and Amsterdam, and, on occasion, St. Petersburg and other remote capital markets of Europe. Eight American railroads were quoted from the Amsterdam Beurs, one (the Baltimore & Ohio) from Berlin, but none from Vienna or Paris. Some 25 American railroads were carried daily in the London *Times* report for the London stock market. With this wealth of data available, our comparisons are confined to Erie railroad stock and Southern Pacific stock as priced each day on the London, Amsterdam, and New York stock exchanges at weekly intervals over the period October 1906 to June 1908.

The results of measuring the price differences for the various securities across the several markets in these financial crises spanning nearly two centuries are shown in Table 8.1. This shows the average and the variance of the absolute price differences as a percentage of the average of each pair of prices in order to compare the effects of transactions costs in each market and between the two markets on price differences. The remaining statistics – the standard deviation, the maximum difference that was observed, the minimum difference, the range of the differences, and then, for good measure, the autoregressive moving-average time-series model that best describes the dynamic pattern of the differences – are calculated for

[16] Franco Bonelli, "The 1907 Financial Crisis in Italy: A Peculiar Case of the Lender of Last Resort in Action," in C. Kindleberger and P. Laffargue, eds., *Financial Crises: Theory, History, and Policy* (Cambridge University Press, 1982), pp. 51–3.

the percentage actual price differences. These are the precise statistical measures that reflect the concepts of transaction costs, delays in information, and the degree to which arbitrage is carried out. Other measures might be devised to reflect other aspects of integration (e.g., longest run of observations greater than one standard deviation from the average difference), but these seem to cover the most obvious dimensions of integration across each pair of markets.[17]

Panels A–D for the eighteenth century show essentially the same values in each crisis episode for the averages, variances, standard deviations, ranges, and ARMA patterns. The exceptions to this observation are that the ranges were always greater for East India stock than for Bank of England stock and that the ranges for both were noticeably greater in the 1793 crisis. This is evidence that market integration may, in fact, have been breaking down at the end of the eighteenth century in the face of the political disturbances that disrupted trade and communications between the two markets. Otherwise, little change occurred in the degree of integration of these two markets.

Only one case of an ARMA process of (0, 0) order occurs for the eighteenth-century panics: Bank of England stock in the 1763 crisis. Because that crisis was focused on speculation in East India Company stock, it is not surprising that the ARMA for price differences in East India shares is not (0, 0) but (1, 0), indicating a one-period lag process at work in the price differences. Is this evidence of well-integrated markets by the middle of the eighteenth century? In the preceding chapter, an ARMA model other than (0, 0) was considered an indicator of lack of market integration; so by that standard the prevalence of ARMA (1, 0) models is an indicator that market integration was not complete in the eighteenth century. But perhaps different standards should be applied to the case of price differences between two markets for a stock under speculative attack in a financial panic

---

[17] The Amsterdam prices were adjusted before taking the difference from the London price. The adjustment arises from the discovery that Amsterdam prices were consistently higher than London prices. This led to the determination that the Amsterdam prices were time prices, and the London prices were spot. Larry Neal, "Efficient Markets in the Eighteenth Century? The Amsterdam and London Stock Exchanges," *Business and Economic History*, 11(1982), pp. 81–100. A regression equation was estimated relating the excess of the Amsterdam price over the London price to the number of days until the next payment of dividends. This equation was then used to calculate Amsterdam prices adjusted to their "spot" equivalents. The adjustment reduced the average difference found (Amsterdam spot prices were lower on average than Amsterdam time prices for both stocks) and reduced the order of the estimated ARMA models. But the variance, standard deviation, and range of differences were largely unaffected by this adjustment.

TABLE 8.1
Summary statistics on stock market integration
in the eighteenth- and nineteenth-century crises

Eighteenth Century: Bank of England and East India Company shares quoted on the Amsterdam and London stock exchanges (average and variance are for percentage absolute price differences; remaining statistics are for percentage actual differences)

A. The crisis of 1745 (biweekly, June 1744 - June 1747)

Name	Avg	Var	SD	Max	Min	Range	ARMA
Bank	1.00	0.52	1.19	3.78	-2.92	6.71	(3,0)
E. India	1.35	1.29	1.71	7.01	-4.62	11.63	(1,0)

B. The crisis of 1763 (biweekly, June 1761 - June 1764)

Name	Avg	Var	SD	Max	Min	Range	ARMA
Bank	1.06	0.87	1.36	4.93	-2.29	7.23	(0,0)
E. India	1.45	1.37	1.82	4.99	-3.38	8.37	(1,0)

C. The crisis of 1772 (biweekly, January 1772 - January 1775)

Name	Avg	Var	SD	Max	Min	Range	ARMA
Bank	0.71	0.27	0.80	1.57	-2.60	4.17	(1,0)
E. India	1.59	1.53	1.95	5.61	-4.58	10.19	(1,1)

D. The crisis of 1793 (biweekly, December 1791 - December 1794)

Name	Avg	Var	SD	Max	Min	Range	ARMA
Bank	1.180	1.822	1.671	8.751	-2.685	11.436	(1,1)
E. India	1.342	2.706	2.078	9.156	-8.923	18.079	(1,1)

Source: For London, *The Course of the Exchange* (appearing semiweekly, with daily prices); for Amsterdam, J. G. van Dillen, "Effectenkoersen aan de Amsterdamsche Beurs 1723-1794," *Economische-Historische Jaarboek*, 17 (1931), pp. 1-46 (from the *Amsterdamsche Courant*, sampled fortnightly).

that is spreading from one market to the other. It would seem reasonable that in these specially selected episodes, a panic spreading from one center to another would mean that information was flowing from one to the other, so that price differences, especially in the shares under the severest attack by investors scrambling to cover speculative positions, might be autoregressive. Finding an ARMA model with a non-zero moving-average process [such as the (1, 1) model in 1793], on the other hand, would imply that some element other than lagged information flows was at work. The (1, 1) model for the 1793 crisis implies that markets were less well integrated then than in the earlier three crises, on this reasoning. Our other, traditional, indicators of market integration also indicate that the 1793 crisis was more disruptive; so this helps support the interpretation that, in the context of variables used and the episodes chosen here, (1, 0) models demonstrate a greater degree of market integration than do (1, 1) models.

But this interpretation can be checked another way, namely, by calibrat-

TABLE 8.1 (continued)
Summary statistics on stock market integration
in the eighteenth- and nineteenth-century crises

Nineteenth Century: French *rentes* and American railroad stocks quoted on the Amsterdam, London, New York, and Paris stock exchanges (average and variance are for absolute percentage differences of prices in the two markets compared; remaining statistics are for percentage actual differences.)

E. The crisis of 1825 (weekly, July 1824 - July 1826)
(French *rentes*, 5% and 3%, compared in London and Paris)

Name	Avg	Var	SD	Max	Min	Range	ARMA
5 % rente	0.58	0.53	0.92	4.68	-3.51	8.18	(0,1)
3 % rente	0.84	0.83	1.18	3.92	-1.48	5.41	(0,1)

F. The crisis of 1873 (weekly, July 1872 - July 1874)
i) French *rentes*, 5% and 3%, compared in London and Paris

Name	Avg	Var	SD	Max	Min	Range	ARMA
5 % rente	1.50	1.00	1.10	1.48	-5.19	6.67	(1,2)
3 % rente	1.76	1.03	1.05	0.51	-4.18	4.69	(3,0)

ii) American railroad stocks, the Erie and the Illinois Central, compared in London and New York

Name	Avg	Var	SD	Max	Min	Range	ARMA
Erie	2.10	4.85	2.85	9.68	-4.49	14.17	(3,0)
Ill. Cen.	1.80	3.36	2.56	9.80	-7.78	17.58	(1,1)

G. The crisis of 1907 (weekly, July 1906 - July 1908)
i) Stock of the Erie railroad, compared in London, Amsterdam, and New York

Pair	Avg	Var	SD	Max	Min	Range	ARMA
L - NY	3.19	4.73	2.75	11.58	-8.83	20.41	(4,1)
Am - NY	2.25	5.84	2.78	15.46	-3.13	18.59	(2,2)
L - Am	1.82	1.48	1.99	5.00	-5.71	10.71	(2,1)

ii) Stock of the Southern Pacific railroad, compared in London, Amsterdam, and New York

Pair	Avg	Var	SD	Max	Min	Range	ARMA
L - NY	2.56	1.73	1.41	7.62	-0.93	8.54	(1,1)
Am - NY	1.10	0.88	1.44	4.89	-4.82	9.72	(0,0)
L - Am	2.64	1.73	1.42	9.29	-0.93	10.21	(1,1)

Source: **1825:** London: *The Times*, Thursday issue or closest match to Paris quote. Paris: *Le Moniteur Universel*, Thursday issue or closest business day.
1873: London: *The Times*, Thursday issue or closest match to either Paris or New York quote. Paris: *Le Figaro*, Thursday issue or closest business day. New York: *The Commercial and Financial Chronicle*, monthly summary.
1907: London, Amsterdam, and New York: *The Times*, Thursday issue or closest match to New York or Amsterdam quote.

ing our measures of the eighteenth-century panics against comparable measures for the nineteenth century. Those results are shown in panels E–G of Table 8.1, and they make the mid-eighteenth-century results look quite respectable, indeed. The average differences in price levels between the various markets of the nineteenth century were much the same right through to 1907. In fact, the largest difference found occurred in 1907 (for

Erie stock compared on the London and New York exchanges). The variances are also similar, except that those for American railroad stocks in the nineteenth century are substantially higher. The standard deviations (recall that these are for the absolute percentage differences) are also quite uniform by security and time period, save for the American railroad stocks. Their standard deviations are double the levels for French rentes in the 1873 crisis and remain high for Erie stock in the 1907 panic. The range of differences for the nineteenth-century securities were also much the same as in the eighteenth century, with the exception of those for American railroad stocks in the 1873 crisis and Erie stock in 1907. The possible range of differences should decrease as the speed of communication of prices between two markets increases; so our quantitative evidence indicates that only the speeding up of communications over the nearly two centuries under consideration had any effect in improving the integration of European capital markets. And that improvement could be easily offset in the case of volatile stocks (Erie in 1907) and uncertainties of exchange rates when governmental policies changed (American securities in 1873). But the improvement of communications did not improve integration to the extent that all possible profit opportunities from arbitrage were eliminated.

In the ARMA models calculated for the nineteenth century, we find no random walk until we get to the 1907 panic. Even there the random walk appears in only one of the six possible cases (three markets and two stocks are compared). Even worse is the finding that for the 1873 crisis the estimated coefficients for the ARMA models (not shown in the table) for each security – French 3% and 5% rentes, Erie and Illinois Central stock – indicate that the ARMA process was explosive, rather than dampened! That might be conceivable if a rational bubble were in progress in one market and not in the other for the same stock, but that situation hardly seems likely if the markets were better integrated than in the eighteenth century.

In sum, the evidence is that the Amsterdam and London capital markets of the eighteenth century were closely integrated, even by the standards of the early twentieth century, and they were well integrated even during financial crises that affected one market more severely than the other, according to contemporary accounts. That was true, of course, only for the securities that were listed in both markets. For other securities that were listed and actively traded in one market, but not in the other, integration obviously could have taken place through trading first in one of the commonly listed securities and then in any of the locally traded securities. The ease of integration would then be improved by increasing the number of commonly listed securities. Those did begin to grow in the nineteenth century, especially after the middle of the century, with first London and then Paris joining Amsterdam as markets where foreign securities could be locally traded.[18] But the degree of integration does not seem to have made much progress in terms of decreasing the average difference in prices and eliminating systematic patterns of price differences.

Fritz Machlup noted that use of the term "integration" in economic discussion did not occur regularly until 1948; previous references to the concept in the twentieth century normally spoke of "disintegration," because that was the dominant feature of the international economy after World War I.[19] Today, the European Community has made only limited progress toward its initial goal of capital market integration. Even when capital movements across national boundaries are permitted with relatively certain exchange rates, the acquisition of foreign securities or the sale of domestic securities to foreigners may be subject to governmental restrictions and controls.[20] The situation has progressed little since the Segré report of 1966 found that very few European securities were even listed on stock exchanges outside the home country for the European company and concluded that little progress had been made toward the desirable goal of pan-European capital markets.[21] The latest assessment of European capital markets was very negative, by contrast with the New York market: "Bloc trades (10,000 shares or more) in European markets often have to be implemented over days or even weeks to avoid disrupting the market. And because of fixed commissions and stamp duties or bourse taxes, transactions can be very expensive."[22] All this, of course, is but a specific example of the uniqueness of the international economic integration that had been achieved by the outbreak of World War I and how far we remain from that condition today.

[18] In 1855, the Amsterdam Beurs listed officially 87 securities, only 14 of which were domestic, and 2 colonial; three-fourths of those, however, were government bonds. By January 1914, the number had grown prodigiously to 1,796, of which 691 were domestic, 840 foreign, and 265 colonial. Of the foreign securities, 194 were issued by North American railroads. Ludger Brenninkmeyer, *Die Amsterdamer Effektenboerse* (Berlin: Emil Ebering, 1920), pp. 178–83. By contrast, we may note that in 1983, only 294 foreign stocks were listed in the United States, up sharply from 99 in 1979. *Business Week*, 24 July 1984, p. 101.

[19] Machlup, *A History of Thought*, pp. 4–12.

[20] Ibid., p. 17.

[21] European Economic Community, *The Development of a European Capital Market* (Brussels: EEC, 1966.)

[22] *Business Week*, 24 July 1984, p. 102.

9. The capital markets during revolutions, war, and peace

In February 1793, after war had been declared by the French revolutionary government against both England and Spain, and the Dutch "patriot" party was attempting its own revolution in Amsterdam in sympathy, the great Anglo-Dutch merchant banker Henry Hope removed himself from Amsterdam to London. He returned briefly in December when it appeared that the first invasion of the Austrian Netherlands had been defeated. But on 17 October 1794, as French troops were poised at the River Maas for the final offensive into Holland, he crossed over to England permanently, with John Williams Hope, while other members of the firm fled to Germany. The two remaining members, Pierre Labouchère and Alexander Baring, made their escape on 18 January 1795. Henry Hope carried with him 372 valuable paintings, insured for £26,000. Without selling his recently completed country seat at Welgelegen or his warehouse and office in central Amsterdam, he arranged for purchase of the East Sheen estate near Richmond and a palatial London residence that he began to expand in order to accommodate his collection of art.[1]

This is only one example, albeit one of the largest and best-documented examples, of the displacement of capital from the European continent in front of the advancing French Revolution and its armies. The revolutionaries had abolished traditional property rights, including feudal obligations and seigneurial dues, and they disrupted customary channels of trade. Hope and his family, already having strong financial ties with England, were able to transfer their movable wealth nearly intact. So, too, we should imagine, were most merchant bankers able to avoid the capital losses implied by the revolution, and perhaps many were able eventually, as were the Hopes, to profit from the new opportunities provided by war finance. Other merchants were less favorably placed and did less well. Certainly the nobility were desperate to liquidate and salvage what they could of their estates, as well as to save their lives. The emigrés had to turn to the

---

[1] Marten J. Buist, *At Spes Non Fractra, Hope & Co. 1770–1815* (The Hague: Nijhoff, 1974), pp. 48–50, passim.

international merchant bankers of the time and use the existing international capital markets to remove the liquid part of their property beyond the reach of French Revolutionary arms.

There is good reason to believe that they were successful to a much greater degree than previously suspected, largely because the international capital markets of the time were larger and better organized than previously thought. Moreover, these capital movements from the Continent to Britain explain succinctly why the British industrial revolution took place during that period, despite the significant pressures of war expenditures and British government subsidies to Continental allies taking place at the same time. The return of emigré capital to the Continent from England when peace was restored also helps explain the depression of British industry and incomes from 1815 through the financial crisis of 1825, although the role of British speculators also was important.

This thesis is by no means new – it is perhaps impossible to say anything new about these epochal events without being foolish – but it has been ignored increasingly as political history and economic history have become more and more nationalistic in interest and focus. As we have become more impressed in the 1980s by the transmission of international financial disturbances in increasingly well integrated capital markets, it is clearly time to review and reassess the importance that international capital movements may have had in the past. But even at the time of the "Bullion Report" in 1811, evidence was noted regarding the significance of capital movements by those who would defend the Bank of England from the barbs of the Bullion Committee. The sizes of anticipated capital flows out of Great Britain played a key role in the Bank of England's restriction on the specie convertibility of its notes in 1797. The large and sudden movements of foreign capital out of British government funds in 1817 were the major concerns of the Bank officials who wished to delay resumption of full convertibility in 1819. Those concerns about the early role of capital movements deserve to be taken more seriously than they traditionally have been by economic historians.

To make the argument, it is useful to examine a few examples of how specific individuals managed to liquidate at least some of their assets on the Continent and to invest them abroad. This will show that their concerns were compelling and that they were able to use the existing network for remittances effectively and to modify it as the governments of France and England changed monetary regimes, introduced exchange controls, and altered property rights. Then we shall review the evidence provided by twice-weekly foreign exchange rates and daily government security prices to show the possible effects (and lack of effects at times) of those capital movements. Finally, I shall argue that this evidence links together the British industrial revolution and the French Revolution in a logical and compelling way, helping to explain the paper pound in 1797, the "Continental System" that Napoleon created from 1803 to 1813, and the resumption of the gold standard by Britain from 1819 to 1821.

Business historians have recently published several case studies showing the ability of individuals and firms of uncertain nationality to move their fortunes surreptitiously or overtly in those perilous and (for some) profitable times. Four of the more striking cases that illustrate the process and indicate its possible importance are, in chronological order, the move of the banker Walter Boyd from Paris to London on 23 September 1792,[2] the flight of Henry Hope, as described earlier, in October 1794,[3] the plans of the Du Pont family in 1797 to migrate from France to the United States, a move that eventually was completed at the end of 1799,[4] and, finally, the arrival of the young Nathan Meyer Rothschild in Manchester from Frankfurt in 1799.[5] These are but a few of the most famous and best-documented cases of the cosmopolitan bourgeoisie of the late eighteenth century. These prosperous, intelligent, and energetic individuals who became displaced by the effects of revolution, war, and recovery from 1789 to 1825[6] responded by developing new ways to transfer their claims on capital in real terms and to maintain control of distant assets.[7]

Walter Boyd

Walter Boyd was a Scot. Like John Law a century earlier, he migrated first to London, where he made useful contacts, then moved to the Low Coun-

---

[2] S. R. Cope, *Walter Boyd, A Merchant Banker in the Age of Napoleon* (London: Alan Sutton, 1983).

[3] Buist, *At Spes Non Fractra.*

[4] Ambrose Saricks, *Pierre Samuel Du Pont de Nemours* (Lawrence: University of Kansas Press, 1965).

[5] Richard Davis, *The English Rothschilds* (London: Collins, 1983).

[6] The latter date is determined by the dates of the Latin American revolutions for independence from Spain and the speculative surge that took place in both the Paris and London stock markets in that year, as well as the changes in the Bank of England's financial role that followed.

[7] For more examples and a fascinating discussion of the role of this class in nineteenth-century economic history, see Charles A. Jones, *International Business in the Nineteenth Century: The Rise and Fall of a Cosmopolitan Bourgeoisie* (New York University Press, 1987).

tries to begin his business career (but in Brussels rather than Amsterdam), and then founded a very successful bank in Paris – Boyd, Ker & Cie – whereby he made his fortune. The bank's prosperity was based on remittance facilities in London (through the firms of Robert and Charles Herries), Brussels (through Edouard Walckiers and the firm of Veuve Nettine & Fils), Amsterdam (Henry Hope), and Hamburg (John Parish). As the revolution took its course, Boyd's facilities were utilized more and more by the aristocracy to rearrange and relocate their assets.[8]

In March 1791 he saw the former Austrian ambassador to France, Count Mercy-Argenteau, draw down most of his balance of 871,000 livres in Boyd, Ker & Cie to finance the purchase of Three Per Cent Consols through the house of Harman, Hoare & Co. in London. Mercy-Argenteau had left Paris at the end of 1790, his royalist sympathies being well known, and from Brussels was trying to salvage what property he could. Income from his French estates fell because of the suppression of feudal rights, and the French paper currency known as the assignat was falling on the foreign exchanges.[9] Count Mercy-Argenteau was a very wealthy man, with estates in France, holdings in the Austrian Netherlands, and a plantation in Santo Domingo. He also owned large amounts of French securities. His actions to convert his French assets into British assets certainly were not limited to the direct purchase of British consols, but could take a variety of indirect routes as well. At the end (he died in August 1794 while on a trip to London to negotiate on behalf of the "Imperial Loans" being promoted by Boyd), only his purchase of English consols was an unqualified success. His failures in other ventures were due to his inexperience in managing financial and mercantile assets and his reluctance to accept his losses in assignats or to rely on commodity merchants to handle his affairs in a blind trust. His principal French financial advisor, the marquis de Laborde, was beheaded on 18 April 1794.

Boyd also had English customers who during April to July 1792 speculated on a rise in the assignat by purchasing either French securities or assignats directly. The British authorities thought that was weakening the sterling exchange, and in January 1793 they made assignats void in Britain.[10] Boyd, in fact, managed to raise capital for his new London firm, Boyd, Benfield & Co., begun on 15 March 1793, by selling Paul Benfield

---

[8] Cope, *Walter Boyd*, chap. 1–2, passim.

[9] The efforts of Mercy-Argenteau to liquidate his French wealth and move it to London or Belgium are described in H.E.B., "Flight of Capital from Revolutionary France," *American Historical Review*, 41(July 1936), pp. 710–23.

[10] Cope, *Walter Boyd*, p. 25.

three blocks of French life annuities held by his Paris bank for nearly £80,000. Benfield, in turn, was an outstanding example of the wealthy nabob returning from a career of dubious morality but undoubted profitability in India. His return to England was prompted by the arrival of Cornwallis in India and the tightened control over country trade imposed on freewheeling English merchants who were not in the East India Company's formal structure. But much like Hope in Amsterdam, confronted with a new, hostile regime, Benfield had difficulties in transferring his Indian wealth back to England without using the exchange facilities of the East India Company. He may have been ill-advised in the long run to take Boyd's offer of French assets, but that may have seemed less risky than trying to maintain his claim on assets in India.

Boyd's experience in facilitating international transfers and his awareness of the eagerness of Continental investors to deal in the London market no doubt underlay his arguments to William Pitt in 1794 that the British government should underwrite a £6 million loan to Austria. He argued that a considerable part of the loan would be remitted to London from foreign countries, presumably from merchants and nobles throughout the territories ruled by the Habsburgs. The firm of Veuve Nettine & Fils in Brussels, where Boyd had begun his career, was the leading firm engaged in remittances from the Austrian Netherlands to Vienna.[11] Boyd argued that the loan should be issued in London rather than abroad because no other place had such important connections with every other country, and because remittance of the proceeds to the Austrian armies would be easier from London than from elsewhere.[12] The taking up of the loan by foreigners acting through their attorneys in London would be identical with the case of capital flight illustrated in Figure 9.1, and the remittance of proceeds could operate exactly as in Figure 10.1, with the British government becoming the drawee, using bills drawn by Boyd and Benfield to make payments in the Habsburg Empire for the military services they were importing.

In December 1794, Pitt signed the agreement as Boyd wished, and by February 1795 he was using against his critics, especially the Bank of England,[13] Boyd's arguments about Continental investors taking up a large part of the so-called Imperial Loans. The Austrians signed off in May

[11] P. G. M. Dickson, *Finance and Government under Maria Theresa, 1740–1780* (Oxford University Press, 1987), Vol. 2, pp. 182–3.
[12] Cope, *Walter Boyd*, p. 48.
[13] Ibid., p. 63.

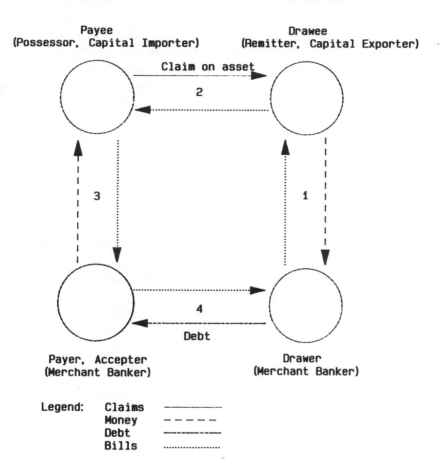

Figure 9.1. The foreign bill of exchange as a means of payment in capital flight.

1795, and remittances then began. The scale those remittances reached in a few months no doubt accounted for the 7% fall of the British pound relative to Hamburg in the summer of 1795.[14]

Boyd then became the major contractor, or entrepreneur, in the terminology of the time, for the large loans that Pitt was forced to float for the British government in 1795, 1796, and 1797. The inability of the market to support the issues of 1796 and 1797 meant liquidity constraints for Boyd

[14] Ibid., p. 70 (cf. Figure 9.2).

and eventual failure of Boyd, Benfield & Co. in March 1799. After the Peace of Amiens (March 1802), Boyd returned to Paris to negotiate for recovery of the assets of his Paris firm. A fresh outbreak of war put an end to those efforts and further confined him to the Continent without resources. When peace did come, he was able to recover a good part of his French assets, which had risen in value, and eventually to pay off his English creditors. Returning to England at the end of 1814, his fortunes recovered sufficiently that by the time of his death in 1837 he had acquired an estate worth over £200,000. Such were the vagaries of fortune for one of the more *unlucky* participants in the new era of government finance.[15]

Henry Hope

Henry Hope had written to Boyd in the summer of 1794 inquiring if Boyd would assist in urging the British government to open its ports to Dutch ships returning with colonial goods and allow them to reexport without penalty. That would avoid the risk of capture of their cargoes by the French in the event the Revolutionary forces captured Holland. The grand pensionary of Holland, when asked his opinion of that proposal by the British government, replied that it would be better for the English to seize Dutch cargoes "in order to leave to the Hopes and other over-grown capitalists of this country no other chance for saving their property than the giving or at least lending a part of it to supply the wants of the Government."[16] Though removed to London, where English business had to be done through the Baring firm, and reduced to a minimal staff in Amsterdam, Hope managed to continue his underwriting business. That was done through partners who remained in Amsterdam, through contacts in Hamburg, and through commissioning merchants such as Robert Voûte to act on Hope's behalf.

Following the Peace of Amiens, the firm of Henry Hope remained in London, but furnished part of the capital for a new firm, Hope & Co., which was operated in Amsterdam by John Williams Hope and Pierre Labouchère. That created a unique combination of underwriting facilities for government loans and remittance services in both the London and Amsterdam financial centers. That combination frequently led to anomalous and, to a modern observer, amusing confusions over the sources of savings for financing all the belligerents. For example, Henry Hope & Co.

15 Ibid., chap. 13–14.
16 Buist, *At Spes Non Fractra*, p. 49.

handled the Spanish loan when Spain was fighting against France in 1792–3, but Hope & Co. handled the Spanish loan of 1807 when Span was allied with France.[17]

In the fall of 1807 those tangled connections led to a bizarre incident involving the British warship *Diana,* carrying more than 3.5 million Mexican piastres from Vera Cruz to Portsmouth, coins useful for payment to Wellington's troops and for the English East India Company. Even though the insurance on the *Diana* and its cargo was the largest single risk covered by Lloyd's during the Napoleonic Wars, that transaction accounted for only a small part of the 52.5 million piastres that Hope and Baring managed to take from the Mexican mint over the period 1804–8. The bulk of that treasure ended up in the hands of the French government, through the intermediation of G. J. Ouvrard, Napoleon's financial genius, who relied on the Hope companies to move the Mexican coins from Vera Cruz to Antwerp. Ouvrard himself then managed the transfer from Antwerp to Paris, at least until his imprisonment by Napoleon in 1806.[18] Hope's connections with Baring were useful for getting the use of British warships to transport some of the piastres safely to Europe; their connections with David Parish in Philadelphia (originally from Hamburg) were valuable in establishing an American–Antwerp link in the web of remittances, and the use of their agents Vincent Nolte and A. P. Lestapis, in New Orleans and Vera Cruz, completed the complicated network.[19]

Alexander Baring played a key role in those transactions, convincing the British government that it was an economical way to provide Wellington with his supplies on the Iberian Peninsula. In 1815, Baring was the leading figure in the syndicate of underwriters that marketed the £30 million issue of Three Per Cent Consols (bought by Baring and by Smith, Payne & Smith at 77% of par) needed to subsidize the allies against a Napoleon returned from Elba. Only £1 million of the subsidies raised by that issue was said to have been transferred from London. All the remainder came by remitting from the payments made by eager investors in the British securities located in Amsterdam, Basel, Frankfurt, Hamburg, St. Petersburg,

[17] Buist, *At Spes Non Fractra,* chap. 9–11, gives full details of these various operations.
[18] Ibid., p. 329.
[19] Vincent Nolte, *The Memoirs of Vincent Nolte: Reminiscences in the Period of Anthony Adverse* (New York: G. Howard Watt, 1934), chap. 2–8, gives a colorful account of a junior member of the scheme stationed primarily in New Orleans. Ralph Hidy, *The House of Baring in American Trade and Finance: English Merchant Bankers at Work, 1763–1861* (Cambridge, MA: Harvard University Press, 1949), pp. 35–7, gives a somewhat different account than Buist.

and Vienna.[20] Baring reappeared as a leading witness before the secret committee opposing resumption (and Ricardo) in 1819. His testimony was valued because he had played the leading role in underwriting the first large loan to France in 1817.[21]

Pierre Samuel Du Pont de Nemours and sons

The Du Pont migration was decided on in 1797, and for two years the family prepared for the move, though the elder Du Pont also retained hope for a political role in Napoleon's Consulate. To finance the move, Du Pont started a joint-stock land company to operate in the United States and offered shares in it up to 4 million francs. It appears that he raised only 214,347 francs, and that primarily from the sale of various pieces of real estate – two farms, two houses in Rouen, and the print shop in Paris.[22] In 1801, the younger son, Eleuthère Irénée, returned to France for three months to raise capital for his gunpowder enterprise. He had little difficulty in obtaining the $36,000 he estimated to be necessary, especially because a good part of that was spent on the purchase of machines built in France at the Arsenal to French government specifications and then exported to America.[23] That was a nice example of French capitalists establishing a claim on property abroad even at the end of the Revolutionary period and well past the Reign of Terror.

Nathan Rothschild

The most famous war financier of the period, Nathan Rothschild, arrived in Manchester in 1799 with some £20,000 of capital from his firm and his father's firm in Frankfurt. He quickly prospered in the cotton trade, ordering goods specifically for the central German market served by Frankfurt. In 1806 his marriage to Hannah Cohen allied him with the Anglo-Jewish society that included the Goldsmids and Salomons, wealthy stockjobbers who had been associated with Walter Boyd in the underwriting of Pitt's war

[20] Hidy, *The House of Baring*, p. 53.

[21] See D. C. M. Platt, *Foreign Finance in Continental Europe and the United States, 1815–1870: Quantities, Origins, Functions, and Distribution* (London: Allen & Unwin, 1984), and Stanley Chapman, *The Rise of Merchant Banking* (London: Allen & Unwin, 1984), chap. 2.

[22] Saricks, *Pierre Samuel Du Pont de Nemours*, p. 273.

[23] B. G. du Pont, *E. I. du Pont de Nemours and Company, A History 1802–1902* (Boston: Houghton Mifflin, 1920), p. 12.

loans described earlier.[24] In 1808 he moved to London. It may be that one reason was to oversee the investments of Wilhelm, elector of Hesse, in the British funds. It is known that the elector bought at least £150,000 of Three Per Cent Consols on 18 December 1809, representing reinvestment of the interest due him on his existing holdings![25] As early as June 1803, Nathan Rothschild had written to Harman & Co. inquiring their opinion on the future price of Three Per Cents and placing an order for £5,000 for his father's account. But his father at that time was managing more and more of the elector's financial dealings, and that order may well have been for the elector's account. As one of the major providers of mercenaries for the British forces on the Continent, the elector was in constant receipt of sterling payments, payments that were sequestered when Napoleon's troops took over direct control of Hesse in 1806.[26]

In 1811, Nathan's younger brother James moved to Paris, apparently to be the recipient of gold smuggled across from England, presumably by Nathan.[27] Thus began the development of a unique linking of remittance paths across the belligerent states of Europe. By 1814, Nathan Rothschild was in fact playing the role in the British government's war finances that Walter Boyd had sought to play for Pitt in the early stages of the wars. John Robert Herries, the commissary general for Wellington's army (and son of Charles Herries, who was a partner in the firm that originally employed Walter Boyd), reported that "through the agency of Mr Rothschild . . . the Chest in the South of France was furnished with French gold from Holland by shipments at Helvoetsluys so rapidly and completely that the Commissary General was abundantly supplied for all his wants without having to negotiate a bill; and from that time no Military Debt [the source] of so much loss and embarrassment [in the Peninsula] was created on the Continent."[28] From Herries's testimony it appears that Rothschild was the entrepreneur and merchant banker who succeeded at the end of the Napoleonic Wars in accomplishing what Walter Boyd had attempted and failed to do at the start of the French Revolutionary Wars – finance the war

---

[24] Davis, *The English Rothschilds*, pp. 23–5.
[25] Egon Corti, *The Rise of the House of Rothschild*, translated from German by Brian and Beatrix Lunn (New York: Grosset & Dunlap, 1928), p. 79.
[26] Davis, *The English Rothschilds*, p. 28.
[27] Anka Muhlstein, *James de Rothschild, Une métamorphose, une légende* (Paris: Gallimard, 1981), pp. 17–18.
[28] Davis, *The English Rothschilds*, p. 30, quoting from BL Add. Mss. 57367, ff. 12–26, a memorandum from J. C. Herries to Lord Liverpool and Nicholas Vansittart on 12 June 1816.

against France with the resources of the Continent mobilized through the London capital market.

The transfer problem of Britain
in the Napoleonic Wars

In an intervention made during the Bullion Report debate, Herries went much further than simply lauding the efforts of one man; he described in more general, analytical terms the technique of British war finance:

Although it is by no means an ordinary case, it is certainly a possible one, that a nation may expend abroad much more than it can immediately repay by the export of Bullion, or of any other commodities. It may, on the credit of its Government, *raise money in other countries* [emphasis added], to a larger amount, by Bills of Exchange, than the purchasers of those Bills can immediately procure returns for. If the foreign markets are glutted with the produce of the borrowing nation, and Bullion is very scarce and dear in its market (as in such a state of things it would probably be), the foreign purchaser of its bills must expect considerable delay and inconvenience, in bringing back his funds to his own country: still, however, he might advance the money at a corresponding rate of exchange. This is, probably, the case, with respect to our drafts from abroad at this time: – we are borrowing money to carry on our foreign expenditure, at a high rate of interest. It is, however, an advantage, in some degree compensating this extraordinary expence, that the debt, so created, must, ultimately, be discharged in British produce or merchandize; and *it is, therefore, so much foreign capital invested in British industry* [emphasis added].[29]

In other words, the book credit built up by the Amsterdam merchant banker depicted in Figure 9.1 was seen by Herries to be a form of direct investment in British industry, because the only way he could see for the debts of London bankers to be discharged eventually was by the export of British goods. That was a very clever, if self-serving, argument, but it had the merit of being testable against the movements of the exchange rates of the pound against the various currencies on the Continent. The exchange rates were clearly recognized by the merchants and bankers of the time to be determined by fluctuations in Britain's balance of payments. The balance of payments, in turn, was determined both by the balance of trade *and* by the movements of capital.[30]

---

[29] J. M. Herries, *Review of the Controversy reflecting the High Price of Bullion and the State of our Currency* (London: J. Budd, 1811), pp. 44–5.

[30] Great Britain, "Reports from the Secret Committee on the Expediency of The Bank resuming Cash Payments," *British Parliamentary Papers* (London: House of Commons, 5

Both those determinants were influenced sharply at times by the policy measures undertaken by Great Britain or France, whether for economic purposes or for military purposes. At least three factors were recognized by contemporaries: (1) the suspension of gold or silver convertibility by the belligerent powers, with the paper assignat of the French Revolution and the paper pound of 1797–1821 being the dominant examples, (2) the provisioning of large armies at a distance, both by France on the Continent and by England after war resumed in 1803, and (3) the disruption of normal channels of trade by the victories of the French armies and the British navy and, most notably, the Continental Blockade experiment of Napoleon. But contemporaries understandably saw those as transitory disruptions, not as fundamental alterations in the structure of the international financial system of Europe. A fourth factor should be added that even contemporaries saw as fundamental: (4) the alteration of property rights created by the French Revolution and its spread throughout continental Europe. The network of international finance was also altered in as fundamental a fashion as the national economic and political structures of the new nation-states of Europe.

Throughout the period 1793–1825, the exchange rates give us the net outcome, regarding both current and capital accounts, that resulted from public and private actions taken in response to the great events occurring in the political and military spheres, thereby allowing us to gauge the relative importance of public and private initiatives in the international markets. They may also allow us to gauge, in the international sector at least, the relative weight of the British war effort on the private economy. And the perpetual question of the relationship between the industrial revolution taking place in the British economy and the war effort against the French Revolution can also be posed in terms of these data.

The evidence comes from Castaing's *Course of the Exchange,* from the beginning of 1789 through the end of 1810. For the period from 1811 through 1823, the semiweekly usance rates on Hamburg and Paris and prices of gold are taken from *Lloyd's List.* The same sources are used for the prices of Bank of England and East India Company stock, as well as the prices of Three Per Cent Consols and the premia or discounts on East India bonds. These prices of the prime securities of the period provide the most sensitive and detailed barometer possible by which to gauge the financial

April and 6 May 1819), p. 263, "Minutes of the Court of Directors of the Bank of England, 25th March 1819."

pressures created by revolution and war. The courses of the exchanges, both the foreign exchange and the stock exchange, are displayed in Figures 9.2 and 9.3. These are drawn for end-of-month observations from 1789 through 1823.[31]

The exchanges of London on Amsterdam and Hamburg remained impervious to the excitement of the French Revolution until the fall of 1791, when the pound began to weaken gradually on both mercantile centers. The *ecu*, by contrast, gradually weakened in terms of the pound (and, by inference, in terms of both schellingen and schillingen banco in Amsterdam and Hamburg) from the beginning of 1789 until November 1791. Its decline became increasingly disturbed in 1790 and 1791, until it reached its lowest value in February and March 1792. Thereafter, until the course of the exchange with Paris was halted in April 1793, the French money of account appreciated erratically, whereas the Amsterdam and Hamburg rates began to show some slight signs of varying in response to the French stimuli.

The weakening of the livre tournois in terms of the pound at a time when the pound itself was weakening relative to Amsterdam and Hamburg reflected persistent balance-of-payments deficits in France. Those could have been caused by either a balance-of-trade deficit or a deficit on capital account or both. Given the expropriation of Church lands and those of the emigrés and the movement of many emigrés in the first instance to Holland or Hamburg, it seems most likely that it was continued capital flight that

---

[31] The units for the Amsterdam rates are schellingen and penningen banco at the Bank of Amsterdam per British pound sterling. The mint par of exchange was 36s. 8d. banco. To get the rate in terms of circulating coin in Amsterdam, one must then multiply by a factor of one plus the agio – the banco money was a money of account, kept at a slight premium, referred to as the agio, over the money of circulation. The agio, however, was maintained at a constant 5% after 1802. The units for the Hamburg rates were schillingen and pfennig banco Flemish per pound sterling. Their mint par of exchange was a slightly lower 34s. 3.5d. Flemish banco. The French currency began as pence per ecu, with the ecu equal to 3 livres tournois and the mint par of exchange 29.2d. after 15 June 1726. After the franc germinal was established in April 1803, the mint par became 25 francs, 20 centimes per pound sterling. On 27 February 1797, the Bank of England announced to the public the suspension of convertibility of its bank notes into specie and the exchanges thereafter reflected the evaluation by the markets of the paper pound in terms of its previous gold equivalent, which then became, practically, a money of account. Finally, we must note the interruption of the course of the exchange with Paris from 2 April 1793, when Britain reciprocated France's declaration of war, until 2 April 1802, when the Treaty of Amiens was finally approved, and the interruption of the exchange with Amsterdam from 20 January 1795 until 30 March 1802. Despite the resumption of hostilities in 1803, the course of the exchanges on both Amsterdam and Paris continued to be reported regularly after March 1802.

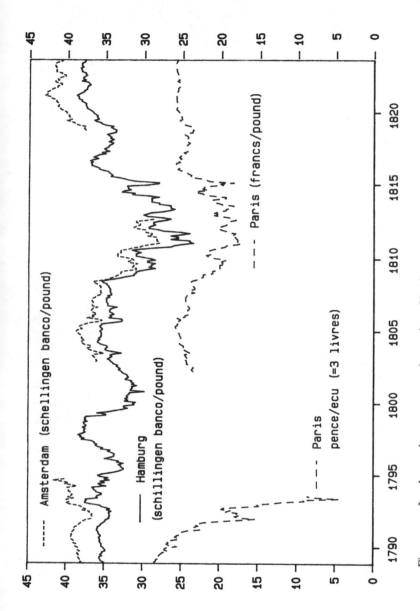

Figure 9.2. London exchange rates on Amsterdam, Hamburg, and Paris, 1789–1823.

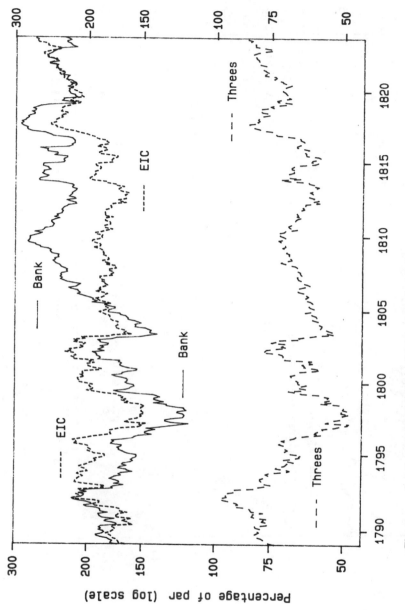

Figure 9.3. London Stock Exchange: Bank of England, East India Company, and Threes, 1798–1823.

was driving down the livre tournois in the initial phase of the French Revolution. Note that the assignat, made legal tender in April 1790, did not affect the exchanges dramatically until its rate of issue accelerated with the exigencies of war finance in April 1792.[32]

The strengthening of the Hamburg exchange in the first months of 1793 may have reflected the destination of some of the emigré capital, but it seems more likely to have reflected the movement of Spanish silver coins from London to Hamburg, where they could be disbursed to Hanover as part of Pitt's subsidization program. The movements of silver to Hamburg in 1794 to pay the Prussian subsidy, on the other hand, had little effect on the Hamburg exchange rate.[33]

The great excitement of 1794 was the bubble in the Amsterdam exchange rate in late September and early October. The decision of the Prussian general Mollendorf in early October to withdraw his troops across the Rhine rather than join up with either the Austrian army or the troops of the duke of York in Holland confirmed the victories of the French general Pichegru and the eventual demise of Holland. In fact, it is not clear that that represented entirely a flight of Dutch capital to England and Hamburg. The few rates we have for the agio in that period show a sharp change to a negative agio on the order of 10%.[34] That implies a run on the Bank of Amsterdam to withdraw accounts and convert them to specie. Even the highest disagio rates observed did not offset the depreciation of banco on the London exchange, however, and so the presumption must be that most of the specie withdrawn from the Bank of Amsterdam left the country for London and, to a lesser extent, Hamburg. But the British funds were also falling in price at that time, as they usually did in times of military adversity.

For the period from February 1795 until April 1802 we have only the usance rate at $2\frac{1}{2}$ months on Hamburg to track the fortunes of war, revolution, and peace. The pound was clearly weaker in Hamburg from late summer 1795 until late spring 1796, when it strengthened greatly, before

[32] Florin Aftalion, *L'économie de la Révolution française* (Paris: Hachette/Pluriel, 1987), pp. 385–7.

[33] John M. Sherwig, *Guineas and Gunpowder: British Foreign Aid in the Wars with France, 1793–1815* (Cambridge, MA: Harvard University Press, 1969), p. 365, and discussion in Chapters 1 and 2.

[34] J. G. van Dillen's table in "Effectenkoersen aan de Amsterdamsche Beurs, 1723–1794," *Economische-Historische Jaarboek*, 17(1931), shows only six dates in the latter half of 1794: July 7, $\frac{7}{16}$ to $\frac{1}{8}$; September 3, -2; November 7, $-9\frac{3}{4}$; November 21, -12 to $-11\frac{1}{2}$; December 5, $-10\frac{1}{2}$ to $-10\frac{1}{4}$; and December 19, $-9\frac{1}{2}$ (p. 46).

lapsing in May. The pound was then fairly stable, until it began to rise in December 1796, continuing well into January 1797. The fall that began in mid-January appears to have been very mild by the standards of previous fluctuations, a tribute perhaps to the effectiveness of the Bank of England's payments of gold in maintaining the stability of the exchanges. Nevertheless, the Bank of England carried out its famous suspension of convertibility of its bank notes into specie in late February 1797.

That suspension of convertibility in late February 1797 was not foreseen in the Hamburg exchange rate, and its response, after fluctuating uncertainly in March through May, was to value the paper pound increasingly above the mint par for the gold pound. Indeed, the international financial pressure caused by the war, according to the exchange-rate barometer, did not affect the British economy until the spring and summer campaigns of 1799. At that time the paper pound fell to permanently lower levels, which were sustained through 1800 and 1801. By contrast, the "funds" fell sharply on announcement of the suspension, probably reflecting the depreciation of the paper pound. They recovered partially in June 1797, but the presuspension levels were not achieved again until the autumn of 1798. The reasons for the suspension of convertibility in February and its confirmation by act of Parliament in May appear obscure. Although there was a run on country banks in Newcastle and Scotland, that could have been met by a fresh issue of Exchequer bills, as had been done successfully in 1793. The 1793 episode, however, had been seen as an internal drain, as depositors in country banks converted to holdings of Bank of England notes and from those bank notes to specie. The 1797 run, by contrast, was clearly seen as risking an external drain of specie abroad, even though the report to Parliament described the crisis in terms of an internal drain arising from the "alarm of Invasion" threatened by the French.[35]

But we should recall that British remittances on the Imperial Loans to Austria were continuing. Although they had caused the exchange on Hamburg to fall below the gold export point in May 1795, the use of offsetting credits in England and bills of exchange by Boyd had restored the exchange rate above the gold export point by March 1796. It was then rising above the gold import point.[36] Perhaps the bank anticipated more pressure on gold reserves when remittances to Austria began again. What is clear is that the return of the French monetary system to a metallic basis in early

35 Great Britain, "Third Report, 21 April 1797 of Committee of Secrecy on the Outstanding Demands of the Bank of England," British Parliamentary Papers, 1797.
36 Ibid., p. 7.

February, when France eliminated the use of paper currency entirely, was going to increase French demand for gold. That obviously would place additional pressure on British gold supplies and on the British techniques of war finance. There is little doubt that that was the intent, in part, of the French authorities. In other words, the paper money experiment of the assignats, which had repeated John Law's experiment of 1719–20, was going to be succeeded by a restoration of gold convertibility, repeating the French experience of 1720–1. The Bank of England anticipated sharp pressure on the London exchanges, similar to that experienced in November 1720. It is useful to note that in both cases, the pressure came hardly at all from English investors shifting their assets to Paris, but mainly from Continental merchants shifting their credits out of London and into Paris.

All three exchange rates showed a slight rise in the value of the paper pound during the resumption of peacetime trading in 1802, and that continued to be the case until the disturbances of 1805. (French currency was then the franc germinal and was quoted in francs and centimes per pound; so its rate moved directly, instead of inversely, with those of Amsterdam and Hamburg.[37]) It appears that resumption of the course of exchange between London and Amsterdam was at the initiative of the Dutch. A report in the London *Times* of 1802 commented as follows:

The Dutch have already taken advantage of the termination of hostilities, so far as to send hither gin, flax, butter, cheese, rags, skins, tanned leather, madder, and Rhenish wines in large quantities. . . . The exports from London to Holland are few. . . . A regular course of the exchange does not yet take place between the two countries, but the Dutch receive immediate payment in hard cash for a great part of the articles of provisions, &c. which we purchase from them.[38]

The rates all slipped in the fall of 1805 and remained low in 1806 and 1807. The next major decline in the paper pound occurred in the fall of 1808, when the massive expenditures of the Peninsular Campaign were added to the subsidies to the Continental allies, which continued despite

[37] In 1802 only, the Amsterdam exchange was on "current florins," because the Bank of Amsterdam had not returned to full operation. From the start of 1803 onward there was no special notation on the Amsterdam quotes, and the levels indicate they were again in schellingen banco. It is interesting that Posthumus shows the rates in Amsterdam for bills drawn on London to be in florins as early as 16 February 1801 and to switch to schellingen banco by 29 November 1802. Nicholas Posthumus, *Inquiry into the History of Prices in Holland* (Leiden: E. J. Brill, 1946), Vol. 1, p. 614.
[38] London *Times*, 1 February 1802, p. 3, col. 2.

TABLE 9.1
Mint pars of exchange

Paris on London	25 francs and 21 cents for one pound in standard gold
Paris on Amsterdam	56 1/2 deniers Dutch currency in Amsterdam for 3 francs in Paris
Paris on Hamburg	100 marks banco in Hamburg for 188 francs in Paris
London on Paris	25 francs and 20 cents for one pound in standard gold
London on Amsterdam, banco	36 shillings and 8 pence Flemish per pound sterling
London on Amsterdam, current	11 florins and 4.5 stivers per pound sterling
London on Hamburg	34 shillings and 3.5 pence Flemish banco per pound sterling

Source: Great Britain, "Reports from the Secret Committee on the Expediency of The Bank resuming Cash Payments," *British Parliamentary Papers* (London: House of Commons, 5 April and 6 May 1819), second report, pp. 363-4, appendix C.7, C.8.

their ineffectiveness. The rates continued to fall in 1809, but firmed up in the period April through September of 1810.

The final trade crisis precipitated by Napoleon's harsh enforcement of the Continental Blockade then appeared clearly in the fall of 1810. Especially pronounced was the fall of the rate on Hamburg, which continued to plummet until April 1811. Thereafter, it was clearly the altering fortunes of war that determined the exchanges, because Paris and Hamburg moved in unison. Especially remarkable was the depression of the pound in both cities during Napoleon's Hundred Days in the spring of 1815.

What can we conclude from these foreign-exchange-rate data for some of the larger issues that have occupied the attention of economic historians studying this period? First, we must recognize that these data are incomplete, because they give only the exchange rates among the monies of account traditionally used in international trade, omitting the intermediate rates that determined rates of exchange between circulating monies. For example, the price of gold in terms of the paper pound changed periodically in the interval 1797–1821, as did the price of silver relative to gold in London and Hamburg. The agio rate (the premium of bank deposits over circulating coins) at the Bank of Amsterdam fluctuated violently in 1794. The assignat depreciated at an accelerating rate relative to the livre tournois, even during the interval when it was made legal tender. But after 1802 the agio remained a constant 5% at the Bank of Amsterdam, the

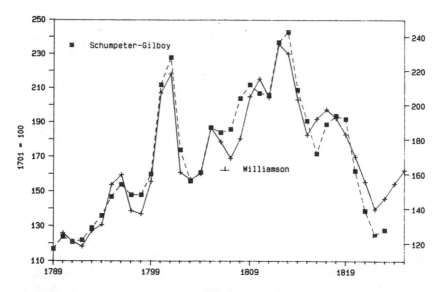

Figure 9.4. British price indexes, 1789–1823 (data of Schumpeter-Gilboy and Williamson).

assignat had been eliminated, and the Bank of England maintained the price of gold at fairly constant rates. So the omission of those intermediate rates may not materially affect our general impressions.

Second, we must recognize that the domestic price level in Britain was affected by the vicissitudes of war finance as well and may have played an independent role in causing the fluctuations we have described in the stock market and in the foreign exchange rates. Figure 9.4 shows two of the general price indexes developed by economic historians for this period – the Schumpter-Gilboy and the Williamson indexes. Advocates of the importance of inflationary forces in this period note the rise from 1792 to 1813 – nearly 3% annually. That was a low rate by our modern standards, and a low rate compared with any other paper-currency regime of the eighteenth century. But it was a high rate by British standards for previous wars of the eighteenth century, all conducted under a de facto gold standard. Doubters of the importance of war inflation for the period 1789–1815 as a whole note the importance of two episodes in creating the price rise, and they note that both episodes, one at the turn of the eighteenth century during a succession of bad harvests, and one at the peak of Wellington's campaigns on the Continent, were associated with real supply shocks and were short-lived. This view of the course of domestic inflation is consistent with the view expressed here that fluctuations in the exchange rates were episodic and tended to disappear in the absence of major reversals in military or political events – until 1808. Thereafter, the fluctuations were larger and showed no tendency to dampen quickly. There definitely was a change in the effect of British war financing on the exchanges – or a change in the British financial techniques, as will be argued in the next chapter.

Moreover, that kind of volatility continued after the war and dominated in the testimony of the witnesses before the secret committees of the House of Commons and House of Lords in 1819. The bullionist argued that the volatility was due to excessive issues of notes by the Bank of England, but a large part, as the leading merchant bankers testified, must have been due to deliberate movements of large sums of capital back and forth between London and the Continent as political opportunities shifted and provisions for the funding of government debts and reparations were altered. That was the continuing legacy in the financial sphere of the operations of the Continental subsidies begun by Pitt and continued at increasingly higher levels by his successors. It would be very strange if the military shocks and financial innovations imposed by the British and French governments on the international capital markets that had arisen over the course of the eighteenth century had no repercussions for the real economy of Britain as it entered the nineteenth century.

The evidence of the stock and foreign exchanges, combined with our qualitative evidence from the activities of the financiers and international middlemen of the era, indicates that the capital flows during the period of the Napoleonic Wars were on a much larger scale than ever before and were predominantly from the Continent to England, at least until the Continental System was imposed by Napoleon in 1806. What effects did the events of Continental revolution, war on a global scale, diversion of foreign trade, peace, and restoration have on the direction and dimensions of capital flows within the European economy? How did the deteriorating assignat, the innovation of the paper pound, and the creation of the franc germinal affect the capital flows? And what effect did all those have on the course of British industrialization under way at the time? Clearly, a more determined analytical effort is required than has yet been undertaken by economic historians.

10. A tale of two revolutions: international capital flows, 1792–1815

The key historical event for the transformation of the international financial system in the period 1789–1825 was the success of Napoleon's Continental System, which disrupted the traditional British techniques for financing wars on the European continent, as it was intended to do. After 1808, when Napoleon perfected his Continental System, the exchanges of Britain with the Continent fluctuated violently, and from then on the government funds behaved quite differently. Instead of all three major stocks declining gradually in concert, the stocks of the Bank of England and the East India Company began to rise, with sharp fluctuations, whereas the Three Per Cents remained stable. How did the Continental System cause that regime change in the British financial markets?

The British success in fighting European wars had begun with the aid of William III's Dutch financiers in the War of the Grand Alliance (1688–97)[1] and continued through the Seven Years' War (1756–63).[2] Figure 10.1 shows how the network of trade credit created by widespread use of the foreign bill of exchange was exploited by the British government to finance its armies on the European continent during the eighteenth century. The Exchequer purchased from London merchants bills of exchange that were drawn on their correspondents abroad, then sent the bills to the British quartermaster abroad, who used them locally to hire troops and purchase supplies. Because British manufactured goods and colonial reexports were in high demand in Europe, the bills drawn in London were accepted readily by the European merchants, who used them to pay for imports from Britain. British woolens were thus transformed into Hessian mercenaries fighting the French, at least when the British war effort was successful.[3] That

---

[1] P. G. M. Dickson, *The Financial Revolution in England: A Study in the Development of Public Credit, 1688–1756* (London: Macmillan, 1967).

[2] Larry Neal, "Interpreting Power and Profit in Economic History: A Case Study of the Seven Years War," *Journal of Economic History,* 37(March 1977), pp. 20–35.

[3] Adam Smith, *Wealth of Nations* (London: 1776; reprinted New York: Random House, 1937), described this system at the outset of Book IV, "Principle of the Mercantile System" (pp. 410–14 in the Modern Library edition of 1937).

LONDON   AMSTERDAM

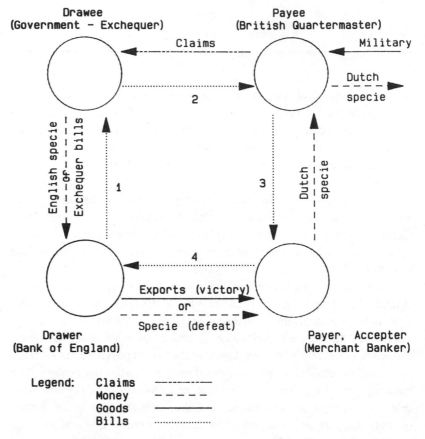

Figure 10.1. The foreign bill of exchange as a means of payment on the Continent in time of war.

sequence describes well the initial stages of the finance techniques employed by Britain in the war against Revolutionary France, 1793–1802, with the major difference that Britain's Continental allies were continually losing. As they lost battles against the French armies, so British merchants lost markets for their exports, and the bills of exchange drawn on London had to be extinguished increasingly by means of specie.

Pitt began his "First Coalition" against the French by hiring mercenaries from Hesse and subsidizing troops from Prussia, calculating his sums in

TABLE 10.1
Trade balances during war and revolution
(annual averages in millions of pounds)

Date	Imports	Exports	Reexports	Balance of trade
1784-86	20.4	12.7	2.7	-5.0
1794-96	34.3	21.8	6.9	-5.6
1804-06	50.6	37.5	8.3	-4.8
1814-16	64.7	44.5	16.1	-4.1
1824-26	57.0	35.3	8.1	-13.6

Source: Ralph Davis, *The Industrial Revolution and British Overseas Trade* (Leicester, UK: Leicester University Press, 1979), p. 86. Davis did not give the calculated balance of trade (exports + reexports - imports) stating "The differences of 5 per cent or more that appear in carefully calculated aggregates of import and export totals made by different scholars are so large that the possible error swamps the balancing figure that is aimed at" (p. 85). *Caveat lector!*

terms of a fixed number of pounds sterling per soldier provided.[4] British exports and reexports rose (Table 10.1). The loss of Holland at the end of 1794 made that traditional form of conducting war on the Continent impracticable, and the conclusion of a separate peace by Austria, in which the French were ceded Belgium in exchange for Austria's annexation of Venice, brought the war to a humiliating close. The continued defeats of British allies and mercenaries meant loss of markets for British goods, as well as military losses. The loss of markets shows up in Table 10.1 as a slackened rate of exports until the Treaty of Amiens in 1802. That provided a breathing spell for Britain and its sometime allies, and the volume of trade increased sharply between Britain and the Continent. But the peace treaty also allowed Napoleon to consolidate his political power.

The fresh outbreak of war in 1803 brought new subsidies from Britain to the Continent, the real transfer of which relied on increasing trade with Hamburg. That, however, was brought to an ignominious halt by the Continental Blockade, as Napoleon pursued a policy designed to undermine British financing of the Third Coalition in much the way the First

[4] Foot soldiers were rented in 1793 from Hesse-Kassel at £7 14s. each, and cavalrymen at £19 5s. each. John M. Sherwig, *Guineas and Gunpowder: British Foreign Aid in the Wars with France, 1793–1815* (Cambridge, MA: Harvard University Press, 1969), p. 18.

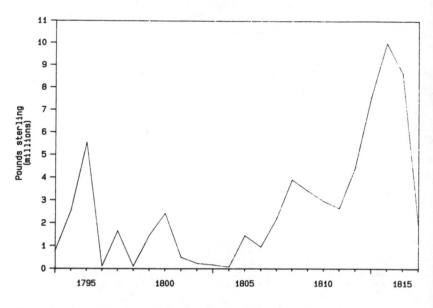

Figure 10.2. British subsidy payments to the Continent, 1793–1816.

Coalition had been undone.[5] In terms of Figure 10.1, Napoleon sought to undermine the acceptance on the Continent of bills of exchange drawn on London by making it very difficult to import British goods to the Continent. He could think of no other reason why merchant bankers on the Continent would be willing to accept London bills. Napoleon made his blockade effective by occupying Hamburg in November 1806. The British subsidies to the Continent (Figure 10.2) virtually ceased.[6] The pound weakened relative to the franc, the Dutch guilder, and the Hamburg pound Flemish, although the dramatic fall did not occur until 1808. (See Figure 9.2, where the fall in 1808 is seen to have been preceded by a short appreciation in the pound sterling, a sign of a liquidity scramble in London, as discussed in Chapter 4.) All this is evidence that the intended

[5] Cunningham gave an extended argument that this was done consciously by Napoleon on the basis of the analysis provided by J. H. Marnière, the chevalier de Guer, whose pamphlet, "Etat de la situation des finance de l'Angleterre et de la banque de Londres au juin 1802," is reprinted at the end of her work. Audrey Cunningham, *British Credit in the Last Napoleonic War* (Cambridge University Press, 1910).

[6] Sherwig, *Guineas and Gunpowder*, pp. 366–7, recorded the low point of subsidies at only £83,303 to Hesse-Kassel in 1804, and thereafter subsidies were paid in an ever wider arc, including eventually Sweden, Sicily, and Spain. (Note the inconsistency with his graph on p. 369, which shows lows in 1804 *and* 1806.)

effects of the blockade on British trade were occurring. Contemporary observers recognized that as well. In his testimony to the Bullion Committee in 1810, J. L. Greffulhe argued that the interruption of trade with the Continent had caused the exchanges to fall, not excessive issues of note by the Bank of England.[7]

If the Continental Blockade worked as intended to hamper British exports to the Continent, it did not succeed in halting Britain's financial support for its allied armies against Napoleon. The eventual failure of Napoleon's economic attack on the financial structure of Britain is evident from the continued strength of the government stocks on the London Stock Exchange (see Figure 9.3). The causes of that failure have been attributed to Britain's renewed overseas trade in 1811 (mainly to new markets in Spanish America) and to alternate routes to European markets through the Baltic and the Mediterranean.[8] In the preceding chapter we saw that Herries attributed the failure basically to the willingness of Continental merchant bankers to build up their credits on London, anticipating eventual victory by Britain and its allies and a resumption of British exports. The ultimate failure of the Continental System, of course, lay in the eventual military defeat of France, but that was due less to a resurgence in British trade than to strictly military factors, especially Napoleon's disastrous 1812 campaign in Russia.

Rather than the rise of illicit trade, or the increase in short-term trade credit given to Britain, then, it seems more reasonable to attribute the blockade's failure in financial terms to offsetting capital movements – investment by Continental merchants and aristocrats in the British funds. The blockade failed in economic terms because of a shift of resources within the British manufacturing sector away from light industry devoted to exports of consumer goods and into heavy industry devoted to production of military goods for Wellington's army in the Peninsular Campaign. The reallocation of manufacturing effort within the British economy was surely aided, if perhaps only indirectly, by the infusion of foreign capital. The structural change in British manufacturing that resulted was necessary to accomplish the eventual military victory on the Continent. British (mostly Scottish, Irish, and Welsh) troops, not Hessians, had to be recruited,

---

[7] See S. Cock, *An Examination of the Report of the Bullion Committee* (London: J. Dennett, 1810). Cock, a Liverpool agent, argued that far from driving up the price of gold, the bank's increased issue of notes helped keep down its price, because the notes substituted for gold as a means of payment in domestic trade.

[8] Eli F. Heckscher, *The Continental System: An Economic Interpretation* (Oxford University Press, 1922).

equipped, sent abroad, and resupplied from home. The financial side of the new British military policy began in 1808 with massive direct payments to Wellington's troops in the Peninsular Campaign. As we saw in the preceding chapter, that transformation of military financing had nearly as great an impact on the foreign exchanges as did the more famous trade crisis of 1810–11. Not until the resumption of the gold standard in 1821 were the foreign exchanges to regain the stability they had displayed from 1721 through 1789.

That sea change in the British economy, caused by the failure of the eighteenth-century financial strategy of Britain for European wars, was reflected as well in the reorganization of the London stock market that followed the crisis of 1810. The *Course of the Exchange* expanded its listings beyond government stocks to include stocks of waterworks, canals, toll roads, and mines. The London Stock Exchange adopted its first rule book for member brokers and jobbers in 1812.[9] Afterward, the entire financial payments network of the British Empire became established in a much more cosmopolitan way, providing the basis for the British imperium of the nineteenth century.

The French Revolution and the Continental System

Tables 10.2 and 10.3 present data on the importance of the foreign holdings of that part of the British national debt administered by the Bank of England – which was the overwhelming part of the debt, because it included all the new debt issues, especially of the Three Per Cent Consols. These were the holdings of foreigners still resident on the Continent or in America in areas under French occupation or French Revolutionary rule. That is, they were the holdings that were sequestered by the bank, which held the dividends due as well. The origins of these holdings go back to February 1794, when Parliament passed an act that prevented any money or effects owned by residents of France that were currently "in the hands of His Majesty's subjects" from being given to them.[10] The justification was that the French Revolutionary government had just passed an act to expropriate all foreign goods belonging to French residents in order to help finance the

---

[9] E. Victor Morgan and W. A. Thomas, *The Stock Exchange: Its History and Functions* (London: Elek Books, 1962), p. 75.

[10] 34 Geo. III, cap. 9. The act was reprinted by Sheila Lambert, ed., *House of Commons Sessional Papers of the Eighteenth Century. Vol. 92: Bills, 1794* (Wilmington, DE: Scholarly Resources, 1975), pp. 1–16.

TABLE 10.2
Foreign holdings of English national debt
(nominal value in pounds sterling)

A. May 1801

DEBT	DUTCH	N'LANDS	SWISS	ITALIAN	FRENCH	GERMANY	TOTAL
Threes	7,278,312	717,987	627,017	517,681	135,897	3,553,463	12,830,357
Reduced 3%	1,407,364	289,016	82,089	38,649	6,890	107,402	1,931,410
Fours	520,966	56,998	50,852	9,025	3,075	169,975	810,891
3%, 1726	75,183	22,137	1,600	1,000	0	2,500	102,420
Navy, 5%	32,804	2,505	15,060	2,011	0	89,265	141,645
Fives, 1797	80,830	4,814	8,182	2,457	776	15,682	112,741
Imperial, 3%	15,550	13,900	9,648	17,059	0	60,079	116,236
Irish, 5%	1,600	0	7,500	0	0	0	9,100
Bank Stock	1,127,748	71,537	58,127	42,153	5,372	82,719	1,387,656
Total	10,540,357	1,178,894	860,075	630,035	152,010	4,081,085	17,442,456
Total Annuity	4,084	276	1,710	1,432	226	1,811	9,539

Source: Bank of England, "Amount of Stock and Annuities in the Names of Foreigners. May 1801," in *Accounts Presented to Parliament, 1802-1819,* SED/8395, Bank of England Archives, p. 20.

TABLE 10.2 (continued)
Foreign holdings of English national debt
(nominal value in pounds sterling)

B. December 1806

DEBT	DUTCH	N'LANDS	FRENCH	SWISS	ITALIAN	GERMANY	RUSSIA	HANOVER	TOTAL
Threes	5,887,591	550,351	230,653	612,819	636,532	2,434,094	239,010	367,955	10,959,005
Reduced 3%	1,580,809	159,287	6,537	68,709	44,825	139,630	50,863	19,239	2,069,899
Fours	376,231	48,535	11,897	38,850	6,745	322,869	2,800	4,915	812,842
3%, 1726	92,484	1,000	0	700	0	6,193	0	0	100,377
Navy, 5%	64,146	7,782	6,470	15,046	4,642	110,880	7,000	562	216,528
Fives, 1797	29,847	512	72	4,355	416	5,193	2,445	625	43,465
Imperial, 3%	8,350	12,066	1,860	13,648	459	23,138	8,000	0	67,521
Irish, 5%	2,100	0	0	1,000	0	5,112	0	0	8,212
Bank Stock	800,019	52,503	3,203	63,646	32,098	77,590	3,000	555	1,032,614
Total	8,841,577	832,036	260,692	818,773	725,717	3,124,699	313,118	393,851	15,310,463
Total Annuity	3,355	819	57	696	525	2,786	200	0	8,438

Source: Bank of England, *Accounts Presented to Parliament, 1802-1819*, SED/8395, Bank of England Archives, p. 21. Title of account is "Amount of Stock and Annuities in the Names of Foreigners," 17 December 1806." Eight nationalities are distinguished: Dutch, Netherlands, French, Swiss, Italian, Russian, Hanover, Germany, and Other Powers. Nine stocks are mentioned: "3 per cent Cons., Reduced, 4 per Cent, 3 pCent 1726, 5 pCent Navy, 5 pCent 1797, Imperial 3 pCent, Irish 5pCent, and Bank Stock." Four annuities: "Long anns., 28 years Ann., Imp. Ann. 25 Yrs, and Irish Annuities 15 Years." The account is noted as "By order of and for the Governor," with no mention of being submitted to Parliament or being ordered by Parliament. There is a note on "3 per Cent" total for Hanover that £1,100,000 "on the Account of the Lords of the Regency of Hanover not included."

TABLE 10.2 (continued)
Foreign holdings of English national debt
(nominal value in pounds sterling)

C. November 1810

DEBT	DUTCH	FRENCH	GERMANY	HANOVER	SWISS	SPAIN	RUSSIA	AMERICA	TOTAL
Threes	5,265,354	1,205,234	1,129,647	354,203	725,932	863,607	246,633	348,660	10,139,270
Reduced 3%	1,403,503	347,079	54,038	18,689	60,352	316,920	60,873	24,363	2,285,817
Fours	310,151	51,074	178,843	4,443	35,230	205,621	2,700	8,125	796,187
3%, 1726	61,436	7,588	0	0	700	0	0	100	69,824
Navy, 5%	56,291	32,438	6,670	700	4,815	100,115	3,911	47,501	252,441
Fives, 1797	27,268	5,018	3,639	425	4,256	0	0	428	41,034
Imperial, 3%	7,083	13,904	0	0	13,903	53,500	0	5,280	93,670
Irish, 5%	0	0	0	0	4,600	0	0	2,000	6,600
Bank Stock	643,523	65,567	55,138	200	64,671	26,979	0	1,998	858,076
Total	7,774,609	1,727,902	1,427,975	378,660	914,459	1,566,742	314,117	438,455	14,542,919
Total Annuity	3,050	588	336	21	827	866	0	75	5,763

Source: Bank of England, *Accounts Presented to Parliament, 1802-1819*, SED/8395, Bank of England Archives, p. 78.

TABLE 10.3

An account of the total amount of foreign property in the British funds, on 24 November 1810, and also a half yearly account on 28 February and 31 August in each year, to 31 August 1818, inclusive

Date		Total of stocks	Terminable annuities
1810:	24 November	14,566,994	5,763
1811:	31 August	14,707,527	5,786
1812:	29 February	14,862,676	5,797
	30 August	14,919,997	5,717
1813:	27 February	15,217,705	5,558
	31 August	15,319,107	5,758
1814:	28 February	15,839,176	5,758
	31 August	15,900,341	5,832
1815:	28 February	15,878,290	6,111
	31 August	16,629,959	6,427
1816:	29 February	17,334,458	6,363
	31 August	17,235,150	6,511
1817:	1 March	15,892,711	6,130
	30 August	13,305,397	5,583
1818:	28 February	12,729,618	5,764
	31 August	12,486,913	5,791

Source: Great Britain, "Reports from the Secret Committee on the Expediency of The Bank resuming Cash Payments," *British Parliamentary Papers* (London, House of Commons, 5 April and 6 May 1819), appendix to second report, No. 43, p. 354.

war against England and Austria. So if their monies or effects were returned to them in the course of normal trade, they would be confiscated by the Revolutionary government. The British confiscation, by law-abiding contrast, preserved title to the monies or effects of the private individuals resident in France "or in any Country, territory, or place" under the control of the French Revolutionary government so that they could eventually have the benefit of their property.

In the meantime, however, special commissioners appointed for the task had control of their assets. An act passed in April 1794 "for more effectually preserving the money or effects . . . for the benefit of the individual owners" required these commissioners to pay the assets so acquired into an account at the Bank of England. The commissioners were then ordered that "all the monies to arise . . . shall from time to time be laid out in the purchase of Three Pounds *per centum* Consolidated Annuities, or in any other of the Public Funds transferrable at the Bank of England."[11] The "effects" of foreigners so applied to the purchase of the national debt for the duration of the hostilities included the payments of marine insurance claims on ships and cargoes lost since the outbreak of hostilities by merchants under the rule of French Revolutionaries. The scope of that act widened as the success of the French troops continued on the Continent and as other powers took up alliances with Napoleon.

The holdings of Americans, for example, had grown considerably after the Seven Years' War, especially among wealthy Americans in the southern colonies. (George Washington held stock in the Bank of England throughout the War for American Independence.) But American holdings were not included in the bank's accounts until the "Jefferson embargo" took effect in January 1808. At that time, their remaining investments in English government stocks were frozen as well and added to the total. The changing pattern of the sequestered holdings of British national debt by foreigners, reflecting the shifts in the fortunes of war from 1801 to 1810, is displayed in Figures 10.3–10.5. One notes the overwhelming importance of the Dutch holdings in each period and the increasing number of nationalities represented in 1806 and 1810 as Napoleon's armies spread over the Continent and his influence extended to Russia and the United States. Figure 10.6 shows the changing totals sequestered from 1801 to 1819, expressed both in the book values reported by the bank to Parliament and in the current market values determined by the price of Three Per Cent Consols on the London Stock Exchange.

But the preceding discussion demonstrates that the investments by foreigners in English government stocks were primarily by those not yet subject to expropriation of their capital by the forces of the French Revolution. So the figures in Table 10.2 must be scaled up by some unknown factor, perhaps three or five for the early years, but surely not less than two at any time. In January 1807, the principal of the unredeemed debt administered by the bank was calculated at £550,441,393. So the December 1806 sequestered holdings of foreigners were merely 2.8% of the total debt, and only a bit under 3.2% of the Three Per Cents. Scaling these up by a factor of three, we arrive at a rough guess that 8% to 10% of British national debt was held by foreigners.

Moreover, to these numbers must be added holdings acquired by recent

[11] Ibid., p. 161.

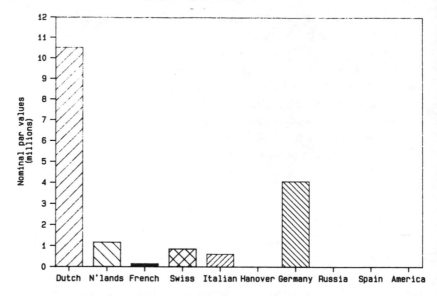

Figure 10.3. Foreign holdings of English national debt, 1801 (transfer books at Bank of England).

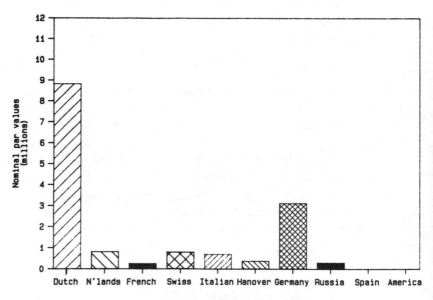

Figure 10.4. Foreign holdings of English national debt, 1806 (transfer books at Bank of England).

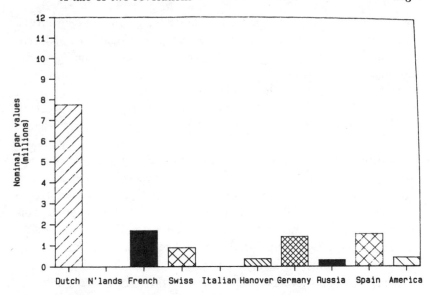

Figure 10.5. Foreign holdings of English national debt, 1810 (transfer books at Bank of England).

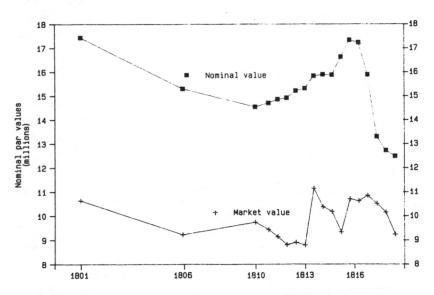

Figure 10.6. Foreign holdings of English national debt, 1801–18 (transfer books at Bank of England).

immigrants, whose flight from the Revolution took them to English ports. On becoming resident in England, their holdings would earn dividends without restriction, and so they would not be included in the bank's accounting of foreign owners. The immigrants in England who had come directly from France were few in number (fewer than 10,000 were counted in London in 1797, and over half of those were clergy),[12] but the argument really applies more to Dutch and German merchants and aristocrats than to French.

Another element of British war finance that reduced the burden of debt was the importance of unpaid dividends. Parliament received a full accounting from the bank, shortly after the revolution, of the amounts due but not paid to owners of the government securities transferable at the bank (which was all debt except that owed to the East India Company and the South Sea Company). In the year ending 31 December 1789, the bank paid out over £8 million in quarterly dividends. But it left unpaid another £2,624,709.[13] Most of those had arisen from the estates of deceased individuals who apparently died intestate, and some dated back to the first half of the eighteenth century.[14] Needless to say, the government quickly took advantage of those accumulated forfeitures to reduce its debt service to the bank.

Finally, we must return to the point made by Herries (see footnote 29 in Chapter 9) that bills of exchange drawn on London and held by foreign merchants who could not obtain British goods with them, for whatever reason, represented so much investment in British industry. That view of the transfer process allows us to reinterpret the shocks to London exchange rates in terms of their effects on foreign investment in British industry. Herries's argument was that if Britain initiated its transfer of real resources to its Continental allies by selling bills of exchange to them, so long as they deferred realizing those bills by purchasing imports from Britain with them, they had invested in Britain. So, by that argument, the initial financial transfer of bills on London by the British government to Continental quartermasters in 1793 using the remittance facilities of Walter Boyd,

12 Lambert, *House of Commons. Vol. 104: Reports and Papers, 1796–97*, p. 339.
13 Lambert, *House of Commons. Vol. 81: Reports and Papers, 1790–91*, pp. 1–3.
14 The bulk of Volume 81 is devoted to a listing of the names and addresses of the "proprietors" in the funds transferred at the Bank of England and the South Sea House whose dividends had not been paid at the last dividend date, when the first dividend was missed, an how many times the dividend had been missed. The number of accounts at the bank was 7,479 (p. 201). The total of unpaid dividends that year was £77,527, and at the South Sea House another £70,249 (p. 179).

instead of increasing British exports of consumer goods to the Continent, led to foreign merchants building up their accounts with London merchant bankers. When the pound was made inconvertible in 1797, those foreign balances held in Britain were locked in, for if they had been withdrawn through foreign bills of exchange they would have lost value by the resulting fall in the London exchange rate. The British "Orders in Council" blockaded the French ports and the Continental ports the French occupied. The French, for their part, confiscated any foreign goods found at their ports. The two warring powers combined forces to keep foreign merchants from realizing their British investments by imports to the Continent.

The foreign merchants most affected were precisely those located in the prosperous regions north and east of Revolutionary France – the United Provinces of the Netherlands, the Austrian Netherlands, the conglomeration of political units that made up the Rhineland, Hesse, Switzerland, Hanover, and so on. As the French troops moved successively into those regions, they brought not only liberty, equality, and fraternity but also higher taxes, conscription, loss or uncertainty of existing property rights, and secularization. The economic effect was devastating in the short run and did not ameliorate much when the initial Revolutionary governments were replaced by more conservative authorities concerned to maintain the new set of property rights. The reason was the increasing pressure of Napoleon's military enterprise on the lands outside France proper. Those territories continually saw their taxes increased and remitted to France and their real transfer burden magnified by the high tariffs France imposed even against its satellite kingdoms.[15] The benefits of the Continental System to some of the French manufacturing sectors were not shared by the rest of the Continent under French suzerainty. Moreover, they suffered, as did France, from the disruption caused by the British blockade of the Atlantic and Asian trade that had brought great prosperity to the port cities of northwestern Europe in the eighteenth century.[16]

After the Treaty of Amiens in 1802, British exports to the Continent

[15] See T. C. W. Blanning, *The French Revolution in Germany: Occupation and Resistance in the Rhineland, 1792–1802* (Oxford: Clarendon Press, 1983), for an enlightening contrast of a prosperous, lightly taxed *ancien régime* in the Rhineland with a depopulated, heavily taxed, and rebellious area actually incorporated within the French tariff wall, which cut it off from its natural markets on the right bank of the Rhine.

[16] Points made by François Crouzet, "Wars, Blockade, and Economic Change in Europe, 1792–1815," *Journal of Economic History*, 24(December 1964), pp. 567–88. Crouzet did not inquire, however, how merchants and manufacturers in the rest of Europe might have protected themselves, other than by migrating to France.

rose, and the paper pound strengthened. That could imply a return of foreign capital, and a real transfer through the trade account. If so, the fresh outbreak of war in 1803 hampered that return flow, and the Continental Blockade in 1805 put an end to it. Despite the reigning orthodoxy of Heckscher[17] and Crouzet[18] that the blockade hurt France more than Britain, there is mounting evidence that that interpretation has been overdrawn. Jeffrey Frankel, for example, has shown that the American embargo of 1808, which was complementary to (and perhaps coordinated with) the Continental Blockade, affected the British terms of trade much more adversely than it did the American terms of trade.[19] Geoffrey Ellis has shown that downriver traffic on the upper Rhine rose dramatically during the blockade period, whereas upriver traffic fell, which is consistent with a rise in the upper Rhine's gross barter terms of trade.[20] So the blockade was effective in limiting British trade with the Continent, but that turned out not to be effective in limiting British finance. The ineffectiveness, however, was not due to the inability of Napoleon's measures to restrict trade flows. Rather, it was due to the substitution of capital flows for the previous trade flows.

Foreign capital in Britain, locked in because of the Continental Blockade, could be directed to investments in ironworks, canals, port improvements, toll roads, and the like. In fact, Herries continued his testimony in 1810 by pointing out the large increase in the number of bills approved by Parliament for creation of toll roads, canals, docks, waterworks, and the like since the suspension of convertibility. Rather than British government spending crowding out private investment, it was redirecting it. The evidence of asset price movements in the capital markets (see Figure 9.3) indicates that there is a prima facie case that rather than British government war expenditures crowding out private domestic investment, the dominant effect at times was that revolutionary measures by the French government "crowded in" flight capital to Britain.[21] Especially marked was the rise in

17 Heckscher, *The Continental System*.
18 François Crouzet, *l'Economie Britannique et le Blocus Continental, 1806–1813*, 2 vols. (Paris: Presses Universitaires de France, 1958).
19 Jeffrey A. Frankel, "The 1808–1809 Embargo Against Great Britain," *Journal of Economic History*, 42(June 1982), pp. 291–307.
20 Geoffrey Ellis, *Napoleon's Continental Blockade: The Case of Alsace* (Oxford: Clarendon Press, 1981), pp. 276–7.
21 This ties into the current debate over the effects of war finance on the course of British industrialization, renewed by Jeffrey G. Williamson, "Why Was British Growth So Slow During the Industrial Revolution?" *Journal of Economic History*, 44(September 1984), pp.

the Three Per Cent Consols after the French Revolution took a turn to radicalism in 1791 and before the outbreak of war in 1793. The failure of the subsidized troops of Britain's Continental allies to stop the advances of the French Revolutionary armies led to continued falls in all three stocks. That was dramatically interrupted in December 1794, but that is merely evidence that the wealthy Dutch, and foreign merchants liquidating their stores in Amsterdam, were investing in the English funds as a first haven for their flight capital.

For the period after February 1797 and the advent of the paper pound ("paper pound" refers to the restriction of convertibility of Bank of England notes into gold bullion or coin during the period 1797–1821), we find no more evidence of prolonged decline in any of the three stocks shown. Rather, the picture is of gradual improvement in each, with severe setbacks on two occasions: (1) the resumption of hostilities with France in 1803 and (2) the crisis caused by the Continental Blockade imposed in 1807 and completed with the Jefferson embargo in 1808. This picture conforms well with that already noted by Norman Silberling in his classic article on British war finance in that period.[22] Silberling noted that the yield on consols rose from slightly under 4% in 1793 to nearly 6% when the bank suspended convertibility. Thereafter the yield was always lower, falling rapidly until 1802 and then fluctuating between 4.5% and 5.25% to the end of the war. Interest rates on Exchequer bills and yields on stock of a London dock company followed much the same course.

The stability of the price of consols and the rise in price of Bank of England and East India Company stock not only aided the financing of the war effort but also promoted the shift from rural to urban factories in consumer goods, mechanization in agriculture, and the rise of heavy industry in South Wales, Scotland, and the Midlands. The anomaly that such rapid structural change was accompanied by only slow rates of growth of per capita product was due to the disruptions of demobilization on British labor markets and the postwar return of both foreign capital and British speculative capital to the Continent. But the return flow of capital was

687–712, and rebutted by Carol E. Heim and Philip Mirowski, "Interest Rates and Crowding-Out During Britain's Industrial Revolution," *Journal of Economic History*, 47(March 1987), pp. 117–39. Compare the significant reduction in the amount of British borrowing calculated by Joel Mokyr, "Has the Industrial Revolution Been Crowded Out? Some Reflections on Crafts and Williamson," *Explorations in Economic History*, 24(July 1987), pp. 293–319.

[22] Norman J. Silberling, "British Financial Experience, 1790–1830," *Review of Economics and Statistics*, 1(1919), pp. 282–97.

much less than the original outflow, mainly because as capital left to be invested in underpriced assets on the Continent (or to reacquire emigré property), the pound, still inconvertible, would depreciate. D. C. M. Platt found as well that most of the French debt issues after the war to pay reparations and restore the monarchy was taken up in France, even though the Barings took the lead in underwriting it on the London market.[23] By the time the pound was restored to full convertibility in 1821, the net movement of foreign capital over the previous quarter century of revolution and war had left Britain supreme in terms of industrialization, international trade, and capital concentration until the end of the nineteenth century.

The British industrial revolution

The changes in the patterns of international capital movements that oc-curred under the impact of wars and revolutions two centuries ago had a larger significance, however, than simply setting the stage for the nine-teenth-century drama of financial imperialism, for it is precisely that period of economic development that must be understood in order to unravel the mystery of the industrial revolution in Great Britain. According to earlier economic historians, that occurred much earlier and was brought to fruition by the war effort,[24] or it occurred immediately after the War for American Independence and continued during the Napoleonic Wars,[25] or it occurred immediately after 1815.[26] According to the most recent economic histo-rians, however, it occurred after 1830 and perhaps was delayed by the wars of 1793–1815. I shall argue, on the contrary, that it occurred precisely during and because of the Napoleonic Wars. The argument depends, of course, on assigning a much larger role to the international capital markets of the time than had previously been reported.[27]

23 D. C. M. Platt, *Foreign Finance in Continental Europe and the United States, 1815–1870: Quantities, Origins, Functions, and Distribution* (London: Allen & Unwin, 1984), chap. 1.
24 T. S. Ashton, *The Industrial Revolution, 1760–1830* (Oxford University Press, 1948); David Landes, *The Unbound Prometheus* (Cambridge University Press, 1969).
25 W. W. Rostow, *The Stages of Economic Growth* (Cambridge University Press, 1961); Brinley Thomas, "Escaping from Constraints: The Industrial Revolution in a Malthusian Context," *Journal of Interdisciplinary History*, 15(Spring 1985), 729–53.
26 N. F. R. Crafts, *British Economic Growth during the Industrial Revolution* (Oxford: Clarendon Press, 1985); Jeffrey G. Williamson, *Did British Capitalism Breed Inequality?* (London: Allen & Unwin, 1985).
27 Although there is an implicit appreciation of the role they must have played in the little-known treatment by Fritz Machlup, "The Transfer Problem: Theme and Four Variations," in F. Machlup, ed., *International Payments, Debts, and Gold*, 2nd ed. (New York University Press, 1975), pp. 374–95.

TABLE 10.4
British economic growth during war and revolution

A. Real output (% per year)

Date	Real output	Real output per head	Real commodity output	Real private sector output
1700-1760	0.69	0.31	0.64	0.60
1760-1780	0.70	0.01	0.61	0.66
1780-1801	1.32	0.35	1.35	1.26
1801-1831	1.97	0.52	2.18	2.07

B. Savings and investment

Date	S_{gp}/Y	I_{gpdcf}/Y	I_f/Y
1761-1770	10.0	5.9	0.64
1771-1780	11.6	6.4	0.51
1781-1790	15.3	7.7	1.34
1791-1800	20.5	8.3	0.88
1801-1810	13.5	8.0	-1.12
1811-1820	19.7	9.7	2.55
1821-1830	12.1	11.0	2.66

Notes: S_{gp} = gross private saving; I_{gpdcf} = gross private domestic capital formation; I_f = private foreign investment by Great Britain.

Source: N. F. R. Crafts, "British Economic Growth, 1700-1850; Some Difficulties of Interpretation," Explorations in Economic History, 24 (July 1987), pp. 246, 248.

The current weight of evidence is that the rate of growth of the British economy was respectable, but slow, by the standards of modern economic growth, until 1820 or 1830. Nicholas Crafts's summary of the evidence is given in Table 10.4.[28] This shows that real output per capita grew at respectable, but clearly low, preindustrial rates in the first half of the eighteenth century, stagnated during the 1760–80 period, recovered to preindustrial rates during 1780–1801, and then accelerated noticeably in the period 1801–31. The rates of 1% annually that are associated with

[28] N. F. R. Crafts, "British Economic Growth, 1700–1850: Some Difficulties of Interpretation," Explorations in Economic History, 24(July 1987), pp. 246, 248.

modern economic growth, however, did not appear until after 1830. Crafts regarded that as a natural maturation process given the low weight of cotton textiles in the manufacturing sector until after 1830 and the absence of productivity growth in the rest of the manufacturing sector. Moreover, he found continued increases in labor productivity in the agricultural sector that released labor to the more productive leading sectors in manufacturing. There are problems with Crafts's explanation, and it has been attacked by Jeffrey Williamson[29] and Joel Mokyr[30] on different grounds. The difficulty worth mentioning here is that Crafts did not explain how resources were shifted from traditional manufacturing into the new leading sectors that were emerging in heavy industry. Investment in heavy industry clearly got a major boost from wartime demands, and its existence after the war provided the basis for ever cheaper capital goods. Those, in turn, facilitated the spread of modern manufacturing techniques throughout the British manufacturing sector, and to an increasing extent those techniques were reaching the American and Continental manufacturing sectors as well. How did that happen in Crafts's portrayal of the transformation process?

Panel B of Table 10.4 shows the course of the savings and investment ratios during that critical period, as calculated by Crafts. Savings includes all real domestic capital formation, net foreign investment, and change in government indebtedness. Investment is just domestic capital formation. On the basis of these calculations, the investment behavior showed a steady rise throughout the period, whereas the savings ratio fluctuated wildly. Most of the fluctuation was in government debt, but some was caused by variations in the ratio of net foreign investment by the British. Crafts did not consider the possibility of variations in foreign absorption of British government indebtedness as an explanation for the erratic course of the savings rate, preferring to relate it to the equally erratic course of inflation (see Figure 9.4). But once we recognize the importance of foreign savings in absorbing the British government indebtedness, then the shocks to foreign investors from the misfortunes of revolution and war make plausible the fluctuations in their contribution to British savings on that scale. The net foreign investment figures, on the other hand, make it appear that Britain had net foreign disinvestment only in the period 1801–10, and the preceding decade of revolution and war had caused only a slowing down of British net investment abroad, which resumed on a large

29 Jeffrey G. Williamson, "Debating the Industrial Revolution," *Explorations in Economic History*, 24(July 1987), pp. 269–92.
30 Mokyr, "Has the Industrial Revolution Been Crowded Out?"

scale in the decades 1811–20 and 1821–30. These are unreliable figures, to say the least, because they were calculated on very rough estimates of the current trade balance and the equally rough assumption that the current trade balance was offset by net capital flows. Other items that might offset the trade balance were loss of reserves, unrecorded specie flows, services, short-term capital flows in the form of trade credits, and, of course, "errors and omissions"! But because these estimates of net capital formation have been made, it is useful to refer back to another set of unreliable figures, shown in Table 10.1. These are Ralph Davis's careful calculations of trade flows in current prices at benchmark intervals within that period. The table also presents the implied balance of trade, something Davis refused to do. But such as they are, these do indicate persistent balance-of-trade deficits for Britain in that period, although they fell relative to growing national income. The odd thing was the sharp rise in the trade deficit in 1824–6, which may not seem so odd if we recall the stock market boom of 1824–5, which was led by speculation on Latin American mining stocks, fueled by capital imports from the former Spanish colonies (see Chapter 8).

Wartime demands were mentioned earlier as a possible explanation for the structural transformation of British industry that Crafts did not explain. Jeffrey Williamson, however, argued that those government requirements crowded out private investment and therefore slowed down the overall investment process.[31] The impact of crowding out may have been less than he calculated originally, a point he conceded to Joel Mokyr's recalculations, and it may not have affected the real interest rate on government securities, a point he conceded to Heim and Mirowski,[32] but Williamson nevertheless maintained that crowding out of private investment by rising government debt still was substantial. If nothing else, it may have driven up the risk premium attached to nongovernmental debt, so that real interest rates for private investment still increased and slowed down economic growth. Moreover, Williamson pointed out that the more other scholars discredited his crowding-out thesis, the more burden they took on for themselves to explain why British growth was so slow during the period 1760–1820.[33] That is precisely a challenge we can accept using our understanding of the extent, depth, and resilience of the international capital markets of the time. The crowding-out thesis of Ashton-Mill-Williamson is

[31] Williamson, "Why Was British Growth So Slow During the Industrial Revolution?"
[32] Heim and Mirowski, "Interest Rates and Crowding-Out During Britain's Industrial Revolution."
[33] Williamson, "Debating the Industrial Revolution," pp. 287–90.

constrained by the extent of foreign investment in British debt during the wars, and the slow growth is explained by the effectiveness of the trade restrictions imposed by Napoleon's Continental System and Jefferson's embargo from 1808 to 1814 and the return of capital to the Continent from 1815 to 1825.

To sum up, the purported crowding-out effect of increased British government debt to finance the wars against France has been greatly reduced from the figure first given by Williamson. Most important in reducing its size is the fact that the Three Per Cent Consols consistently sold at less than 60% of par throughout the war period; so the nominal size of the debt used by Williamson overstated the actual money sums by over two-thirds. Next in importance is the phenomenon of intestate individuals forfeiting their dividends and *de facto* reducing the government's debt. Next we must take into account that the effects of foreigners resident in France or territory controlled by French armies were systematically invested in Three Per Cents. The effect of alert merchants and rentiers liquidating their Continental assets and placing them in secure and liquid British government securities was of unknown magnitude, but it probably had a greater effect than the actual expropriations.

A critical role in producing these asymmetrical effects of the beginning of war and the ending of war on capital flows between Britain and the Continent was played by the financial innovation of the "paper pound" in 1797. That innovation was initially merely a technical response to the fundamental changes in property rights being wrought on the Continent by the French Revolution. Its persistence well past the postwar shocks of reparations and reconstruction, until 1821, however, gave it a significance that is worth pondering anew in our current era of flexible exchange rates and pressures for stabilizing them. Moreover, the quarter century of a floating pound sterling from 1797 to 1821 helps us discern an economically logical link between the French Revolution and the British industrial revolution.

11. The Amsterdam and London stock markets, 1800–25

London definitively replaced Amsterdam as the financial center of Europe during the period of war and revolution discussed in the preceding two chapters. Acworth described it thusly:

In 1792, Great Britain held a subordinate position in the financial system of Europe, the London money-market had yet to come into its own, and the movement of capital was still into and not out of England. In 1815, though the fact was scarcely appreciated at the time, the situation had radically changed. Amsterdam had fallen; and London had not only taken its place as the predominant financial market of Europe, but was able to play the part in a way that dwarfed the earlier efforts of the Dutch city.[1]

Not surprisingly, the stock exchanges in both cities underwent substantial reorganizations in that period. Those in London reflected not only the growth in the volume of the traditional assets traded, the government funds, but also the growth in the number of traders and in a variety of new assets. New buildings were constructed to house the exchange's activities. Amsterdam, by contrast, found its numbers reduced, its financial assets reduced in number and quality, and its activities devoted increasingly to real estate transactions. In the course of that historic transformation of the two markets, it is not surprising that the tight links that had been established and maintained for a century between the two markets were substantially loosened. And it is not surprising that a rampant and expanding London market should forge new links that would secure its dominance in world finance through the next century.

The London Stock Exchange, 1792–1825

The loan contracting for each successive year's issue of new government debt after 1796, when Boyd and Benfield received preferential treatment, pitted competing syndicates of underwriters against each other. They com-

---

[1] William Acworth, *Financial Reconstruction in England, 1815–1822* (London: P. S. King & Son, 1925), pp. 81–2.

peted by steadily increasing their respective numbers, so that when David
Ricardo's group finally won the contract for the 1807 loans, his subscription list had 222 names.[2] The successful bidder received the loan on terms
less than the market price of the separate securities and could make a very
large "contractor's bonus" if the market price were depressed before the
subscription and rose afterward. Although the members of the losing syndicates might want to sell short and launch a "bear" attack against the
government stocks after the loan was awarded, whereas the members of the
winning group would try to stimulate a "bull" market to increase their
profits, all members of the competing syndicates wanted to depress the
stock before the new subscription. The activities of the "Commissioners
for the Reduction of the National Debt" played a useful role in keeping up
the price of the old stocks in the face of concerted, but short-lived, bear
attacks. They were charged to buy £1 million (cash) of government debt
annually in 1786 when they were established, and £16 million by 1815.
Although their purchases in total were quite steady (a daily limit was
imposed that was only marginally above the average purchase needed to
fulfill their annual quota), they were shifted toward the particular stock or
stocks that were selling at the lowest price. So their role in promoting the
liquidity and the efficiency of the London market in government debt
should not be minimized.[3]

On 7 January 1801 the Committee of Proprietors of the group of brokers
who had been using the London Stock Exchange building in Threadneedle
Street since 1773 resolved to convert it into a "Subscription Room" and
restrict access to elected members. That was followed by a move by other
brokers, not fortunate enough to be on the Committee of Proprietors, to
construct a new, larger building and move the stock exchange there. The
foundation stone has this inscription:

On the 18th of May in the year 1801, . . . the first stone of this building, erected
by private subscription for transaction of business in the public funds, was
laid. . . . At this year, the first of the union between Great Britain and Ireland, the
public funded debt had accumulated in five successive reigns to £552,730,924. The
inviolate faith of the British nation, and the principles of the constitution, sanction
and ensure the property embarked in this undertaking. May the blessing of the
constitution be secured to the latest posterity.[4]

[2] E. Victor Morgan and W. A. Thomas, *The Stock Exchange: Its History and Functions*
(London: Elek Books, 1962), p. 50.
[3] Ibid., pp. 54–6. Morgan and Thomas minimized the "grooming effect" the commissioners
had, but did not take into account the effect of shifting purchases among the various
annuities.
[4] Ibid., p. 71.

The new building began operation in March 1802, but it was not until 1811 that the Committee for General Purposes decided to codify the regulations of the stock exchange, producing the first rule book in 1812. It was also after the new building was put in use that the *Course of the Exchange,* then being published by Wetenhall and Sheffield, was issued "by authority of the Stock Exchange Committee," apparently replacing the "Gentlemen of the Stock-Exchange" who had appointed Wetenhall to publish the official price list in 1786.[5] With the first issue of 1811, the character of Wetenhall's price list changed dramatically, even though it continued to appear only on Tuesdays and Fridays and to bear the name of Wetenhall as publisher until the end of the nineteenth century. The list was more than doubled in size, and in addition to the quotations of British funds and other securities, only 20 in number, there were added American securities, canals, docks, insurance, and waterworks. Before 1824, however, the combined paid-up capital of the domestic companies traded on the London Stock Exchange was only £34 million, compared with the public debt of over £800 million. It was not until the speculative years of 1824 and 1825 that the capital of joint-stock companies rose sharply, and that movement was cut short by the crash of 1825.[6]

At the end of the war in 1815, the return flow of capital began nearly at once from Britain to the Continent. The two famous merchant banking houses of Baring and Rothschild were preeminent at the start. The Barings handled the finance for the army of occupation and for the reparations payments by France to the allies. They absorbed the London firm of Henry Hope when he died, but largely ignored the Amsterdam firm.[7] Meanwhile, Nathan Rothschild, in London, became the financier to the Holy Alliance, utilizing as he saw fit his brothers in Frankfurt, Paris, Vienna, and Naples. The Rothschilds greatly outdistanced the Barings in the scale of their foreign loans, and they bypassed Amsterdam entirely.[8]

The Amsterdam stock exchange, 1792–1825

The decline of the Amsterdam capital market became visible to all in 1793, when the French declared war on the Dutch Republic. In truth, it does not

---

[5] See Chapter 2, this volume; *Course of the Exchange* (3 November 1786 and 29 July 1803).

[6] Morgan and Thomas, *The Stock Exchange,* p. 83, who took their information from Henry English, *A Complete View of the Joint Stock Companies formed during 1824 and 1825* (London: Boosey & Sons, 1827).

[7] Marten J. Buist, *At Spes Non Fractra: Hope & Co., 1700–1815, Merchant Bankers and Diplomats at Work* (The Hague: Nijhoff, 1974), chapters 12 and 13.

[8] Stanley Chapman, *The Rise of Merchant Banking* (London: Allen & Unwin, 1984), chap. 2.

seem to have recovered well from the shock of the financial panic of 1772–3. Under the pressure of a declining Dutch East India Company (see Chapter 6), and especially the disastrous effects of the fourth Anglo-Dutch war (1780–4), the market in financial assets stagnated, much like the rest of the Dutch economy in that period. The establishment of the Batavian Republic in 1795, though it elicited the publication of the Amsterdam stock market's official price list, also increased the demands of the domestic government on participants in the securities market, squeezing out, in the process, the amounts available to foreign governments. The remaining foreign loans were earmarked for Napoleonic France, even when they were issued nominally on behalf of one of the satellite states.[9] The Batavian and French periods completed the reorientation of the Amsterdam stock exchange from foreign to domestic securities.[10]

Amsterdam suffered from the annulment of debts contracted under the *ancien régime* governments, especially by France, inflation in Austria, and increased taxation and resort to capital levies in the kingdom of Holland. The new, improved tax systems in place throughout Europe after 1815, the legacy of a quarter century of war and revolution, were to be exploited by lenders operating in the capital markets of London and Paris, not Amsterdam. Worse, the transference of Dutch techniques of finance to industrial capitalism were to take place elsewhere.[11]

Moreover, the operation of the Amsterdam market was inhibited by the continuation under Willem I of regulations imposed under the Batavian Republic. So far as we know, the first attempt at self-regulation in Amsterdam was the formation of the Collegie tot Nut des Obligatiehandels at some time around 1787. But even that seems to have been desultory, because the publication of a price current under its direction is not known until 1795 – under the newly formed Batavian Republic. Even then, the motivation appears to have been more to verify to all debtholders that the wild swings in the traded values of their securities were, in fact, occurring.[12] Under such wide price ranges, brokers could engage in gross abuses of the fiduciary trust given them by their clients. It was not until 1833 that enough business was again being directed through the Amster-

9   James C. Riley, *International Government Finance and the Amsterdam Capital Market, 1740–1815* (Cambridge University Press, 1980), pp. 195–8.
10 Johann de Vries, *Een Eeuw vol Effecten, Historische schets van de Vereiniging voor de Effectenhandel en de Amsterdamse Effectenbeurs, 1876–1976* (Amsterdam: Vereniging voor de Effectenhandel, 1976), p. 32.
11 Riley, *International Government Finance*, pp. 242–9.
12 de Vries, *Een Eeuw vol Effecten*, pp. 45–6.

dam exchange that some members of the Collegie tot Nut des Obligatiehandels decided to start the *Nieuwe Handel-Societeit,* which also issued standard price quotes, rather than the uncertain ranges favored by the
collegie.[13] And it was not until 1848 that a new building was completed to
house the exchange. In 1824 the old building of Henrik de Keyser, which
had housed the Amsterdam exchange since 1611, was observed to be
settling dangerously. The brokers moved to a wooden auxiliary market
building, where they did business while exposed to wind and weather. The
new building plan was not approved until 1840, and even though it was
occupied in 1845, it remained without a roof until 1848.[14] There could not
be a more appropriate metaphor to evoke the decline of the Amsterdam
capital market.

Integration of the London and Amsterdam stock exchanges

Nevertheless, the Amsterdam exchange did resume in 1802, with the sign-
ing of the Treaty of Amiens, the *termijnhandel* or forward purchases of
English securities. It was a pathetic reminder of a once-blooming traffic.
Nevertheless, it remained in place even as the war resumed and continued
steadily on to the end of our period. The results of this diminished trade
were reported faithfully in the *Amsterdamsche Prys-courant der effecten.*
These quotes, combined with the spot quotations we have from Wetenhall's
Course of the Exchange (through 1810) and *Lloyd's List* (through 1823),
enable us to replicate for that period of disruption the tests of market
integration we used earlier for the eighteenth century (see Chapter 7).

Table 11.1 summarizes the results in a form analogous to that used in
Tables 7.4 and 7.5. Two striking differences appear immediately: One
concerns the very low coefficients of determination (R^2) for each subperiod
from 1802 to 1825 compared with those in the periods from 1723 to 1794,
despite roughly comparable numbers of observations in the two cases.
More disturbing is the presence of serial correlation, which requires some
major adjustments in each case to estimate the coefficients. (The size of the
adjustment in each case can be gauged by the first-order autocorrelation
coefficient, r, which is given below the summary statistics for each period.) Both features indicate that our specification of the differences between
the Amsterdam prices (time) and London prices (spot), which captures

[13] Ibid., p. 46.
[14] Ibid., pp. 20, 38.

TABLE 11.1
Summary of regression results, Three Per Cent Consols, Amsterdam-London price
differences[1]

	DAYSDIVD[2]	AMEXPM[3]	PAYTIME[4]	Constant	R^2	DW Observations
1802-07[5]						
	.006	-.046	.002	.052	.02	2.31
	(2.32)[6]	(-1.17)	(1.05)	(0.38)		301
	(adjusted for serial correlation, rho=0.525)					
1808-09[5]						
	.003	-.018	-0.003	0.019	-.02	2.15
	(0.50)	(-0.38)	(-1.05)	(0.11)		103
	(adjusted for serial correlation, rho=0.795)					
1814-18[5]						
	.008	-.013	0.007	-.171	.07	2.12
	(3.77)	(-1.22)	(2.90)	(-.93)		240
	(adjusted for serial correlation, rho=0.379)					
1819-25[5]						
	.005	-.028	-.001	.232	.02	2.12
	(2.92)	(-1.22)	(-.36)	(1.53)		373
	(adjusted for serial correlation, rho=0.449)					

Note: All regressions are ordinary least squares.

[1] Dependent variable is Amsterdam - London price on same day.
[2] DAYSDIVD = days to next dividend payment.
[3] AMEXPM = changes in the exchange rate.
[4] PAYTIME = whether the London price was with (0)
      or ex dividend (1).
[5] Subperiods:
      1802-07 [Peace of Amiens, Continental Blockade]
      1808-09 [Peninsular War]
      1814-18 [Peace, war, final peace]
      1819-25 [Resumption of gold standard]
[6] t-statistics are in parentheses under respective coefficients.

Source: See text.

only the strictly technical reasons for time–spot differentials, is sadly
inadequate for the Napoleonic period. Other factors, less technical but
more important, were moving the differentials. Clearly, the difficulties of
communication were greater with the disruption of mail service, and the
uncertainties of a war characterized by major battles in distant arenas
created irregular and large shocks in the information flows to each market.
Examination of the residuals from each regression indicates that the major

battles did create clusters of positive residuals, meaning that the Amsterdam prices of the English securities rose well above their predicted levels on receiving news of most battles. But they also rose above the predicted level at rescounter dates, indicating that when the Amsterdam traders cleared their accounts with each other, there remained excess demand for British securities.

It may be worth remarking that the best regression results are not for the postwar period, when mail service was resumed and the battles were over, but are found for the most disturbed period, 1814–18. Perhaps this is due to regression bias caused by extreme observations in 1815, when Napoleon terrorized the allies for the famous Hundred Days before Waterloo. But it is possible that the weakness of the government in Amsterdam in the early years of Willem I (installed as monarch of both the United Provinces and the Austrian Netherlands by the first Congress of Vienna in 1814) permitted the Amsterdam market to operate more effectively than when it was under French rule. Ironically, the stabilization of his rule, and of the foreign exchanges with England, served to impair rather than improve the integration of the two capital markets.

Conclusion

These regression results reinforce our impressions from the divergent histories of the world's two leading stock exchanges during the first quarter of the nineteenth century. The great financial conflict, as well as military and political conflict, between France and Great Britain that occurred during the Napoleonic period caused disintegration of the cosmopolitan markets in goods and securities that had arisen in western Europe at the end of the seventeenth century. The postwar period, with Great Britain dominant in industrial and financial capabilities and a German nation emerging from the welter of political units that had existed under the *ancien régime,* saw the start of a gradual process of reintegration of those markets. But the process was not one of simply returning to prewar and prerevolution practices of cosmopolitan merchants, bankers, and brokers. Rather, international markets gradually emerged. In those markets, the enhanced fiscal powers of the secular states on the Continent could be used to guarantee their financial obligations and to place them with investors, both domestic and foreign, through the facilities of the London and Paris capital markets. Gradually, those national markets became integrated, especially after the communications revolution brought by the telegraph and then the telephone. But that did not occur until the second half of the nineteenth century.

Today's movement from recently integrated international capital markets to an emerging global and cosmopolitan capital market seems to be re-creating, three centuries later, the conditions for the free transfer of private assets that existed for most of the eighteenth century in western Europe. And today's innovations are being implemented by the activities of multi-national joint-stock companies, linking the lives and fortunes of bankers, merchants, and industrialists across the capitalist world. The multinational firms of the United States, Japan, Great Britain, and Europe are the inher-itors of the East India companies of the English, Dutch, and French, whose activities in the seventeenth century began the cosmopolitan capital mar-kets described in this book. They are only now fulfilling that legacy.

Appendix: End-of-month share prices

Bank of England

30 April 1709 to 31 December 1823
close of day, last trading day of month

East India Company

30 April 1709 to 31 December 1823
close of day, last trading day of month

South Sea Company

29 September 1711 to 31 December 1789
close of day, last trading day of month

Three Per Cent Consols

31 August 1753 to 31 December 1789
close of day, last trading day of month

Note: Daily prices for these and a number of other stocks, as well as the exchange rates and all other stock market data used in this book, are available on magnetic tape from Inter-University Consortium for Political and Social Research, P. O. Box 1248, Ann Arbor, MI 48106, U.S.A.

mo	dd	year	Bank	EIC	SSea	Consols
4	30	1709	119.250	117.250		
5	31	1709	134.000	129.000		
6	30	1709	128.500	126.500		
7	30	1709	128.000	131.250		
8	31	1709	128.750	131.250		
9	30	1709	128.500	133.500		
10	31	1709	119.500	130.750		
11	30	1709	118.250	131.250		
12	31	1709	112.000	127.000		
1	31	1710	118.000	131.000		
2	28	1710	127.000	140.000		
3	31	1710	122.250	136.250		
4	29	1710	122.250	135.000		
5	31	1710	124.000	137.250		
6	30	1710	118.750	136.250		
7	31	1710	113.750	126.500		
8	31	1710	111.750	124.250		
9	30	1710	109.250	124.250		
10	31	1710	98.250	113.500		
11	30	1710	105.750	124.000		
12	30	1710	101.000	118.000		
1	31	1711	103.000	121.250		
2	28	1711	103.750	120.750		
3	31	1711	102.750	121.750		
4	30	1711	101.500	118.500		

mo	dd	year	Bank	EIC	SSea	Consols
9	30	1713	124.750	124.000	92.625	
10	31	1713	123.000	123.000	92.000	
11	30	1713	124.625	126.000	93.875	
12	31	1713	124.750	123.250	91.000	
1	30	1714	121.250	119.000	86.250	
2	27	1714	121.000	117.750	85.500	
3	31	1714	117.750	118.000	84.250	
4	30	1714	121.000	123.000	87.250	
5	31	1714	120.750	123.500	87.750	
6	30	1714	123.750	123.500	86.000	
7	31	1714	122.500	124.000	85.250	
8	31	1714	132.750	134.750	97.000	
9	30	1714	129.750	135.500	95.875	
10	30	1714	127.250	136.000	95.625	
11	30	1714	128.000	138.000	97.000	
12	31	1714	129.750	134.000	97.375	
1	31	1715	133.000	134.000	95.875	
2	28	1715	133.750	134.250	94.000	
3	31	1715	129.250	135.500	95.000	
4	30	1715	130.750	141.000	99.375	
5	31	1715	131.700	142.500	101.000	
6	30	1715	131.750	138.250	98.875	
7	30	1715	128.000	132.500	94.250	
8	31	1715	131.500	137.000	97.625	
9	30	1715	125.500	134.000	93.500	

5	31	1711	104.250	117.250	
6	30	1711	105.000	125.250	
7	31	1711	103.750	116.750	
8	31	1711	101.500	109.250	
9	29	1711	110.500	121.000	72.000
10	31	1711	108.750	124.000	75.500
11	30	1711	111.250	128.250	78.250
12	31	1711	108.500	123.000	75.000
1	31	1712	110.500	120.500	75.000
2	29	1712	112.750	118.750	74.000
3	31	1712	108.000	114.500	72.000
4	30	1712	111.500	117.000	74.500
5	31	1712	117.000	118.000	80.000
6	30	1712	112.700	110.750	78.750
7	31	1712	113.000	108.250	78.250
8	30	1712	116.000	114.000	77.250
9	30	1712	113.750	114.500	76.500
10	31	1712	115.000	116.000	78.500
11	29	1712	115.750	119.000	79.250
12	31	1712	123.250	126.500	86.250
1	31	1713	121.750	123.000	84.000
2	28	1713	122.500	120.750	83.250
3	31	1713	124.750	124.250	86.750
4	30	1713	122.500	122.500	91.000
5	30	1713	123.750	123.500	92.250
6	30	1713	126.500	124.000	95.000
7	31	1713	127.500	123.250	93.500
8	31	1713	130.000	127.000	93.750

10	31	1715	119.500	129.250	89.250
11	30	1715	123.250	135.500	94.750
12	31	1715	127.250	134.250	94.000
1	31	1716	124.250	131.750	92.750
2	29	1716	130.500	136.250	95.750
3	31	1716	129.250	139.250	97.000
4	30	1716	131.000	144.000	101.000
5	31	1716	133.500	147.750	102.250
6	30	1716	134.000	144.000	96.125
7	31	1716	137.125	144.250	97.375
8	31	1716	138.625	149.750	98.625
9	29	1716	139.500	159.500	100.875
10	31	1716	141.750	172.500	106.250
11	30	1716	135.000	171.250	104.125
12	31	1716	137.625	165.500	103.625
1	31	1717	137.500	168.250	103.125
2	28	1717	136.000	166.000	100.625
3	30	1717	132.500	169.000	101.000
4	30	1717	135.000	174.000	104.500
5	31	1717	139.000	186.750	107.750
6	29	1717	147.500	187.500	109.500
7	31	1717	149.500	196.000	111.000
8	31	1717	150.500	196.000	112.375
9	30	1717	147.700	196.000	111.500
10	31	1717	146.000	197.250	112.500
11	30	1717	140.750	199.000	114.000
12	31	1717	156.250	207.500	118.875
1	31	1718	156.250	208.250	119.000

mo	dd	year	Bank	EIC	SSea	Consols
2	28	1718	159.750	216.000	118.375	
3	31	1718	151.250	210.000	112.875	
4	30	1718	151.000	212.750	116.875	
5	31	1718	149.500	211.000	116.750	
6	30	1718	147.250	204.000	112.625	
7	31	1718	150.750	203.000	113.000	
8	30	1718	150.250	194.750	108.875	
9	30	1718	144.000	191.000	107.500	
10	31	1718	142.250	188.000	106.500	
11	29	1718	145.500	197.000	109.875	
12	31	1718	155.500	212.000	118.750	
1	31	1719	157.250	213.250	118.625	
2	28	1719	156.750	210.250	117.500	
3	31	1719	144.000	195.500	110.375	
4	30	1719	145.500	199.500	115.500	
5	30	1719	147.500	197.500	114.875	
6	30	1719	152.750	197.000	117.000	
7	31	1719	143.250	191.250	113.500	
8	31	1719	148.000	194.000	115.625	
9	30	1719	142.250	192.000	116.500	
10	31	1719	141.500	191.200	116.125	
11	30	1719	149.000	196.000	122.750	
12	31	1719	150.250	200.000	128.000	
1	30	1720	153.750	205.250	130.500	
2	29	1720	153.500	212.000	173.250	

mo	dd	year	Bank	EIC	SSea	Consols
7	31	1722	117.250	137.500	91.000	
8	31	1722	117.000	136.500	89.125	
9	29	1722	115.500	125.500	85.750	
10	31	1722	115.500	133.500	93.625	
11	30	1722	114.500	132.500	94.000	
12	31	1722	116.500	134.000	100.500	
1	31	1723	117.000	128.500	95.625	
2	28	1723	118.000	125.750	97.000	
3	30	1723	116.000	129.000	101.375	
4	30	1723	117.250	127.750	97.500	
5	31	1723	117.000	132.500	101.500	
6	29	1723	118.000	134.000	100.875	
7	31	1723	119.750	129.000	105.500	
8	31	1723	121.500	131.500	108.625	
9	30	1723	120.000	137.000	111.500	
10	31	1723	120.000	136.000	111.250	
11	30	1723	121.250	138.000	113.375	
12	31	1723	128.000	141.500	116.750	
1	31	1724	126.750	144.000	114.500	
2	29	1724	129.250	148.000	116.625	
3	31	1724	128.500	149.750	118.125	
4	30	1724	126.500	146.000	117.500	
5	30	1724	128.250	149.000	120.000	
6	30	1724	130.500	150.750	121.750	
7	31	1724	132.750	145.250	118.500	

Month	Day	Year			
8	31	1724	131.625	144.500	116.625
9	30	1724	129.250	148.000	118.000
10	31	1724	129.250	149.750	119.125
11	30	1724	132.750	152.500	121.625
12	31	1724	132.500	152.000	121.875
1	30	1725	132.250	147.750	118.375
2	27	1725	133.250	150.500	118.875
3	31	1725	129.875	150.750	118.750
4	30	1725	133.000	159.000	122.000
5	31	1725	133.375	165.000	122.500
6	30	1725	135.000	168.000	122.750
7	31	1725	135.750	169.500	120.750
8	31	1725	138.250	179.500	123.250
9	30	1725	132.750	166.000	120.125
10	30	1725	133.000	167.750	121.250
11	30	1725	131.250	166.750	121.250
12	31	1725	128.250	159.000	117.750
1	31	1726	124.000	149.750	108.750
2	28	1726	124.000	145.750	103.000
3	31	1726	123.500	150.500	105.500
4	30	1726	124.000	149.500	103.625
5	31	1726	122.250	148.250	102.000
6	30	1726	125.000	150.000	104.000
7	30	1726	126.750	148.500	103.875
8	31	1726	126.750	147.500	104.250
9	30	1726	127.250	147.000	104.250
10	31	1726	120.750	133.000	99.000
11	30	1726	119.500	132.000	98.500

Month	Day	Year			
3	31	1720	150.000	230.000	310.000
4	30	1720	156.000	235.000	342.000
5	31	1720	210.000	290.000	595.000
6	30	1720	240.000	420.000	950.000
7	30	1720	233.000	365.000	850.000
8	31	1720	226.000	345.000	810.000
9	30	1720	215.000	180.000	310.000
10	31	1720	142.000	165.000	210.000
11	30	1720	145.000	165.000	194.000
12	31	1720	147.000	170.000	200.000
1	31	1721	141.000	142.000	200.000
2	28	1721	138.000	142.000	200.000
3	31	1721	129.000	139.000	140.000
4	29	1721	131.500	137.000	139.000
5	31	1721	129.500	134.500	130.000
6	30	1721	129.500	140.500	124.500
7	31	1721	135.000	150.000	146.000
8	31	1721	138.000	144.000	140.000
9	30	1721	125.500	136.500	95.250
10	31	1721	123.000	141.500	96.000
11	30	1721	124.500	141.250	96.750
12	30	1721	125.000	143.750	98.500
1	31	1722	122.500	141.500	99.000
2	28	1722	120.000	140.750	96.750
3	31	1722	115.500	138.750	90.250
4	30	1722	113.750	139.000	90.000
5	31	1722	116.000	138.500	90.750
6	30	1722	118.250	142.000	91.000

mo	dd	year	Bank	EIC	SSea	Consols
12	31	1726	118.000	130.750	96.500	
1	31	1727	124.250	138.750	100.875	
2	28	1727	125.250	142.500	100.125	
3	31	1727	125.500	138.750	98.500	
4	29	1727	126.250	151.000	104.500	
5	31	1727	131.500	169.500	113.750	
6	30	1727	131.750	168.250	113.625	
7	31	1727	133.000	164.750	110.875	
8	31	1727	133.125	162.500	110.000	
9	30	1727	133.000	162.000	109.750	
10	31	1727	129.000	159.000	108.250	
11	30	1727	130.500	162.500	108.000	
12	30	1727	131.000	160.500	106.125	
1	31	1728	139.500	173.000	108.125	
2	29	1728	138.750	170.250	105.625	
3	30	1728	138.250	173.250	106.625	
4	30	1728	136.250	174.250	107.375	
5	31	1728	136.000	172.750	106.500	
6	29	1728	133.750	169.500	104.625	
7	31	1728	133.250	161.500	100.500	
8	31	1728	137.250	171.000	103.500	
9	30	1728	137.000	171.000	103.000	
10	31	1728	134.000	171.500	102.875	
11	30	1728	133.500	167.000	100.625	
12	31	1728	131.750	163.750	98.125	

mo	dd	year	Bank	EIC	SSea	Consols
5	31	1731	145.500	195.875	101.750	
6	30	1731	146.750	197.000	102.875	
7	31	1731	147.000	194.750	103.250	
8	31	1731	149.000	194.250	103.500	
9	30	1731	148.750	186.000	103.250	
10	30	1731	145.750	174.500	102.000	
11	30	1731	148.000	179.500	103.500	
12	31	1731	149.000	181.750	102.500	
1	31	1732	149.500	178.000	102.000	
2	29	1732	149.625	177.000	98.250	
3	31	1732	150.500	175.250	98.250	
4	29	1732	147.750	178.000	98.625	
5	31	1732	147.750	178.125	98.750	
6	30	1732	148.250	169.000	97.750	
7	31	1732	151.000	165.500	100.000	
8	31	1732	152.750	157.250	104.875	
9	30	1732	151.000	156.875	104.500	
10	31	1732	149.875	155.250	104.000	
11	30	1732	149.875	154.000	104.375	
12	30	1732	150.000	156.750	105.125	
1	31	1733	151.250	160.750	105.125	
2	28	1733	151.000	159.625	102.375	
3	31	1733	150.750	158.375	102.500	
4	30	1733	149.000	160.750	102.500	
5	31	1733	150.875	162.500	104.500	

Month	Day	Year			
1	31	1729	134.500	164.250	99.250
2	28	1729	136.000	165.000	97.375
3	31	1729	136.500	165.500	97.625
4	30	1729	135.000	169.000	98.375
5	31	1729	136.000	171.250	100.125
6	30	1729	137.250	178.250	102.625
7	31	1729	139.000	176.500	101.500
8	30	1729	139.250	177.250	102.000
9	30	1729	139.375	177.500	101.750
10	31	1729	137.000	179.250	102.250
11	29	1729	138.000	183.250	103.250
12	31	1729	139.000	187.250	105.250
1	31	1730	139.750	182.500	104.875
2	28	1730	139.500	180.500	101.375
3	31	1730	145.000	186.750	102.750
4	30	1730	141.250	188.250	102.875
5	30	1730	140.750	189.125	103.125
6	30	1730	143.375	192.500	104.375
7	31	1730	142.000	184.500	103.625
8	31	1730	144.000	183.750	102.750
9	30	1730	144.500	189.250	103.375
10	31	1730	142.625	189.125	103.625
11	30	1730	143.625	190.500	104.000
12	31	1730	144.000	190.875	104.000
1	30	1731	144.000	188.500	103.500
2	27	1731	144.750	192.000	101.000
3	31	1731	147.750	197.250	103.000
4	30	1731	147.000	199.000	103.375

Month	Day	Year			
6	30	1733	151.000	167.500	106.375
7	31	1733	149.500	158.500	104.625
8	31	1733	145.250	152.000	84.000
9	29	1733	144.000	150.500	80.000
10	31	1733	130.500	139.500	72.500
11	30	1733	131.500	137.000	74.125
12	31	1733	136.000	138.750	79.750
1	31	1734	133.000	136.000	77.000
2	28	1734	132.500	136.250	75.250
3	30	1734	132.500	135.875	73.875
4	30	1734	131.250	137.250	75.500
5	31	1734	134.000	142.500	76.000
6	29	1734	137.000	147.000	81.000
7	31	1734	137.250	141.500	79.750
8	31	1734	138.250	143.000	79.750
9	30	1734	140.000	146.000	81.750
10	31	1734	135.750	142.000	79.500
11	30	1734	137.000	144.500	81.500
12	31	1734	139.500	149.000	83.500
1	31	1735	139.500	145.000	84.000
2	28	1735	140.750	148.250	82.750
3	31	1735	141.250	149.750	82.875
4	30	1735	138.000	149.000	83.250
5	31	1735	138.250	149.000	82.750
6	30	1735	136.250	147.000	80.250
7	31	1735	139.250	146.000	83.125
8	30	1735	140.250	146.750	81.750
9	30	1735	142.375	149.500	83.000

mo	dd	year	Bank	EIC	SSea	Consols
10	31	1735	142.250	159.000	86.500	
11	29	1735	146.750	167.000	93.125	
12	31	1735	146.500	169.000	93.500	
1	31	1736	148.000	169.000	95.000	
2	28	1736	149.000	174.500	95.875	
3	31	1736	150.500	175.500	98.250	
4	30	1736	147.500	174.500	97.500	
5	31	1736	148.000	176.500	99.000	
6	30	1736	149.125	177.500	99.750	
7	31	1736	149.625	171.750	99.000	
8	31	1736	151.250	178.500	99.500	
9	30	1736	151.500	181.500	100.000	
10	30	1736	148.750	178.500	100.000	
11	30	1736	149.250	179.000	100.000	
12	31	1736	148.250	178.500	100.250	
1	31	1737	149.125	177.500	101.500	
2	28	1737	151.625	179.750	102.625	
3	31	1737	143.000	176.500	98.000	
4	30	1737	145.125	182.250	104.000	
5	31	1737	147.250	181.500	103.750	
6	30	1737	145.750	182.000	103.750	
7	30	1737	144.000	174.500	103.000	
8	31	1737	145.500	177.500	101.500	
9	30	1737	145.750	177.000	101.750	
10	31	1737	143.000	177.500	102.000	

mo	dd	year	Bank	EIC	SSea	Consols
3	31	1740	141.500	158.750	99.125	
4	30	1740	140.250	159.000	99.500	
5	31	1740	142.000	162.000	101.000	
6	30	1740	143.125	163.000	100.000	
7	31	1740	143.250	159.250	101.500	
8	30	1740	144.000	160.250	101.000	
9	30	1740	140.000	153.500	95.500	
10	31	1740	138.000	153.500	96.000	
11	29	1740	139.000	155.500	98.250	
12	31	1740	138.750	155.500	98.750	
1	31	1741	140.500	155.000	101.750	
2	28	1741	143.000	156.500	101.125	
3	31	1741	142.000	156.000	101.750	
4	30	1741	143.000	163.250	104.250	
5	30	1741	140.375	159.000	102.625	
6	30	1741	141.500	159.500	103.000	
7	31	1741	141.375	156.500	103.750	
8	31	1741	141.000	156.000	101.875	
9	30	1741	141.750	157.500	103.750	
10	31	1741	140.750	159.000	104.500	
11	30	1741	138.500	160.000	105.250	
12	31	1741	135.500	159.250	104.250	
1	30	1742	136.250	156.500	104.375	
2	27	1742	136.250	157.500	103.125	
3	31	1742	139.500	159.000	105.500	

M	D	Year	Price 1	Price 2	Price 3
4	30	1742	138.000	159.250	106.000
5	31	1742	139.750	162.000	113.125
6	30	1742	142.500	172.000	109.000
7	31	1742	142.000	174.000	110.500
8	31	1742	142.000	171.000	108.500
9	30	1742	142.250	171.750	109.125
10	30	1742	140.500	174.750	110.250
11	30	1742	143.000	179.500	111.125
12	31	1742	143.000	179.750	111.750
1	31	1743	145.250	176.000	112.250
2	28	1743	146.000	178.000	110.500
3	31	1743	147.000	180.250	110.000
4	30	1743	146.500	186.000	112.000
5	31	1743	148.250	194.500	115.250
6	30	1743	144.500	188.500	113.000
7	30	1743	147.875	189.000	114.750
8	31	1743	147.250	186.000	111.000
9	30	1743	148.625	188.000	111.500
10	31	1743	146.500	194.000	113.250
11	30	1743	146.500	194.000	112.000
12	31	1743	147.500	197.500	113.250
1	31	1744	148.250	194.000	113.500
2	29	1744	146.000	181.000	106.000
3	31	1744	143.000	169.750	103.000
4	30	1744	141.625	171.500	105.000
5	31	1744	142.500	172.250	105.750
6	30	1744	144.000	179.000	108.000
7	31	1744	147.000	178.250	109.750

M	D	Year	Price 1	Price 2	Price 3
11	30	1737	142.750	177.250	102.250
12	31	1737	142.875	177.000	101.750
1	31	1738	142.250	175.500	102.500
2	28	1738	142.250	176.000	101.250
3	31	1738	141.750	173.750	100.125
4	29	1738	139.000	169.500	99.000
5	31	1738	142.500	173.500	101.500
6	30	1738	141.625	169.500	100.500
7	31	1738	138.500	161.000	97.250
8	31	1738	143.750	171.500	102.000
9	30	1738	145.000	171.500	103.000
10	31	1738	142.750	172.500	103.500
11	30	1738	143.000	173.750	103.875
12	30	1738	142.625	173.250	104.000
1	31	1739	143.375	170.250	103.500
2	28	1739	143.500	168.500	99.875
3	31	1739	144.500	169.250	100.750
4	30	1739	141.000	166.500	99.250
5	31	1739	142.125	169.000	99.625
6	30	1739	137.500	158.500	94.500
7	31	1739	137.000	153.000	94.000
8	31	1739	138.250	153.750	93.000
9	29	1739	139.250	155.000	94.000
10	31	1739	135.500	152.500	93.000
11	30	1739	138.500	158.000	96.500
12	31	1739	139.000	159.000	97.250
1	31	1740	138.750	154.000	96.750
2	29	1740	139.750	155.000	95.125

mo	dd	year	Bank	EIC	SSea	Consols
8	31	1744	147.000	176.875	108.500	
9	29	1744	148.000	178.500	108.500	
10	31	1744	144.625	180.750	109.500	
11	30	1744	145.000	184.750	112.000	
12	31	1744	145.000	184.000	112.000	
1	31	1745	144.750	179.500	109.500	
2	28	1745	146.625	182.000	106.250	
3	30	1745	147.000	182.750	107.000	
4	30	1745	145.500	186.750	110.500	
5	31	1745	146.875	187.500	109.000	
6	29	1745	146.875	186.500	109.750	
7	31	1745	144.500	178.250	107.750	
8	31	1745	143.000	174.000	103.000	
9	30	1745	141.500	169.500	100.000	
10	31	1745	138.500	172.500	100.500	
11	30	1745	133.750	169.500	98.000	
12	31	1745	125.750	163.500	91.000	
1	31	1746	123.000	155.500	94.125	
2	28	1746	119.500	155.750	89.750	
3	31	1746	117.500	156.500	91.000	
4	30	1746	124.750	166.000	97.500	
5	31	1746	125.250	168.000	97.250	
6	30	1746	127.500	174.000	100.125	
7	31	1746	133.250	177.750	105.500	
8	30	1746	136.500	183.000	106.000	

mo	dd	year	Bank	EIC	SSea	Consols
1	31	1749	128.000	174.250	107.250	
2	28	1749	129.625	174.750	107.000	
3	31	1749	131.500	176.750	106.750	
4	29	1749	129.000	177.000	107.500	
5	31	1749	135.000	188.000	114.750	
6	30	1749	136.250	186.500	115.250	
7	31	1749	137.375	185.750	116.000	
8	31	1749	140.250	190.250	116.000	
9	30	1749	140.500	190.875	116.750	
10	31	1749	137.625	190.500	115.250	
11	30	1749	134.000	187.000	109.250	
12	30	1749	133.000	188.250	110.250	
1	31	1750	134.000	187.000	111.125	
2	28	1750	133.375	188.000	110.000	
3	31	1750	134.250	187.000	110.000	
4	29	1750	131.750	185.500	109.500	
5	31	1750	133.250	184.000	112.000	
6	30	1750	133.875	187.000	113.000	
7	31	1750	134.000	184.000	112.250	
8	31	1750	135.265	185.500	111.750	
9	29	1750	135.750	184.750	112.500	
10	31	1750	133.500	185.750	113.750	
11	30	1750	135.250	187.500	113.750	
12	31	1750	136.500	188.750	112.000	
1	31	1751	135.500	184.500	111.750	

Month	Day	Year			
2	28	1751	136.750	185.750	110.000
3	30	1751	139.250	187.500	112.125
4	30	1751	137.125	188.750	113.000
5	31	1751	138.250	193.000	115.000
6	29	1751	141.500	195.000	115.500
7	31	1751	139.750	182.750	113.000
8	31	1751	141.000	186.500	114.750
9	30	1751	142.000	187.250	115.500
10	31	1751	139.250	188.000	115.125
11	30	1751	140.750	190.250	117.000
12	31	1751	141.875	190.750	117.250
1	31	1752	143.750	187.250	117.625
2	29	1752	144.125	186.250	116.000
3	31	1752	145.000	186.750	117.000
4	30	1752	143.750	188.750	118.125
5	30	1752	146.250	190.000	120.000
6	30	1752	147.000	193.000	120.750
7	31	1752	147.375	187.000	122.000
8	31	1752	146.250	189.000	121.125
9	30	1752	147.250	192.000	122.500
10	31	1752	143.250	192.000	122.500
11	30	1752	142.250	194.500	122.750
12	30	1752	143.875	196.875	123.500
1	31	1753	143.750	192.000	122.500
2	28	1753	143.500	193.500	120.875
3	31	1753	143.250	194.000	120.750
4	30	1753	140.500	194.000	120.875
5	31	1753	139.875	196.000	120.750

Month	Day	Year			
9	30	1746	134.750	183.500	106.750
10	31	1746	131.000	180.500	103.000
11	29	1746	126.500	175.500	102.000
12	31	1746	128.750	180.000	105.000
1	31	1747	127.000	175.750	103.000
2	28	1747	128.000	174.500	101.000
3	31	1747	128.500	173.500	101.250
4	30	1747	126.750	154.000	105.000
5	30	1747	126.500	152.750	102.000
6	30	1747	125.250	159.750	102.500
7	31	1747	125.750	156.250	103.500
8	31	1747	125.500	161.000	102.500
9	30	1747	125.500	160.000	160.250
10	31	1747	121.625	159.875	99.375
11	30	1747	119.500	161.500	100.500
12	31	1747	120.750	163.500	106.000
1	30	1748	120.000	160.000	100.000
2	29	1748	119.250	160.750	94.500
3	31	1748	117.750	157.500	91.000
4	30	1748	125.000	173.500	105.500
5	31	1748	126.000	178.000	107.000
6	30	1748	128.500	184.000	110.250
7	30	1748	127.000	178.500	110.000
8	31	1748	127.625	179.875	107.000
9	30	1748	129.000	182.000	106.250
10	31	1748	127.000	177.500	105.500
11	30	1748	126.750	178.500	107.250
12	31	1748	125.750	177.000	105.250

mo	dd	year	Bank	EIC	SSea	Consols
11	30	1757	119.000	141.500	103.500	91.250
12	31	1757	117.000	139.500	103.000	90.750
1	31	1758	118.750	138.500	103.000	90.500
2	28	1758	121.000	149.000	104.000	92.500
3	31	1758	124.000	148.000	106.250	94.000
4	29	1758	119.500	147.250	105.375	94.000
5	31	1758	121.500	147.000	105.250	95.625
6	30	1758	122.000	146.000	108.000	96.750
7	31	1758	119.500	137.000	108.000	92.750
8	31	1758	118.750	133.250	102.000	91.875
9	30	1758	118.625	135.500	102.500	90.750
10	31	1758	117.000	134.250	100.250	89.750
11	30	1758	117.250	136.500	100.250	90.750
12	30	1758	116.750	136.000	100.500	89.750
1	31	1759	117.000	134.000	100.500	88.500
2	28	1759	116.750	134.250	97.000	86.750
3	31	1759	116.500	132.000	95.250	83.750
4	30	1759	113.000	129.250	94.000	81.250
5	31	1759	111.250	128.500	93.000	79.500
6	30	1759	111.000	125.750	93.000	79.250
7	31	1759	110.125	121.500	92.000	77.875
8	31	1759	112.750	125.000	93.750	81.750
9	29	1759	112.750	126.250	94.500	82.125
10	31	1759	111.375	130.500	94.000	81.750
11	30	1759	113.250	134.500	96.000	86.000

mo	dd	year	Bank	EIC	SSea	Consols
6	30	1753	138.000	197.000	121.750	
7	31	1753	137.500	192.500	122.500	
8	31	1753	137.500	192.250	120.250	105.125
9	29	1753	138.750	192.500	120.250	104.750
10	31	1753	135.750	191.750	119.500	104.125
11	30	1753	136.000	193.250	120.500	104.500
12	31	1753	135.625	193.875	121.625	103.875
1	31	1754	133.500	189.000	121.000	103.625
2	28	1754	134.125	187.750	119.000	102.625
3	30	1754	134.125	186.500	118.000	102.250
4	30	1754	132.750	191.250	119.000	103.250
5	31	1754	134.250	190.750	119.125	104.250
6	29	1754	134.000	193.000	119.500	104.500
7	31	1754	133.750	187.500	119.500	104.625
8	31	1754	134.000	187.750	117.875	104.125
9	30	1754	133.750	187.500	116.500	103.000
10	31	1754	130.875	185.500	116.500	102.875
11	30	1754	132.250	183.750	116.250	103.000
12	31	1754	133.250	185.250	117.000	103.875
1	31	1755	130.000	175.500	114.000	102.000
2	28	1755	130.625	177.000	113.000	100.250
3	31	1755	129.250	173.000	112.250	98.625
4	30	1755	126.250	172.750	110.000	97.625
5	31	1755	127.250	175.000	111.500	99.750
6	30	1755	126.375	175.000	111.000	98.875

Mo	Day	Year				
7	31	1755	123.500	167.000	103.875	93.125
8	30	1755	122.625	166.000	103.000	92.125
9	30	1755	123.500	167.250	104.250	93.500
10	31	1755	120.000	165.750	104.500	90.625
11	29	1755	122.500	148.500	104.000	91.250
12	31	1755	122.500	148.750	105.500	92.750
1	31	1756	120.000	141.750	104.750	88.875
2	28	1756	120.500	142.750	101.500	89.250
3	31	1756	120.500	142.500	101.500	89.500
4	30	1756	118.000	142.000	102.500	90.750
5	31	1756	117.000	138.750	101.250	89.500
6	30	1756	116.500	137.000	100.250	89.250
7	31	1756	117.000	133.750	101.000	88.750
8	31	1756	117.500	133.250	99.000	89.250
9	30	1756	117.750	133.250	99.750	89.500
10	30	1756	115.250	133.750	99.750	88.375
11	30	1756	115.250	134.500	100.250	88.500
12	31	1756	115.500	136.000	100.375	88.500
1	31	1757	116.000	133.000	101.000	86.750
2	28	1757	118.000	136.250	99.500	87.750
3	31	1757	119.250	139.250	101.000	90.125
4	30	1757	117.000	139.500	100.250	89.125
5	31	1757	119.750	142.000	101.500	90.000
6	30	1757	119.500	133.000	102.250	90.000
7	30	1757	119.500	133.500	102.000	88.875
8	31	1757	120.250	134.500	102.250	89.625
9	30	1757	121.250	141.500	103.000	91.500
10	31	1757	119.750	140.500	104.000	91.000
12	31	1759	114.000	141.000	97.000	84.500
1	31	1760	111.000	133.500	95.000	80.000
2	29	1760	110.000	133.750	90.250	80.250
3	31	1760	111.250	137.000	91.500	82.125
4	30	1760	109.625	137.500	92.500	82.500
5	31	1760	109.750	137.000	92.750	82.500
6	30	1760	110.750	140.000	94.625	84.250
7	31	1760	111.000	136.000	94.500	83.750
8	30	1760	111.750	139.000	93.750	83.625
9	30	1760	111.750	140.500	93.000	82.750
10	31	1760	110.000	142.250	93.500	83.000
11	29	1760	107.500	139.000	91.000	78.750
12	31	1760	106.750	140.000	90.000	75.625
1	31	1761	106.000	136.750	87.250	73.250
2	28	1761	104.500	134.500	85.500	73.625
3	31	1761	107.500	137.000	87.000	77.625
4	30	1761	115.000	143.000	98.250	88.000
5	30	1761	116.000	144.250	97.000	88.000
6	30	1761	114.750	143.000	96.000	85.750
7	31	1761	113.250	141.500	95.000	79.500
8	31	1761	110.000	134.000	95.000	77.500
9	30	1761	111.250	133.000	89.500	73.250
10	31	1761	104.250	128.500	84.500	71.875
11	30	1761	102.500	125.000	83.000	70.375
12	31	1761	95.750	123.500	77.000	66.500
1	30	1762	93.750	112.000	76.000	61.875
2	27	1762	95.250	114.500	74.250	68.000
3	31	1762	96.750	117.000	77.000	70.000

mo	dd	year	Bank	EIC	SSea	Consols
4	30	1762	97.000	117.250	78.000	69.500
5	31	1762	97.000	118.500	79.500	72.500
6	30	1762	97.500	118.000	80.000	72.000
7	31	1762	99.250	122.000	80.000	75.250
8	31	1762	109.000	140.000	87.000	85.750
9	30	1762	112.500	142.000	90.000	83.500
10	30	1762	108.500	140.000	90.500	81.125
11	30	1762	114.000	153.500	98.000	86.250
12	31	1762	119.250	161.750	102.750	92.500
1	31	1763	119.500	158.000	101.500	89.750
2	28	1763	129.500	173.000	103.000	94.375
3	31	1763	131.500	170.000	106.250	94.875
4	30	1763	125.000	172.000	106.500	94.375
5	31	1763	124.750	170.500	104.000	93.625
6	30	1763	122.125	173.500	104.000	93.500
7	30	1763	118.750	163.000	104.000	90.250
8	31	1763	117.000	162.000	95.500	87.250
9	30	1763	116.000	156.500	93.750	81.500
10	31	1763	111.000	154.500	92.000	83.500
11	30	1763	113.375	155.250	94.000	85.875
12	31	1763	113.250	162.000	93.500	85.500
1	31	1764	113.500	156.750	93.250	83.875
2	29	1764	116.500	157.250	94.000	85.125
3	31	1764	118.250	152.500	95.000	85.250
4	30	1764	116.500	153.500	95.500	87.500

mo	dd	year	Bank	EIC	SSea	Consols
9	30	1766	138.500	223.500	104.000	89.375
10	31	1766	136.750	221.250	104.125	89.000
11	29	1766	136.250	219.500	103.500	89.375
12	31	1766	137.250	223.750	104.000	90.125
1	31	1767	143.000	230.750	103.000	89.250
2	28	1767	142.500	233.000	103.500	89.000
3	31	1767	142.250	246.000	101.750	88.875
4	30	1767	142.000	259.000	104.000	89.000
5	30	1767	145.000	244.500	104.500	88.625
6	30	1767	148.000	251.000	106.000	89.125
7	31	1767	145.750	252.750	103.250	87.375
8	31	1767	148.000	271.000	103.750	88.250
9	30	1767	159.250	264.250	104.750	88.375
10	31	1767	156.500	269.000	105.500	88.875
11	30	1767	158.000	262.500	108.000	90.375
12	31	1767	160.250	265.250	109.000	92.625
1	30	1768	162.750	262.250	106.750	90.625
2	29	1768	164.000	266.500	108.000	91.500
3	31	1768	167.125	274.750	109.000	92.750
4	30	1768	167.000	268.250	109.000	93.750
5	31	1768	169.500	273.000	111.000	94.375
6	30	1768	169.000	277.750	109.250	94.500
7	30	1768	164.750	266.000	105.500	89.750
8	31	1768	167.000	274.500	105.750	90.250
9	30	1768	163.500	274.500	104.000	88.375

5	31	1764	114.250	148.000	96.000	86.000
6	30	1764	113.000	151.000	95.250	86.250
7	31	1764	113.375	146.000	95.000	84.875
8	31	1764	113.500	146.500	93.000	83.000
9	29	1764	122.500	145.750	92.000	83.000
10	31	1764	122.000	148.250	94.000	84.125
11	30	1764	122.375	150.500	95.375	84.250
12	31	1764	127.000	156.500	96.500	88.250
1	31	1765	126.750	151.750	96.500	85.625
2	28	1765	129.750	151.000	97.250	87.125
3	30	1765	130.500	153.000	98.125	88.000
4	30	1765	127.875	154.500	100.250	87.625
5	31	1765	128.000	155.000	100.000	87.375
6	29	1765	129.750	159.500	103.000	88.625
7	31	1765	133.250	156.500	102.000	87.875
8	31	1765	136.500	160.000	104.000	89.750
9	30	1765	137.500	164.500	105.500	92.250
10	31	1765	136.250	164.250	104.750	91.875
11	30	1765	135.250	165.000	104.750	91.500
12	31	1765	135.125	167.000	105.250	91.875
1	31	1766	135.250	165.500	104.000	89.375
2	28	1766	134.750	164.750	102.000	88.250
3	31	1766	136.250	163.000	102.500	89.125
4	30	1766	132.750	178.500	102.500	89.375
5	31	1766	136.000	188.750	102.500	90.000
6	30	1766	136.250	187.375	102.250	90.750
7	31	1766	135.000	214.000	100.750	87.875
8	30	1766	138.000	206.000	104.000	89.875

10	31	1768	159.000	272.500	104.500	87.750
11	30	1768	160.250	270.000	104.500	88.625
12	31	1768	161.625	276.500	106.000	90.000
1	31	1769	162.500	274.500	103.250	88.250
2	28	1769	164.500	275.000	103.250	88.125
3	31	1769	165.750	276.500	103.750	89.000
4	29	1769	164.250	273.750	103.125	88.625
5	31	1769	167.250	230.000	105.250	89.625
6	30	1769	166.500	241.000	105.000	89.750
7	31	1769	167.125	230.250	105.000	89.750
8	31	1769	168.500	228.000	104.000	89.250
9	30	1769	162.500	226.000	103.500	88.000
10	31	1769	160.625	224.250	103.250	88.375
11	30	1769	151.500	219.000	102.000	85.500
12	30	1769	153.500	219.000	102.500	86.375
1	31	1770	150.000	205.500	99.000	83.875
2	28	1770	153.500	219.750	99.250	85.500
3	31	1770	152.750	226.750	97.750	85.875
4	30	1770	151.750	226.500	98.000	86.750
5	31	1770	154.000	229.500	100.000	87.000
6	30	1770	149.750	222.750	99.500	85.250
7	31	1770	149.875	217.500	99.750	84.000
8	31	1770	153.000	218.500	98.875	84.875
9	29	1770	139.250	196.250	98.875	78.500
10	31	1770	136.500	194.000	92.000	79.000
11	30	1770	133.000	183.500	89.000	78.000
12	31	1770	131.750	185.500	91.000	78.250
1	31	1771	148.000	214.000	91.000	84.375

mo	dd	year	Bank	EIC	SSea	Consols
7	31	1775	141.875	151.000	95.250	87.750
8	31	1775	143.125	153.500	97.750	88.875
9	30	1775	144.000	155.750	98.000	89.125
10	31	1775	141.000	156.750	97.500	89.000
11	30	1775	143.500	165.000	98.625	89.750
12	30	1775	143.000	166.000	98.250	89.500
1	31	1776	142.250	165.000	96.000	86.875
2	29	1776	142.000	163.250	94.750	86.125
3	30	1776	142.125	161.250	94.875	86.000
4	30	1776	139.500	162.000	94.625	85.500
5	31	1776	136.875	160.500	94.250	84.625
6	29	1776	138.500	162.750	95.500	84.750
7	31	1776	137.750	159.750	92.000	84.125
8	31	1776	140.500	166.250	93.500	83.750
9	30	1776	140.250	169.000	94.000	83.625
10	31	1776	135.250	164.500	94.750	81.875
11	30	1776	137.250	171.500	91.750	82.125
12	31	1776	138.000	173.000	91.875	81.875
1	31	1777	138.000	168.500	90.000	80.625
2	28	1777	136.500	167.500	90.125	79.375
3	31	1777	136.750	166.000	89.500	78.625
4	30	1777	134.750	165.500	90.500	79.625
5	31	1777	134.125	167.500	93.250	79.250
6	30	1777	132.250	166.500	94.000	79.000
7	31	1777	130.000	157.000	88.250	76.250

mo	dd	year	Bank	EIC	SSea	Consols
2	28	1771	155.500	231.000	96.000	88.000
3	30	1771	147.250	218.000	96.250	85.500
4	30	1771	152.500	228.000	96.250	87.500
5	31	1771	155.500	226.500	100.000	88.750
6	29	1771	155.250	225.750	100.750	89.000
7	31	1771	155.750	216.000	100.500	87.250
8	31	1771	155.250	216.500	100.000	87.375
9	30	1771	150.250	213.750	100.125	86.625
10	31	1771	149.125	217.500	100.000	86.875
11	30	1771	148.000	218.000	99.000	87.000
12	31	1771	150.750	225.000	100.250	88.375
1	31	1772	152.125	218.250	102.000	87.750
2	29	1772	152.500	214.500	99.750	87.875
3	31	1772	153.375	216.000	100.250	88.750
4	30	1772	149.750	213.250	99.750	89.125
5	30	1772	151.375	226.000	99.625	90.000
6	30	1772	149.375	213.750	97.000	89.500
7	31	1772	149.000	212.000	97.625	88.250
8	31	1772	148.500	207.750	97.500	88.500
9	30	1772	148.375	191.000	97.250	88.125
10	31	1772	143.625	182.000	96.000	87.375
11	30	1772	144.500	166.000	96.625	88.125
12	31	1772	143.000	163.500	95.750	88.875
1	30	1773	143.375	161.500	94.000	87.250
2	27	1773	143.750	163.000	94.250	87.375

Mo	Day	Year				
8	30	1777	131.000	161.500	87.750	77.625
9	30	1777	132.000	164.000	88.500	78.000
10	31	1777	130.125	166.250	90.000	79.000
11	29	1777	128.750	167.000	88.750	78.375
12	31	1777	125.000	161.000	83.000	75.125
1	31	1778	119.750	154.000	79.000	71.500
2	28	1778	117.250	144.000	78.250	69.125
3	31	1778	108.250	128.500	70.000	60.250
4	30	1778	106.750	128.500	70.250	60.750
5	30	1778	108.250	134.500	72.500	61.500
6	30	1778	109.250	135.250	73.500	61.750
7	31	1778	109.375	132.250	73.500	61.625
8	31	1778	114.000	137.000	73.500	63.875
9	30	1778	116.000	138.000	73.000	65.875
10	31	1778	113.000	144.000	73.500	65.250
11	30	1778	109.750	140.000	72.500	62.500
12	31	1778	107.750	138.000	71.250	61.500
1	30	1779	109.125	139.500	69.500	61.750
2	27	1779	110.000	140.000	69.750	59.250
3	31	1779	115.000	153.500	70.625	62.000
4	30	1779	115.250	155.500	72.500	63.625
5	31	1779	112.875	151.750	72.750	62.875
6	30	1779	108.000	141.750	72.750	60.750
7	31	1779	108.750	139.250	69.500	60.000
8	31	1779	111.375	140.000	70.750	61.125
9	30	1779	111.750	143.750	71.000	61.250
10	30	1779	110.250	144.500	71.500	61.750
11	30	1779	109.750	144.500	71.000	61.250

Mo	Day	Year				
3	31	1773	143.000	153.000	94.000	86.500
4	30	1773	139.500	147.000	93.000	85.750
5	31	1773	139.250	143.000	93.500	86.250
6	30	1773	141.125	147.250	93.750	87.000
7	31	1773	142.000	150.000	93.750	86.500
8	31	1773	143.250	152.000	94.000	87.000
9	30	1773	143.625	152.500	94.375	87.500
10	30	1773	141.500	146.500	94.125	87.875
11	30	1773	140.250	139.500	94.500	87.500
12	31	1773	140.125	140.250	95.250	87.375
1	31	1774	140.250	139.000	93.250	86.375
2	28	1774	140.625	139.250	93.750	86.625
3	31	1774	140.375	141.750	94.750	86.875
4	30	1774	139.750	145.000	94.625	87.875
5	31	1774	140.625	154.500	95.750	88.000
6	30	1774	142.125	154.000	97.000	88.625
7	30	1774	144.000	149.000	96.250	89.000
8	31	1774	144.500	147.500	96.750	88.375
9	30	1774	145.125	148.000	96.750	89.000
10	31	1774	141.500	147.000	96.500	88.750
11	30	1774	142.875	149.500	98.250	89.875
12	31	1774	145.000	153.750	98.250	91.125
1	31	1775	143.250	153.000	100.000	87.125
2	28	1775	144.625	155.750	98.500	88.500
3	31	1775	144.750	156.250	99.500	88.500
4	29	1775	142.375	155.000	99.250	89.125
5	31	1775	142.625	154.500	98.750	88.750
6	30	1775	141.750	155.000	97.125	88.875

mo	dd	year	Bank	EIC	SSea	Consols.
5	31	1784	115.250	123.000	66.500	58.125
6	30	1784	115.500	122.750	65.000	59.000
7	31	1784	115.750	122.250	65.000	57.250
8	31	1784	117.375	127.000	64.500	55.875
9	30	1784	114.000	126.250	62.000	54.625
10	30	1784	110.750	128.000	62.500	54.875
11	30	1784	112.750	131.000	62.750	56.000
12	31	1784	112.875	136.500	62.750	56.375
1	31	1785	117.250	135.000	64.000	56.250
2	28	1785	115.250	131.000	64.000	55.375
3	31	1785	115.000	133.000	64.000	55.000
4	30	1785	115.500	133.000	64.500	57.500
5	31	1785	116.750	133.250	66.500	57.625
6	30	1785	118.500	136.250	66.500	58.625
7	30	1785	120.750	132.500	66.500	58.125
8	31	1785	122.750	136.500	68.250	58.750
9	30	1785	124.500	143.500	69.500	59.875
10	31	1785	130.750	150.000	71.500	65.375
11	30	1785	139.750	156.250	78.500	70.000
12	31	1785	139.000	161.000	79.000	71.625
1	31	1786	140.500	155.500	81.000	70.500
2	28	1786	140.000	157.500	78.000	70.125
3	31	1786	139.750	159.000	78.000	69.250
4	29	1786	137.500	159.500	78.000	69.875
5	31	1786	146.000	162.750	80.250	74.250

mo	dd	year	Bank	EIC	SSea	Consols
12	31	1779	110.000	145.750	71.500	62.000
1	31	1780	113.000	147.000	71.500	60.750
2	29	1780	114.750	153.250	69.750	60.625
3	31	1780	114.500	155.250	70.500	60.750
4	29	1780	112.000	156.250	72.000	60.750
5	31	1780	111.625	152.000	70.750	61.375
6	30	1780	113.500	153.250	70.250	63.375
7	31	1780	116.250	151.250	71.375	62.250
8	31	1780	115.000	151.500	71.500	61.625
9	30	1780	114.250	149.250	71.000	61.125
10	31	1780	111.250	152.750	71.000	61.125
11	30	1780	110.750	153.250	69.500	61.125
12	30	1780	108.750	152.750	69.500	60.250
1	31	1781	105.750	148.250	69.500	58.125
2	28	1781	108.000	147.000	66.750	58.875
3	31	1781	111.000	147.500	67.000	58.375
4	30	1781	112.000	146.500	68.875	58.625
5	31	1781	113.250	144.250	67.500	58.750
6	30	1781	113.625	149.000	69.000	59.125
7	31	1781	114.125	133.250	66.250	57.250
8	31	1781	113.750	140.000	66.250	57.000
9	29	1781	116.000	138.500	66.000	56.625
10	31	1781	108.500	139.500	65.000	55.875
11	30	1781	112.000	140.250	63.500	57.500
12	31	1781	110.500	139.500	64.000	57.750

	Day	Year				
1	31	1782	111.625	134.500	63.000	55.750
2	28	1782	111.000	132.250	62.250	54.375
3	30	1782	113.250	134.750	62.000	55.625
4	30	1782	114.500	139.000	63.750	59.500
5	31	1782	114.500	138.000	65.500	59.750
6	29	1782	114.750	137.500	65.250	59.875
7	31	1782	113.500	128.250	65.000	57.875
8	31	1782	113.875	127.750	63.500	56.625
9	30	1782	116.500	129.250	64.750	57.750
10	31	1782	114.500	133.250	65.750	57.875
11	30	1782	116.000	133.000	68.000	60.000
12	31	1782	123.500	141.000	68.250	64.875
1	31	1783	133.500	144.500	69.500	68.000
2	28	1783	134.750	142.000	74.000	68.125
3	31	1783	136.750	139.750	76.000	67.875
4	30	1783	133.000	139.000	76.000	67.875
5	31	1783	131.750	139.000	75.000	67.375
6	30	1783	127.250	139.250	75.000	66.500
7	31	1783	127.500	134.250	75.000	62.875
8	30	1783	128.000	139.000	71.000	64.500
9	30	1783	122.250	140.000	71.000	59.625
10	31	1783	117.875	138.000	71.000	58.875
11	29	1783	114.500	120.000	68.000	58.000
12	31	1783	111.750	124.500	68.000	57.000
1	31	1784	112.750	121.500	68.000	56.000
2	28	1784	116.000	124.000	66.000	57.250
3	31	1784	118.750	125.500	65.250	58.000
4	30	1784	116.000	124.000	66.000	58.125

	Day	Year				
6	30	1786	145.250	160.750	81.250	74.375
7	31	1786	150.750	160.500	84.250	75.875
8	31	1786	159.000	167.750	87.500	77.750
9	30	1786	156.000	165.500	85.500	77.375
10	31	1786	149.250	166.500	85.500	76.250
11	30	1786	145.500	166.000	83.500	73.875
12	30	1786	151.000	168.000	82.500	75.375
1	31	1787	151.625	163.250	82.000	73.750
2	28	1787	153.875	164.750	83.250	75.000
3	31	1787	155.250	169.250	85.500	76.250
4	30	1787	154.250	170.250	86.000	77.250
5	31	1787	155.500	171.250	85.750	76.875
6	30	1787	150.000	165.000	85.500	73.750
7	31	1787	147.750	159.000	79.250	70.625
8	31	1787	150.000	159.750	80.500	72.500
9	29	1787	149.500	158.250	80.500	72.250
10	31	1787	152.500	166.000	77.875	75.500
11	30	1787	157.250	176.000	85.250	76.875
12	31	1787	158.000	175.500	86.250	77.375
1	31	1788	161.000	170.250	84.500	75.500
2	29	1788	158.500	167.500	84.625	75.250
3	31	1788	176.750	175.250	84.250	75.625
4	30	1788	172.750	173.000	86.500	75.125
5	31	1788	171.875	170.750	85.500	75.500
6	30	1788	172.000	171.750	85.000	75.250
7	31	1788	174.000	169.000	82.500	74.375
8	30	1788	175.625	166.500	83.125	74.125
9	30	1788	176.250	168.000	82.750	74.625

mo	dd	year	Bank	EIC	SSea	Consols
3		1793	172.500	207.250		76.500
4		1793	167.750	214.000		77.375
5		1793	168.250	213.500		77.000
6		1793	171.500	211.750		77.625
7		1793	177.125	210.750		77.625
8		1793	174.500	208.250		76.000
9		1793	172.250	204.500		74.875
10		1793	166.375	206.750		74.125
11		1793	168.500	211.250		75.375
12		1793	165.750	208.500		73.625
1		1794	156.250	199.500		67.375
2		1794	160.500	200.750		66.000
3		1794	161.750	201.500		67.625
4		1794	162.750	207.000		71.250
5		1794	167.000	208.750		70.625
6		1794	161.250	204.000		68.000
7		1794	165.500	199.750		67.375
8		1794	164.625	198.000		67.000
9		1794	158.000	192.500		64.625
10		1794	155.750	190.500		66.750
11		1794	157.625	193.500		68.500
12		1794	156.000	189.250		65.000
1		1795	153.250	182.750		62.625
2		1795	152.750	181.500		62.750
3		1795	153.000	181.750		62.000

mo	dd	year	Bank	EIC	SSea	Consols
10	31	1788	173.750	170.750	83.250	75.625
11	29	1788	170.000	167.750	82.625	73.875
12	31	1788	170.250	166.250	82.500	74.000
1	31	1789	169.750	162.250	80.500	71.750
2	28	1789	175.625	167.500	83.500	74.000
3	31	1789	175.125	168.000	83.750	74.250
4	30	1789	173.875	168.750	85.750	75.000
5	30	1789	177.000	169.500	86.250	76.125
6	30	1789	179.000	173.500	86.750	77.125
7	31	1789	185.250	174.500	87.500	78.875
8	31	1789	189.500	175.000	88.625	79.250
9	30	1789	190.250	177.750	89.375	80.250
10	31	1789	184.000	179.750	88.125	79.125
11	30	1789	181.750	175.000	87.750	77.875
12	31	1789	183.125	173.500	87.750	78.750
1		1790	187.500	171.000		78.875
2		1790	185.000	171.500		77.375
3		1790	187.250	173.500		79.375
4		1790	185.125	174.250		79.750
5		1790	169.500	155.000		74.750
6		1790	170.125	158.750		74.000
7		1790	173.750	158.500		73.875
8		1790	181.500	164.500		76.750
9		1790	180.000	162.000		76.250
10		1790	172.000	156.250		74.250

Month	Year			
11	1790	184.000	168.750	79.375
12	1790	186.375	171.250	81.125
1	1791	187.000	168.750	80.625
2	1791	187.875	167.500	80.500
3	1791	178.500	160.000	76.250
4	1791	185.750	166.500	81.125
5	1791	186.125	166.250	81.625
6	1791	186.250	166.500	81.750
7	1791	190.000	171.750	83.000
8	1791	200.750	185.500	88.875
9	1791	203.375	193.250	89.250
10	1791	194.750	192.750	87.250
11	1791	196.000	187.000	88.125
12	1791	200.875	186.750	90.500
1	1792	209.250	192.000	93.375
2	1792	215.500	212.000	96.125
3	1792	217.500	216.000	96.500
4	1792	206.500	207.000	92.875
5	1792	204.000	208.000	93.375
6	1792	203.250	212.000	92.750
7	1792	207.500	208.250	93.625
8	1792	201.500	200.500	89.500
9	1792	204.625	209.000	90.125
10	1792	200.375	209.500	90.375
11	1792	173.500	182.000	78.750
12	1792	175.000	184.500	78.875
1	1793	173.000	181.000	75.750
2	1793	163.625	195.000	73.250

Month	Year			
4	1795	159.750	192.750	65.625
5	1795	163.000	195.500	66.500
6	1795	165.000	199.500	67.875
7	1795	168.500	196.250	66.750
8	1795	168.375	198.500	67.625
9	1795	169.875	200.000	68.750
10	1795	166.125	199.250	68.625
11	1795	165.750	204.000	68.250
12	1795	176.000	216.000	70.125
1	1796	175.250	212.250	68.250
2	1796	173.000	212.750	67.750
3	1796	175.000	216.500	69.125
4	1796	164.000	209.000	66.625
5	1796	155.750	199.500	64.375
6	1796	154.500	194.250	63.750
7	1796	151.250	183.250	60.375
8	1796	141.000	175.500	55.500
9	1796	146.250	176.500	57.750
10	1796	146.000	175.750	57.375
11	1796	143.000	177.000	56.375
12	1796	138.250	171.500	55.125
1	1797	145.000	166.500	55.375
2	1797	135.250	151.750	51.875
3	1797	128.000	148.000	50.125
4	1797	121.750	150.500	48.250
5	1797	115.500	144.500	47.875
6	1797	126.500	163.500	54.375
7	1797	131.000	159.500	53.000

mo dd	year	Bank	EIC	SSea	Consols
1	1802	190.500	213.000		68.625
2	1802	190.750	214.750		69.125
3	1802	191.500	215.500		70.625
4	1802	195.000	226.000		76.875
5	1802	183.000	218.000		75.875
6	1802	189.250	220.750		75.250
7	1802	186.000	209.000		71.750
8	1802	183.500	204.000		67.250
9	1802	187.000	208.000		69.375
10	1802	179.500	205.000		68.250
11	1802	178.750	202.500		67.375
12	1802	187.000	216.750		73.375
1	1803	187.000	210.250		70.750
2	1803	189.500	215.500		71.125
3	1803	175.000	201.750		62.125
4	1803	170.500	206.750		63.125
5	1803	150.000	178.000		60.000
6	1803	144.000	173.500		57.250
7	1803	137.000	157.000		52.125
8	1803	142.500	164.000		54.125
9	1803	142.500	162.000		52.500
10	1803	141.500	163.500		53.625
11	1803	144.000	168.500		54.500
12	1803	146.250	171.250		56.125
1	1804	154.500	172.500		55.750

mo dd	year	Bank	EIC	SSea	Consols
8	1797	131.000	159.000		52.375
9	1797	126.500	152.500		49.500
10	1797	119.000	150.500		49.250
11	1797	118.250	148.750		49.250
12	1797	118.000	150.750		49.500
1	1798	119.000	146.500		47.625
2	1798	122.750	147.250		49.875
3	1798	122.250	149.000		49.875
4	1798	116.750	148.500		48.250
5	1798	118.000	149.500		49.500
6	1798	118.500	149.000		49.250
7	1798	125.500	146.250		50.000
8	1798	130.000	148.000		50.000
9	1798	130.000	150.250		50.500
10	1798	139.500	163.500		56.125
11	1798	132.000	160.000		52.625
12	1798	136.250	166.000		54.625
1	1799	139.250	162.000		52.875
2	1799	139.000	166.000		54.000
3	1799	134.750	164.250		53.500
4	1799	137.500	170.000		55.500
5	1799	140.250	170.500		56.000
6	1799	154.000	182.750		61.875
7	1799	168.000	191.000		63.375
8	1799	173.500	200.750		66.625

Year	Month			
1799	9	60.625	195.000	163.000
1799	10	60.750	194.000	159.000
1799	11	63.375	197.000	158.000
1799	12	63.000	198.250	155.000
1800	1	60.375	194.500	155.750
1800	2	63.125	202.000	161.000
1800	3	63.375	209.500	163.000
1800	4	63.250	208.500	161.250
1800	5	64.000	210.500	161.000
1800	6	64.875	211.250	161.750
1800	7	65.000	206.000	166.000
1800	8	65.750	203.500	172.000
1800	9	66.000	208.500	175.000
1800	10	63.750	205.000	165.750
1800	11	63.500	205.750	165.250
1800	12	62.875	205.250	160.750
1801	1	57.625	188.500	153.000
1801	2	55.875	185.500	152.500
1801	3	57.875	194.000	160.000
1801	4	61.250	199.000	165.500
1801	5	61.125	200.000	167.500
1801	6	61.875	201.000	167.750
1801	7	58.500	192.750	166.250
1801	8	60.500	198.000	169.000
1801	9	58.750	193.250	168.000
1801	10	68.125	216.000	189.500
1801	11	67.500	215.000	187.000
1801	12	68.875	218.500	187.250

Year	Month			
1804	2	55.625	170.000	154.000
1804	3	56.500	170.000	154.500
1804	4	56.000	170.500	149.500
1804	5	56.000	169.500	152.250
1804	6	57.125	174.750	155.000
1804	7	58.625	177.000	161.000
1804	8	57.000	176.500	160.500
1804	9	57.250	177.500	161.750
1804	10	57.500	177.750	163.000
1804	11	58.625	181.500	167.500
1804	12	59.500	185.000	168.250
1805	1	61.000	188.000	179.000
1805	2	58.000	184.000	179.250
1805	3	58.125	180.750	178.000
1805	4	58.125	179.000	172.500
1805	5	59.250	181.500	172.500
1805	6	59.750	182.500	179.250
1805	7	58.625	182.500	182.750
1805	8	58.250	177.000	178.500
1805	9	58.750	181.000	196.000
1805	10	59.250	187.000	190.500
1805	11	61.000	189.250	195.000
1805	12	60.250	192.250	194.500
1806	1	60.875	186.000	197.500
1806	2	59.875	183.000	203.000
1806	3	60.625	183.000	208.000
1806	4	60.125	179.750	212.500
1806	5	61.375	183.750	209.000

mo dd	year	Bank	EIC	SSea	Consols
6	1806	211.000	192.000	0.000	63.500
7	1806	212.000	185.500	0.000	64.000
8	1806	219.000	188.000	0.000	62.875
9	1806	222.500	187.000	0.000	63.125
10	1806	213.250	183.000	0.000	61.250
11	1806	212.000	179.500	0.000	59.250
12	1806	208.500	182.250	0.000	60.375
1	1807	218.000	181.500	0.000	62.000
2	1807	225.000	185.500	0.000	62.375
3	1807	228.750	183.000	0.000	62.125
4	1807	233.000	187.500	0.000	63.375
5	1807	230.500	187.500	0.000	63.625
6	1807	233.250	187.750	0.000	63.875
7	1807	231.500	175.000	0.000	62.000
8	1807	232.500	177.000	0.000	62.500
9	1807	231.500	174.250	0.000	62.750
10	1807	224.000	174.000	0.000	62.750
11	1807	225.500	179.000	0.000	63.875
12	1807	224.250	179.000	0.000	64.250
1	1808	227.500	171.500	0.000	63.500
2	1808	232.000	172.500	0.000	63.875
3	1808	233.000	172.000	0.000	64.625
4	1808	234.500	182.250	0.000	66.625
5	1808	239.000	177.500	0.000	68.125
6	1808	240.500	182.500	0.000	69.750

mo dd	year	Bank	EIC	SSea	Consols
11	1810	244.000	184.000	0.000	66.875
12	1810	243.000	183.250	0.000	67.125
1	1811	242.250	178.000	0.000	65.875
2	1811	241.000	176.500	0.000	65.625
3	1811	245.250	178.500	0.000	64.500
4	1811	245.000	182.250	0.000	64.750
5	1811	240.500	183.000	0.000	64.625
6	1811	233.000	182.000	0.000	64.375
7	1811	241.000	175.000	0.000	62.500
8	1811	236.000	184.000	0.000	64.250
9	1811	238.000	182.500	0.000	63.625
10	1811	232.000	183.000	0.000	64.000
11	1811	231.000	184.500	0.000	63.375
12	1811	230.000	183.000	0.000	63.375
1	1812	232.000	182.000	0.000	62.750
2	1812	230.500	177.500	0.000	61.500
3	1812	230.000	176.500	0.000	59.625
4	1812	228.750	176.500	0.000	61.750
5	1812	224.000	175.500	0.000	61.250
6	1812	215.000	176.250	0.000	61.000
7	1812	212.500	164.750	0.000	56.250
8	1812	222.000	169.000	0.000	59.375
9	1812	226.000	167.000	0.000	57.875
10	1812	214.750	163.250	0.000	58.750
11	1812	216.250	163.000	0.000	58.375

Year	Month				
1808	7	68.000	0.000	185.000	243.000
1808	8	65.750	0.000	179.000	239.500
1808	9	66.000	0.000	179.000	240.750
1808	10	67.125	0.000	180.250	235.000
1808	11	66.375	0.000	181.500	236.000
1808	12	66.875	0.000	185.500	235.000
1809	1	66.625	0.000	183.500	244.000
1809	2	67.750	0.000	184.750	245.750
1809	3	67.375	0.000	183.750	247.000
1809	4	67.750	0.000	185.750	245.500
1809	5	68.125	0.000	188.750	249.500
1809	6	69.250	0.000	195.000	260.000
1809	7	68.000	0.000	187.500	260.750
1809	8	68.250	0.000	187.000	267.000
1809	9	68.250	0.000	188.000	268.000
1809	10	69.250	0.000	194.000	277.000
1809	11	70.000	0.000	196.000	279.000
1809	12	70.750	0.000	195.250	277.000
1810	1	67.875	0.000	188.500	276.000
1810	2	67.875	0.000	185.500	275.500
1810	3	68.875	0.000	186.000	276.000
1810	4	70.125	0.000	185.000	269.500
1810	5	70.375	0.000	192.000	262.500
1810	6	71.250	0.000	193.000	258.000
1810	7	68.750	0.000	186.000	269.000
1810	8	68.125	0.000	181.000	257.500
1810	9	64.000	0.000	175.500	255.000
1810	10	66.000	0.000	182.000	254.000
1812	12	58.375	0.000	163.250	223.000
1813	1	59.250	0.000	164.000	221.000
1813	2	58.500	0.000	161.000	219.000
1813	3	59.000	0.000	161.000	219.250
1813	4	59.750	0.000	166.500	217.000
1813	5	58.375	0.000	170.000	214.500
1813	6	57.750	0.000	169.000	213.500
1813	7	57.750	0.000	168.000	218.500
1813	8	56.875	0.000	165.000	219.000
1813	9	58.750	0.000	173.000	217.500
1813	10	58.000	0.000	172.500	219.000
1813	11	61.250	0.000	182.000	228.000
1813	12	61.500	0.000	182.000	237.000
1814	1	66.875	0.000	194.000	262.000
1814	2	70.375	0.000	199.000	263.000
1814	3	62.750	0.000	199.000	261.500
1814	4	67.500	0.000	196.000	252.500
1814	5	67.500	0.000	194.500	249.500
1814	6	67.500	0.000	192.500	256.000
1814	7	67.250	0.000	194.000	258.250
1814	8	65.250	0.000	194.000	256.250
1814	9	65.250	0.000	190.500	254.000
1814	10	64.250	0.000	189.000	246.500
1814	11	66.000	0.000	187.500	249.500
1814	12	66.125	0.000	187.500	250.000
1815	1	65.250	0.000	192.000	257.750
1815	2	63.875	0.000	192.750	257.500
1815	3	58.250	0.000	191.250	257.000

mo dd	year	Bank	EIC	SSea	Consols
4	1815	230.000	175.500	0.000	57.125
5	1815	228.500	176.500	0.000	59.375
6	1815	230.000	177.000	0.000	59.000
7	1815	229.000	175.000	0.000	56.750
8	1815	225.500	171.500	0.000	56.375
9	1815	255.000	171.000	0.000	57.125
10	1815	242.500	178.000	0.000	61.000
11	1815	237.500	189.500	0.000	61.125
12	1815	238.000	189.500	0.000	60.875
1	1816	251.000	186.500	0.000	61.750
2	1816	252.000	181.500	0.000	61.750
3	1816	251.000	181.000	0.000	60.125
4	1816	261.750	184.000	0.000	62.375
5	1816	224.000	191.500	0.000	64.250
6	1816	219.000	188.000	0.000	64.250
7	1816	220.000	180.500	0.000	63.250
8	1816	216.500	179.500	0.000	61.625
9	1816	216.500	182.000	0.000	61.500
10	1816	216.500	181.500	0.000	61.875
11	1816	218.250	189.000	0.000	63.000
12	1816	219.500	193.000	0.000	63.000
1	1817	225.000	193.500	0.000	63.500
2	1817	244.000	199.000	0.000	67.375
3	1817	247.250	202.000	0.000	71.625
4	1817	251.500	208.000	0.000	72.125

mo dd	year	Bank	EIC	SSea	Consols
9	1819	230.500	219.000	0.000	69.500
10	1819	213.500	206.500	0.000	66.500
11	1819	216.250	209.000	0.000	67.625
12	1819	217.000	209.000	0.000	67.000
1	1820	222.500	208.500	0.000	67.875
2	1820	223.000	214.000	0.000	68.250
3	1820	224.500	214.500	0.000	68.625
4	1820	223.500	218.500	0.000	69.500
5	1820	224.500	219.500	0.000	69.625
6	1820	219.500	221.000	0.000	69.875
7	1820	226.000	217.750	0.000	68.500
8	1820	221.000	215.500	0.000	67.500
9	1820	221.500	215.000	0.000	66.250
10	1820	215.500	221.750	0.000	67.875
11	1820	219.000	224.500	0.000	69.375
12	1820	221.000	224.500	0.000	69.625
1	1821	228.000	228.500	0.000	71.500
2	1821	226.500	230.500	0.000	72.875
3	1821	226.000	230.000	0.000	71.875
4	1821	223.500	230.500	0.000	72.375
5	1821	232.750	235.000	0.000	76.750
6	1821	229.750	236.000	0.000	76.625
7	1821	230.000	230.000	0.000	74.375
8	1821	236.000	232.500	0.000	76.000
9	1821	237.000	234.250	0.000	76.375

Month	Year				
5	1817	256.000	213.000	0.000	73.125
6	1817	274.000	217.500	0.000	73.000
7	1817	280.000	230.000	0.000	77.750
8	1817	281.250	231.500	0.000	79.000
9	1817	280.250	239.000	0.000	81.000
10	1817	285.750	239.500	0.000	82.375
11	1817	289.500	246.500	0.000	83.375
12	1817	290.500	247.000	0.000	83.375
1	1818	287.000	240.000	0.000	78.875
2	1818	289.500	240.750	0.000	79.750
3	1818	284.000	240.750	0.000	78.750
4	1818	282.000	236.500	0.000	79.500
5	1818	278.500	231.500	0.000	79.000
6	1818	279.500	232.000	0.000	79.000
7	1818	277.000	233.500	0.000	77.250
8	1818	270.000	225.500	0.000	74.000
9	1818	268.500	225.500	0.000	74.625
10	1818	274.500	233.500	0.000	77.625
11	1818	268.500	232.000	0.000	78.250
12	1818	268.000	233.000	0.000	79.125
1	1819	272.500	232.750	0.000	78.500
2	1819	266.000	229.000	0.000	73.000
3	1819	261.000	222.000	0.000	74.250
4	1819	250.500	220.000	0.000	72.000
5	1819	220.000	211.000	0.000	67.125
6	1819	216.000	210.000	0.000	66.250
7	1819	233.000	222.000	0.000	71.375
8	1819	230.500	219.000	0.000	71.625

Month	Year				
10	1821	238.500	241.000	0.000	77.500
11	1821	239.000	240.000	0.000	77.500
12	1821	235.000	240.000	0.000	77.250
1	1822	238.250	238.500	0.000	76.125
2	1822	249.000	247.000	0.000	78.625
3	1822	249.500	247.000	0.000	79.500
4	1822	237.000	242.000	0.000	78.500
5	1822	240.000	239.000	0.000	79.375
6	1822	242.500	239.500	0.000	79.500
7	1822	251.500	251.000	0.000	80.375
8	1822	252.500	251.000	0.000	80.375
9	1822	252.500	252.250	0.000	81.375
10	1822	251.000	257.000	0.000	82.375
11	1822	246.750	257.500	0.000	81.125
12	1822	246.500	252.000	0.000	79.625
1	1823	241.500	245.000	0.000	76.875
2	1823	239.000	235.500	0.000	73.000
3	1823	236.000	233.000	0.000	74.375
4	1823	214.750	243.500	0.000	77.375
5	1823	219.250	251.500	0.000	80.750
6	1823	221.250	251.500	0.000	80.875
7	1823	222.250	252.000	0.000	80.750
8	1823	226.500	264.250	0.000	82.875
9	1823	226.750	265.750	0.000	83.125
10	1823	221.750	263.750	0.000	82.250
11	1823	224.000	268.000	0.000	84.250
12	1823	230.500	269.000	0.000	84.125

Bibliography

Acworth, William, *Financial Reconstruction in England, 1815–1822* (London: P. S. King & Son, 1925).

Adams, Donald, Jr., "American Neutrality and Prosperity, 1793–1808: A Reconsideration," *Journal of Economic History*, 40(December 1980), pp. 713–37.

Adler, Moshe, "Stardom and Talent," *American Economic Review*, 75(March 1985), pp. 208–18.

Aftalion, Florin, *L'économie de la Révolution Française* (Paris: Hachette/Pluriel, 1987).

Amsterdamsche Courant (14 July 1723–20 December 1794).

Anderson, Adam, *An Historical and Chronological Deduction of the Origin of Commerce, from the earliest accounts*, 4 vols. (London, 1764, continued to 1788 by William Combe and published for the last time in 1801; reprinted New York: Augustus M. Kelley, 1967).

Anderson, J. L., "A Measure of the Effect of British Public Finance, 1793–1815," *Economic History Review*, 27(November 1974), pp. 610–19.

Andreades, A., *History of the Bank of England, 1640–1903*, 4th ed. (New York: Augustus M. Kelley, 1966).

Ansley, Craig F., "An Algorithm for the Exact Likelihood of a Mixed Autoregressive–Moving Average Process," *Biometrika*, 66(1979), pp. 59–65.

Ashton, T. S., *Economic Fluctuations in England, 1700–1800* (Oxford: Clarendon Press, 1959).

An Economic History of England: The Eighteenth Century (London: Methuen, 1966).

The Industrial Revolution, 1760–1830 (Oxford University Press, 1948).

Attman, Artur, *The Bullion Flow between Europe and the East 1000–1750* (Göteborg: Kungl. Vetenskass- och Vitterhets-Samhallet, 1981).

Dutch Enterprise in the World Bullion Trade 1550–1800 (Göteborg: Kungl. Vetenskass- och Vitterhets-Samhallet, 1983).

Bachelier, Louis, "Theory of Speculation," translated by A. James Boness in Paul Cootner, ed., *The Random Character of Stock Market Prices* (Cambridge, MA: Massachusetts Institute of Technology Press, 1964), pp. 17–78.

Berding, Helmut, *Napoleonische Herrschafts- und Gesellschaftspolitik im Königreich Westfalen 1807–1813. Kritische Studien zur Geschichtswissenschaft*, Vol. 7 (Göttingen: Vandenhoeck & Ruprecht, 1973).

Bibliothèque Générale de L'école des Haute Etudes, VIe Section, *Sociétés et Compagnies de Commerce en Orient et dans l'Océan Indien* (Paris: SEVPEN, 1970).

Blanchard, Oliver J., and Mark W. Watson, "Bubbles, Rational Expectations, and Financial Markets," in Paul Wachtel, ed., *Crises in the Economic and Financial Structure* (Lexington, MA: Lexington Books, 1982), pp. 295–315.

Blanning, T. C. W., *The French Revolution in Germany: Occupation and Resistance in the Rhineland, 1792–1802* (Oxford: Clarendon Press, 1983).

Bonelli, Franco, "The 1907 Financial Crisis in Italy: A Peculiar Case of the Lender of Last Resort in Action," in C. Kindleberger and P. Laffargue, eds., *Financial Crises: Theory, History, and Policy* (Cambridge University Press, 1982), pp. 51–65.

Box, G. E. P., and G. M. Jenkins, *Time Series Analysis: Forecasting and Control* (San Francisco: Holden-Day, 1970).

Braudel, Fernand, and Frank Spooner, "Prices in Europe from 1450 to 1750," in E. E. Rich and Charles Wilson, eds., *The Cambridge Economic History of Europe*, Vol. 4 (Cambridge University Press, 1967), pp. 374–486.

Brenninkmeyer, Ludger, *Die Amsterdamer Effektenboerse* (Berlin: Emil Ebering, 1920).

Brezis, Elise, "Non Transitory Effects of International Financial Flows: The Industrial Revolution," unpublished paper, Department of Economics, Massachusetts Institute of Technology, October 1987.

Brigham, Eugene F., *Financial Management*, 4th ed. (New York: Dryden Press, 1985).

Bruijn, J. R., F. S. Gaastra, and I. Schöffer, *Dutch–Asiatic Shipping in the 17th and 18th Centuries*, 3 vols., Grote Serie of *Rijks Geschiedkundige Publicatien*, Vols. 165–7 (The Hague: Nijhoff, 1979–87).

Buist, Marten J., *At Spes Non Fractra, Hope & Co., 1770–1815, Merchant Bankers and Diplomats at Work* (The Hague: Nijhoff, 1974).

Business Week, "The New York Colossus" (24 July 1984), pp. 98–112.

Cannan, Edwin, ed., *The Paper Pound of 1797–1821; The Bullion Report, 8th of June, 1810* (reprinted in New York: Augustus M. Kelley, 1969).

Capefigue, Jean Baptiste, *Histoire des Grandes Opérations Financières: Banques, Bourses, Emprunts . . .* , 4 vols. (Paris: Amyot, 1855–60).

Carswell, John, *The Descent on England* (New York: John Day, 1969).

The South Sea Bubble (London: Cresset Press, 1960).

Carter, Alice Clare, "The Dutch and the English Public Debt in 1777," *Economica*, 20(May 1953), pp. 159–61.

"Dutch Foreign Investment, 1738–1800," *Economica*, 20(November 1953), pp. 322–40.

"Dutch Foreign Investment, 1738–1800, in the Light of the Amsterdam 'Collateral Succesion' Inventories," *Tijdschrift voor Geschiednis*, 66(1953), pp. 27–38.

The English Public Debt in the Eighteenth Century (London: The Historical Association, 1968).

Getting, Spending and Investing in Early Modern Times (Assen: Van Gorcum, 1975).

"The Huguenot Contribution to the Early Years of the Funded Debt, 1694–1714," *Proceedings of the Huguenot Society of London* 19:3(1955), pp. 21–31.

"Note on 'A Note on Yardsticks,'" *Economic History Review*, 2nd series, 12(January 1959), pp. 440–4.

"Transfer of Certain Public Debt Stocks in the London Money Market from 1 January to 31 March 1755," *Bulletin of the Institute of Historical Research*, 28(November 1955), pp. 202–12.

Castaing, John, *The Course of the Exchange* (London: 26 March 1697–30 June 1908).

Chandler, Alfred D., *Strategy and Structure: Chapters in the History of Industrial Enterprise* (Cambridge, MA: Harvard University Press, 1962).

Chapman, Stanley, *The Rise of Merchant Banking* (London: Allen & Unwin, 1984).

Chaudhuri, K. N., *Trade and Civilisation in the Indian Ocean* (Cambridge University Press, 1985).

   The Trading World of Asia and the English East India Company, 1660–1760 (Cambridge University Press, 1978).

Child, Josiah, *A Treatise Concerning the East-India Trade* (London: Robert Boulter, 1681).

Clapham, John, *The Bank of England: A History*, 2 vols. (Cambridge University Press, 1945).

   "Loans and Subsidies in Time of War, 1793–1914," *Economic Journal*, 27(1917), pp. 495–501.

Clark, G. N., *The Colonial Conference between England and the Netherlands in 1613–1615* (Batavia: E. J. Brill, 1951).

Clauder, Anna C., *American Commerce as Affected by the Wars of the French Revolution and Napoleon, 1793–1812* (Clifton, NJ: Augustus M. Kelley, 1972).

Cock, S., *An Examination of the Report of the Bullion Committee* (London: J. Dennett, 1810).

Coornaert, E. L. J., "European Economic Institutions and the New World; the Chartered Companies," in E. E. Rich and C. H. Wilson, eds., *The Cambridge Economic History of Europe. Vol. 4: The Economy of Expanding Europe in the 16th and 17th Centuries* (Cambridge University Press, 1967), pp. 223–74.

Cope, S. R., "The Stock Exchange Revisited: A New Look at the Market in Securities in London in the Eighteenth Century," *Economica*, 45(February 1978), pp. 1–21.

   Walter Boyd, A Merchant Banker in the Age of Napoleon (London: Alan Sutton, 1983).

Corti, Egon, *The Rise of the House of Rothschild*, translated from the German by Brian and Beatrix Lunn (New York: Grosset & Dunlap, 1928).

Cotray, Nicolaas, *Prys-Courant der Effecten, 1795–1825*.

Cottrell, P. L., *Industrial Finance, 1830–1914; The Finance and Organization of English Manufacturing Industry* (New York: Methuen, 1979).

Cowles, Alfred, III, Cowles Commission for Research in Economics, *Common Stock Indexes* (Bloomington, IN: Principia Press, 1939).

Cowles, Virginia, *The Great Swindle: The Story of the South Sea Bubble* (London: Collins, 1960).

Crafts, N. F. R., *British Economic Growth During the Industrial Revolution* (Oxford: Clarendon Press, 1985).

   "British Economic Growth, 1700–1813: A Review of the Evidence," *Economic History Review*, 36(May 1983), pp. 177–99.

   "British Economic Growth, 1700–1850: Some Difficulties of Interpretation," *Explorations in Economic History*, 24(July 1987), pp. 245–68.

Cranfield, G. A., *The Development of the Provincial Newspaper, 1700–1760* (Oxford: Clarendon Press, 1962).

Crouzet, François, *l'Economie Britannique et le Blocus Continental, 1806–1813*, 2 vols. (Paris: Presses Universitaires de France, 1958).

   "Wars, Blockade, and Economic Change in Europe, 1792–1815," *Journal of Economic History*, 24(December 1964), pp. 567–88.

Cunningham, Audrey, *British Credit in the Last Napoleonic War* (Cambridge University Press, 1910).

Dahl, Folke, "Amsterdam – Cradle of English Newspapers," *The Library*, 4(1949), pp. 166–78.

  A Bibliography of English Corantos and Periodical Newsbooks, 1620–1642 (Stockholm: Almqvist & Wiksell, 1953).

da Pinto, Isaac, *Traité sur la Circulation et la Crédit* (Amsterdam: M. M. Rey, 1771).

David, Paul, "Clio and the Economics of QWERTY," *American Economic Review*, 75(May 1985), pp. 332–7.

  Some New Standards for the Economics of Standardization in the Information Age, Center for Economic Policy Research Publication No. 79, Stanford, CA, 1986.

  "'The Battle of the Systems' and the Evolutionary Dynamics of Network Technologies," unpublished manuscript, Stanford University, 1986.

Davies, K. G., "Joint Stock Investment in the Later Seventeenth Century," *Economic History Review*, 2nd series, 4:3(1952), pp. 283–301.

  The Royal African Company (New York: Atheneum, 1970).

Davis, Lance, "The Investment Market, 1870–1914: The Evolution of a National Market," *Journal of Economic History*, 25(September 1965), pp. 355–99.

Davis, Ralph, *The Rise of the Atlantic Economies* (London: Weidenfeld & Nicolson, 1975).

Davis, Richard, *The English Rothschilds* (London: Collins, 1983).

Deane, Phyllis, "The Implications of Early National Income Estimates for the Measurement of Long-Term Economic Growth in the United Kingdom," *Economic Development and Cultural Change*, 3(January 1955), pp. 3–38.

de Jong-Keesing, E. E., *De economische crisis van 1763 te Amsterdam* (Amsterdam: 1939).

de Korte, J. P., *De Jaarlijkse Financiele Verantwoording in de Verenigde Oostindische Compagnie* (The Hague: Nijhoff, 1983).

de la Vega, Joseph, *Confusion de Confusiones*, translated by Hermann Kellenbenz (Amsterdam: 1688; reprinted Boston: Harvard Graduate School of Business, 1957).

de Roover, Raymond, *Evolution de la lettre de change XVIIe–XVIIIe* (Paris: 1953).

  Business, Banking, and Economic Thought in Late Medieval and Early Modern Europe (University of Chicago Press, 1974).

de Vries, Jan, *The Economy of Europe in an Age of Crisis, 1600–1750* (Cambridge University Press, 1976).

de Vries, Johann, *Een Eeuw vol Effecten, Historische schets van de Vereiniging voor de Effectenhandel en de Amsterdamse Effectenbeurs, 1876–1976* (Amsterdam: Vereniging voor de Effectenhandel, 1976).

Diba, Behzad T., and Herschel I. Grossman, "The Impossibility of Rational Bubbles," NBER Working Paper No. 1615, 1985.

Dickson, P. G. M., *The Financial Revolution in England: A Study in the Development of Public Credit, 1688–1756* (London: Macmillan, 1967).

  Finance and Government under Maria Theresa, 1740–1780, 2 vols. (Oxford University Press, 1987).

Downie, J. A., *Robert Harley and the Press: Propaganda and Public Opinion in the Age of Swift and Defoe* (Cambridge University Press, 1979).

DuBois, Armand B., *The English Business Company After the Bubble Act, 1720–1800* (New York: The Commonwealth Fund, 1938).

Duffy, Ian P. H., "The Discount Policy of the Bank of England During the Suspension of Cash Payments, 1797–1821," *Economic History Review*, 35(February 1982), pp. 67–82.

Dufraisse, Roger, "Französische Zollpolitik, Kontinentalsperre und Kontinentalsystem in Deutschland der napoleonischen Zeit," in Helmut Berding and H.-P. Ullmann, eds., *Deutschland zwischen Revolution und Restauration* (Düsseldorf: Droste, 1981), pp. 328–52.

Duguid, Charles, *The Story of the Stock Exchange* (London: Grant Richards, 1901).

du Pont, B. G., *E. I. duPont de Nemours and Company, A History 1802–1902* (Boston: Houghton Mifflin, 1920).

Eagly, Robert, and V. Kerry Smith, "Domestic and International Integration of the London Money Market, 1731–1789," *Journal of Economic History*, 36(March 1976), pp. 198–212.

Earle, Peter, ed., *Essays in European Economic History, 1500–1800* (Oxford: Clarendon Press, 1974).

Ellis, Geoffrey, *Napoleon's Continental Blockade: The Case of Alsace* (Oxford: Clarendon Press, 1981).

English, Henry, *A Complete View of the Joint Stock Companies formed during 1824 and 1825* (London: Boosey & Sons, 1827).

Erleigh, Viscount, *The South Sea Bubble* (New York: G. P. Putnam's Sons, 1933).

European Economic Community, *The Development of a European Capital Market* (Brussels: EEC, 1966).

Fairman, William, *The Stocks Examined and Compared . . . ,* 7th ed. (London: John Richardson, 1824).

Fama, Eugene, "Efficient Capital Markets: A Review of Theory and Empirical Work," *Journal of Finance*, 25(May 1970), pp. 383–423.

Faure, Edgar, *Le Banqueroute de Law* (Paris: Gallimard, 1977).

Fehrenbach, Elisabeth, *Traditionelle Gesellschaft und revolutionaeres Recht. Die Einfuehrung des Code Napoleon in den Rheinbundstaaten* (Göttingen: Vandenhoeck & Ruprecht, 1974).

Feldback, Ole, *India Trade under the Danish Flag 1772–1808* (Copenhagen: Scandinavian Institute of Asian Studies, 1969).

Flood, Robert P., and Peter M. Garber, "Bubbles, Runs and Gold Monetization," in Paul Wachtel, ed., *Crises in the Economic and Financial Structure* (Lexington, MA: Lexington Books, 1982), pp. 275–93.

"Market Fundamentals versus Price-level Bubbles: The First Tests," *Journal of Political Economy*, 88(August 1980), pp. 745–70.

Floud, Roderick, and Donald McCloskey, eds., *The Economic History of Britain Since 1700. Vol. 1: 1700–1860* (Cambridge University Press, 1983).

Frankel, Jeffrey A., "The 1808–1809 Embargo Against Great Britain," *Journal of Economic History*, 42(June 1982), pp. 291–307.

Freke, John, *The Price of the Several Stocks, Annuities, And other Publick Securities, Ec. with the Course of Exchange* (London: 26 March 1714–22 June 1722).

Furber, Holden, *John Company at Work: A Study of European Expansion in India in the Late Eighteenth Century* (Cambridge, MA: Harvard University Press, 1948).

Rival Empires of Trade in the Orient, 1600–1800 (Minneapolis: University of Minnesota Press, 1976).

Gaastra, F. S., "The Exports of Precious Metal from Europe to Asia by the Dutch

East India Company, 1602–1795," in J. F. Richards, ed., *Precious Metals in the Later Medieval and Early Modern Worlds* (Durham, NC: Carolina Academic Press, 1983), pp. 447–75.

Galenson, David W., *Traders, Planters, and Slaves: Market Behavior in Early English America* (Cambridge University Press, 1986).

Gash, Norman, *Lord Liverpool: The Life and Political Career of Robert Banks Jenkinson Second Earl of Liverpool, 1770–1828* (Cambridge, MA: Harvard University Press, 1984).

Gayer, Arthur D., W. W. Rostow, and Anna Jacobson Schwartz, *The Growth and Fluctuation of the British Economy, 1790–1850*, 2 vols. (Oxford: Clarendon Press, 1953).

Gee, Joshua, *The Trade and Navigation of Great Britain* (New York: Augustus M. Kelley, 1969).

Giffen, Robert, *Stock Exchange Securities: An Essay on the General Causes of Fluctuations* (New York: Augustus M. Kelley, 1968).

Glamann, Kristof, *Dutch–Asiatic Trade, 1620–1740*, 2nd ed. (The Hague: Nijhoff, 1981).

Granger, C. W. J., and Paul Newbold, *Forecasting Economic Time Series*, 2nd ed. (Orlando, FL: Academic Press, 1986).

Great Britain, "History of the Earlier Years of the Funded Debt, from 1694 to 1786," *British Parliamentary Papers*, Command Paper 9010, 1898.

  "Report by the Secretary and Comptroller General of the Proceedings of the Commissioners for the Reduction of the National Debt from 1786 to 31st March 1890," *British Parliamentary Papers*, Command Paper 6539, 1891.

  "Reports from the Secret Committee on the Expediency of the Bank resuming Cash Payments," *British Parliamentary Papers* (London: House of Commons, 5 April and 6 May 1819).

  "Third Report, 21 April 1797 of Committee of Secrecy on the Outstanding Demands of the Bank of England," *British Parliamentary Papers*, 1797.

Groeneveld, F. P., *Economische Crisis van het jaar 1720* (Gröningen: Noordhof, 1940).

Hamilton, Earl J., *American Treasure and the Price Revolution in Spain, 1501–1650* (Cambridge, MA: Harvard University Press, 1934).

  Money, Prices, and Wages in Valencia, Aragon and Navarre, 1351–1500 (Cambridge, MA: Harvard University Press, 1936).

  War and Prices in Spain, 1651–1800 (Cambridge, MA: Harvard University Press, 1947).

  "John Law," in *International Encyclopedia of the Social Sciences*, Vol. 9 (New York: Free Press, 1968).

  "John Law of Lauriston: Banker, Gamester, Merchant, Chief?" *American Economic Review*, 57(May 1967), pp. 273–82.

  "Origin and Growth of the National Debt in Western Europe," *American Economic Review*, 37(May 1947), pp. 118–30.

  "The Political Economy of France at the Time of John Law," *History of Political Economy*, 1(January 1969), pp. 123–49.

  "Prices and Wages at Paris under John Law's System," *Quarterly Journal of Economics*, 51(1936–7), pp. 42–70.

Hannan, E. J., and J. Rissanen, "Recursive Estimation of Mixed Autoregressive–Moving Average Order," *Biometrika*, 69(1982), pp. 81–94; "Correction," 70(1983), p. 303.

Harsin, Paul, *Doctrines Monétaires et Financières en France du XVIe au XVIIIe Siecle* (Paris: Libraire Felix Alcan, 1928).

ed., *Dutot: Réflexions politiques sur les finance et le commerce*, 2 vols. (Paris: Les Belles Lettres, 1935).

ed., *John Law: Oeuvres complètes*, 3 vols. (Paris: Sirey, 1934).

"Problème de l'escompte des lettres de change en France aux XVIIe et XVIIIe siècles," *Revue internationale d'histoire de la Banque*, 7(1973), pp. 191–8.

H.E.B., "Flight of Capital from Revolutionary France," *American Historical Review*, 41(July 1936), pp. 710–23.

Heckscher, Eli F., *The Continental System: An Economic Interpretation* (Oxford University Press, 1922).

"A Note on South Sea Finance," *Journal of Economic and Business History*, 3(1931), pp. 321–4.

Heim, Carol E., and Philip Mirowski, "Interest Rates and Crowding-Out During Britain's Industrial Revolution," *Journal of Economic History*, 47(March 1987), pp. 117–39.

Hemmeon, Joseph C., *The History of the British Post Office* (Cambridge, MA: Harvard University Press, 1912).

Herries, J. M., *Review of the Controversy reflecting the High Price of Bullion and the State of our Currency* (London: J. Budd, 1811).

Hidy, Ralph, *The House of Baring in American Trade and Finance: English Merchant Bankers at Work, 1763–1861* (Cambridge, MA: Harvard University Press, 1949).

Hilferding, Rudolf, *Finance Capital: A Study of the Latest Phase of Capitalist Development*, translated by Morris Watnick and Sam Gordon, edited by Tom Bottomore (London: Routledge & Kegan Paul, 1981).

Hoes, H. J., "Voorgeschiedenis en Ontstaan van het Financieele Dagblad, 1796–1943," *Economish- en Sociaal-Historisch Jaarboek*, 49(1986), pp. 1–40.

Hoppit, Julian, *Risk and Failure in English Business, 1700–1800* (Cambridge University Press, 1987).

Houghton, John, *A Collection for Improvement of Husbandry and Trade*, 9 vols. (London: Randall Taylor et al., 1692–1703; republished Westmead, Farnborough, Hants.: Gregg, 1969).

Hueckel, Glenn, "War and the British Economy, 1793–1815: A General Equilibrium Analysis," *Explorations in Economic History*, 10(October 1973), pp. 365–96.

James, John, "The Development of the National Money Market, 1893–1911," *Journal of Economic History*, 36(December 1976), pp. 878–97.

Jones, Charles A., *International Business in the Nineteenth Century: The Rise and Fall of a Cosmopolitan Bourgeoisie* (New York University Press, 1987).

Jones, Robert A., "The Origin and Development of Media of Exchange," *Journal of Political Economy*, 84(August 1976), pp. 757–75.

Keehn, Richard H., "Federal Bank Policy, Bank Market Structure, and Bank Performance: Wisconsin, 1863–1914," *Business History Review*, 48(Spring 1974), pp. 1–27.

Kellenbenz, Hermann, "Introduction," in Joseph de la Vega, *Confusion de Confusiones* (Boston: Harvard Graduate School of Business, 1957).

Keller, Helen, *The Dictionary of Dates* (New York: Macmillan, 1934).

Kindleberger, Charles P., *A Financial History of Western Europe* (London: George Allen & Unwin, 1984).

Manias, Panics and Crashes (New York: Basic Books, 1978).

Kindleberger, Charles, and Pierre Laffargue, eds., *Financial Crises: Theory, History, and Policy* (Cambridge University Press, 1982).

Klein, P. W., *De Trippen in de 17ᵉ eeuw: een studie over het ondernemersgedrag op de Hollandse stapelmarkt* (Assen; The Netherlands: Historische Bibliotheek, 1965).

Koninckx, Christian, *The First and Second Charters of the Swedish East India Company (1731–1766)* (Kortuk, Belgium: Van Ghemmert Publishing, 1980).

Lambert, Sheila, ed., *House of Commons Sessional Papers of the Eighteenth Century* (Wilmington, DE: Scholarly Resources, 1975).

Landes, David, *The Unbound Prometheus* (Cambridge University Press, 1969).

Lavington, F., *The English Capital Market* (New York: Augustus M. Kelley, 1968).

Lee, C. H., *The British Economy Since 1700: A Macroeconomic Perspective* (Cambridge University Press, 1986).

Le Moine de l'Espine, Jacques, *De Koophandel van Amsterdam en andere Nederlandsche stede naar alle gewesten der wereld*, 10th ed. (Amsterdam: J. de Groot, 1801–2).

Levasseur, E., *Recherches Historiques sur le Systeme de Law* (Paris: Guillaumin et Cie, 1854).

Luethy, Herbert, *La Haute Banque Protestante en France de la Révocation de l'Edit de Nantes à la Révolution. Vol. 2: De la Banque aux Finances* (Paris: SEVPEN, 1961).

McCusker, John J., "The Business Press in England before 1775," *The Library, The transactions of the Bibliographical Society*, 6th series, 8:3(September 1986), pp. 205–31.

    European Bills of Entry and Marine Lists: Early Commercial Publications and the Origins of the Business Press (Cambridge, MA: Harvard University Library, 1985).

    Money and Exchange in Europe and America, 1600–1775: A Handbook (Chapel Hill: University of North Carolina Press, 1978).

McCusker, John and Cora Gravesteijn, *Commodity Price-Currents, Exchange Rate Quotes, and General Currents in Early Europe: The Rise of a Commercial and Financial Press*, unpublished manuscript, 1984.

Machlup, Fritz, *A History of Thought on Economic Integration* (New York: Columbia University Press, 1977).

    "The Transfer Problem: Theme and Four Variations," in F. Machlup, ed., *International Payments, Debts, and Gold*, 2nd ed. (New York University Press, 1975), pp. 374–95.

Malkiel, Burton, *A Random Walk Down Wall Street* (New York: Norton, 1973).

Marion, Marcel, *Ce qu'il faut connâitre des crises financières de notre histoire* (Paris: Boivin, 1926).

Mathew, K. S., *Portuguese Trade with India in the Sixteenth Century* (New Delhi: Manohar Publications, 1983).

Mathias, Peter, and M. M. Postan, eds., *The Cambridge Economic History of Europe. Vol. 7: The Industrial Economies: Capital, Labour, and Enterprise, part 1, Britain, France, Germany, and Scandinavia* (Cambridge University Press, 1978).

Michie, Ranald C., "The London and New York Stock Exchanges, 1850–1914," *Journal of Economic History*, 46(March 1986), pp. 171–87.

    "Transfer of Shares in Scotland, 1700–1820," *Business History*, 20(1978), pp. 153–64.

"Options, Concessions, Syndicates, and the Provision of Venture Capital, 1880–1913," *Business History,* 23(1981), pp. 47–164.

Minsky, Hyman, "A Theory of Systematic Fragility," in Edward I. Altman and Arnold W. Sametz, eds., *Financial Crises: Institutions and Markets in a Fragile Environment* (New York: Wiley, 1977), pp. 138–52.

Mirowski, Philip, "The Rise (and Retreat) of a Market: English Joint Stock Shares in the Eighteenth Century," *Journal of Economic History,* 41(September 1981), pp. 559–77.

"What Do Markets Do? Efficiency Tests of the Eighteenth Century London Stock Market," *Explorations in Economic History,* 24(April 1987), pp. 107–29.

Mitchell, B. R., *Abstract of British Historical Statistics* (Cambridge University Press, 1962).

Mokyr, Joel, "Has the Industrial Revolution Been Crowded Out? Some Reflections on Crafts and Williamson," *Explorations in Economic History,* 24(July 1987), pp. 293–319.

Mokyr, Joel, and N. Eugene Savin, "Stagflation in Historical Perspective: The Napoleonic Wars Revisited," *Research in Economic History,* 1(1976), pp. 198–259.

Morgan, E. Victor, and W. A. Thomas, *The Stock Exchange: Its History and Functions* (London: Elek Books, 1962).

Morgenstern, Oskar, *International Financial Transactions and Business Cycles* (Princeton University Press, 1959).

Morineaux, Michel, *Ces Incroyables Gazettes et Fabuleux Metaux* (Cambridge University Press, 1985).

Mortimer, Thomas, *Every Man His Own Broker: Or a Guide to Exchange Alley,* 3rd ed. (London: S. Hooper, 1761).

Muhlstein, Anka, *James de Rothschild, Une métamorphose, une légende* (Paris: Gallimard, 1981).

Mukherjee, Ramkrishna, *The Rise and Fall of the East India Company* (New York: Monthly Review Press, 1974).

Murphy, Antoin E., *Richard Cantillon: Entrepreneur and Economist* (Oxford: Clarendon Press, 1986).

Neal, Larry, "Efficient Markets in the Eighteenth Century? The Amsterdam and London Stock Exchanges," *Business and Economic History,* 11(1982), pp. 81–100.

"Integration of International Capital Markets: Quantitative Evidence from the Eighteenth to Twentieth Centuries," *Journal of Economic History,* 45(June 1985), pp. 219–26.

"The Integration and Efficiency of the London and Amsterdam Stock Markets in the Eighteenth Century," *Journal of Economic History,* 47(March 1987), pp. 97–115.

"Interpreting Power and Profit in Economic History: A Case Study of the Seven Years War," *Journal of Economic History,* 37(March 1977), pp. 20–35.

"Trust Companies and Financial Innovation, 1897–1914," *Business History Review,* 45(Fall 1971), pp. 35–51.

Neal, Larry, and Eric Schubert, "The First Rational Bubbles: A New Look at the Mississippi and South Sea Schemes," unpublished paper, Urbana, IL, 1985.

Nolte, Vincent, *The Memoirs of Vincent Nolte: Reminiscences in the Period of Anthony Adverse* (New York: G. Howard Watt, 1934).

North, Douglass C., *Structure and Change in Economic History* (New York: Norton, 1981).

Officer, Lawrence H., "The Floating Dollar in the Greenback Period: A Test of Theories of Exchange-Rate Determination," *Journal of Economic History*, 41(September 1981), pp. 629–56.

Organisation for Economic Cooperation and Development, *Capital Markets Study* (Paris: OECD, 1967).

Parsons, Brian, "The Behavior of Prices on the London Stock Market in the Early Eighteenth Century," Ph.D. dissertation, University of Chicago, 1974.

Platt, D. C. M., *Foreign Finance in Continental Europe and the United States 1815–1870: Quantities, Origins, Functions, and Distribution* (London: Allen & Unwin, 1984).

Posthumus, Nicholas, *Inquiry into the History of Prices in Holland*, Vol. 1 (Leiden: E. J. Brill, 1946).

Postlethwayt, Malachy, *The Universal Dictionary of Trade and Commerce*, 2 vols. (London: 1774; reprinted New York: Augustus M. Kelley, 1971).

Price, Jacob M., *Capital and Credit in British Overseas Trade: The View from the Chesapeake, 1700–1776* (Cambridge, MA: Harvard University Press, 1980).
    "Notes on Some London Price-Currents, 1667–1715," *Economic History Review*, 2nd series, 7(1954), pp. 240–50.

Ricard, Jean-Pierre, *La Négoce d'Amsterdam: contenant tout ce que doivent savoir les marchands et banquiers, etc.* (Rouen: 1723).

Ricardo, David, *The Principles of Political Economy and Taxation* (London: J. M. Dent & Sons, 1962, reprint of 3rd ed., 1821).

Richards, J. F., ed., *Precious Metals in the Later Medieval and Early Modern Worlds* (Durham, NC: Carolina Academic Press, 1983).

Richards, R. D., "The First Fifty Years of the Bank of England (1694–1744)," in J. G. van Dillen, ed., *History of the Principal Public Banks* (The Hague: Nijhoff, 1934), pp. 201–72.

Riley, James C., *International Government Finance and the Amsterdam Capital Market, 1740–1815* (Cambridge University Press, 1980).
    The Seven Years War and the Old Regime in France: The Economic and Financial Toll (Princeton University Press, 1986).

Robinson, Howard, *The British Post Office: A History* (Princeton University Press, 1948).

Rogers, James E. T., *A History of Agriculture and Prices in England* (Oxford University Press, 1866).
    The First Nine Years of the Bank of England (Oxford University Press, 1887).

Rostow, W. W., *The Stages of Economic Growth* (Cambridge University Press, 1961).

Saricks, Ambrose, *Pierre Samuel Du Pont de Nemours* (Lawrence: University of Kansas Press, 1965).

Sayous, Andre, "Les Repercussions de l'affaire de Law et du South Sea Bubble dans les Provinces Unies," *Bijdragen voor vaderlandsche Geschiednenis en Oudheidkunde*, 8:2(1940), pp. 57–86.

Schama, Simon, "The Exigencies of War and the Politics of Taxation in the Netherlands, 1795–1810," in J. M. Winter, ed., *War and Economic Development* (Cambridge University Press, 1975), pp. 103–37.
    Patriots and Liberators, Revolution in the Netherlands, 1780–1813 (New York: Knopf, 1977).

Schubert, Eric, "The Ties that Bound: Eighteenth Century Market Behavior in Foreign Exchange, International Goods, and Financial Assets," unpublished Ph.D. dissertation, University of Illinois, Urbana-Champaign, 1986.

Scott, William R., *The Constitution and Finance of English, Scottish and Irish Joint-Stock Companies to 1720*, 3 vols. (Cambridge University Press, 1910).

Sedillot, Rene, *Histoire du franc* (Paris: Editions Sirey, 1979).

  Le Franc, Histoire d'une monnaie des origines a nos jours (Paris: Editions Sirey, 1953).

Sherwig, John M., *Guineas and Gunpowder: British Foreign Aid in the Wars with France, 1793–1815* (Cambridge, MA: Harvard University Press, 1969).

Shiller, Robert, "Stock Prices and Social Dynamics," *Brookings Papers on Economic Activity*, No. 2 (1984), pp. 457–98.

Silberling, Norman J., "British Financial Experience, 1790–1830," *Review of Economics and Statistics*, 1(1919), pp. 282–97.

  "Financial and Monetary Policy of Great Britain during the Napoleonic Wars," *Quarterly Journal of Economics*, 38(1923–4), pp. 214–33, 397–439.

Slaven, Anthony, and Derek H. Aldcroft, eds., *Business, Banking, and Urban History: Essays in Honour of S. G. Checkland* (Edinburgh: John Donald Publishers, 1982).

Smart, William, *Economic Annals of the Nineteenth Century, 1801–1820*, Vol. 1 (New York: Augustus M. Kelley, 1964).

Smith, Adam, *Wealth of Nations* (London: 1776; reprinted New York: Random House, 1937).

Smith, Woodruff D., "The Function of Commercial Centers in the Modernization of European Capitalism: Amsterdam as an Information Exchange in the Seventeenth Century," *Journal of Economic History*, 44(December 1984), pp. 985–1005.

Sperling, John G., *The South Sea Company: An Historical Essay and Bibliographical Finding List* (Boston: Harvard Graduate School of Business Administration, 1962).

Spooner, Frank C., *The International Economy and Monetary Movements in France, 1493–1725* (Cambridge, MA: Harvard University Press, 1972).

Steensgaard, Niels, *The Asian Trade Revolution of the Seventeenth Century* (University of Chicago Press, 1974).

Stein, Jerome L., "The Dynamics of Spot and Forward Prices in an Efficient Foreign Exchange Market," *American Economic Review*, 70(September 1980), pp. 565–83.

Stewart, James D., ed., *British Union-Catalogue of Periodicals*, Vol. 1 (London: Butterworth, 1955).

  British Union-Catalogue of Periodicals, Supplement to 1960 (London: Butterworth, 1962).

Stigler, George, *The Organization of Industry* (Homewood, IL: Irwin, 1968).

Sushka, Marie E., and W. Brian Barrett, "Banking Structure and the National Capital Market, 1869–1914," *Journal of Economic History*, 44(June 1984), pp. 463–77.

Sutherland, Lucy S., *The East India Company in Eighteenth-Century Politics* (Oxford: Clarendon Press, 1952).

Thomas, Brinley, "Escaping from Constraints: The Industrial Revolution in a Malthusian Context," *Journal of Interdisciplinary History*, 15(Spring 1985), pp. 729–53.

Tirole, Jean, "On the Possibility of Speculation Under Rational Expectations," *Econometrica*, 50(September 1982), pp. 1163–81.

Tranter, Neil, "The Labour Supply, 1780–1860," in Roderick Floud and Donald N. McCloskey, eds., *The Economic History of Britain since 1700*, Vol. 1 (Cambridge University Press, 1981), pp. 204–26.

van der Wee, Herman, *The Growth of the Antwerp Market*, 3 vols. (The Hague: Nijhoff, 1963).

van Dillen, J. G., "De economische positie en beteknis der Joden in de Republiek en in de Nederlandse koloniale wereld," in H. Brugmans and A. Frank, eds., *Geschiednis der Joden in Nederland* (Amsterdam: Van Holkema & Warendorf, 1940).

"Effectenkoersen aan de Amsterdamsche Beurs, 1723–1794," *Economische-Historische Jaarboek*, 17(1931), pp. 1–46.

Van Klaveren, Jacob, "Rue de Quincampoix und Exchange Alley: Die Spekulationsjahre 1719 und 1720," *Vierteljahrschrift für Sozial- und Wirtschaftsgeschichte*, 48(October 1961), pp. 329–59.

Verlinden, Charles, *The Beginnings of Modern Colonization* (Ithaca, NY: Cornell University Press, 1970).

Vilar, Pierre, *A History of Gold and Money, 1450–1920* (London: Verso, 1976).

Villain, Jean, "Heurs et malheurs de la speculation de 1716 a 1722," *Revue d'histoire moderne et contemporaine*, 4(1957), pp. 121–40.

Vissink, H. G. A., *Economic and Financial Reporting in England and the Netherlands* (Assen, The Netherlands: Van Gorcum, 1985).

West, Kenneth D., "A Specification Test for Speculative Bubbles," Discussion Paper 97, Woodrow Wilson School, Princeton University, 1985.

"Speculative Bubbles and Stock price Volatility," Financial Research Center Memorandum No. 54, Princeton Univeristy, 1984.

Williamson, Jeffrey G., "Debating the Industrial Revolution," *Explorations in Economic History*, 24(July 1987), pp. 269–92.

Did British Capitalism Breed Inequality? (London: Allen & Unwin, 1985).

"Why Was British Growth So Slow During the Industrial Revolution?" *Journal of Economic History*, 44(September 1984), pp. 687–712.

Wilson, Charles, *Anglo-Dutch Commerce and Finance in the Eighteenth Century* (Cambridge University Press, 1941).

"Dutch Investment in Britain in the 17th–19th Centuries," in *Credit Communal de Belgique, Collection Histoire Pro Civitate. No. 58: La Dette Publique aux XVIIIe et XIXe Siècles* (Brussels: 1980).

"Dutch Investment in Eighteenth Century England," *Economic History Review*, 2nd series, 12(January 1959), pp. 434–9.

The Transformation of Europe, 1558–1648 (Berkeley: University of California Press, 1976).

Wright, Chester, and Charles E. Fayle, *A History of Lloyd's from the Founding of Lloyd's Coffee House to the Present Day* (London: Macmillan, 1928).

Index

accepter (of bill of exchange), 6–7, 185, 202
actions, 22, 123; *actions rentières*, 74
Acworth, William, 223
advertisement, 23, 36
agio, 36, 192n, 195, 298
agricultural sector, 220
Aislabie, John, 112
allies, Continental, of Great Britain, 202–3, 205, 214, 217, 225, 229
Amsterdam, 6–8, 10, 16–18, 20–1, 26–31, 37–8, 41–4, 63, 65, 68, 70–2, 79–80, 103–4, 109, 113, 115, 120–1, 132–9, 141–64, 169–71, 174, 177–80, 183–4, 186–7, 190, 192–3, 195, 197, 202, 217, 223, 225–9
Amsterdam market (Beurs), 9, 16, 30, 36, 38, 43, 141–3, 148, 150–1, 153, 163, 168, 170, 174, 179n
Amsterdam prices, 152–3, 229
Amsterdam stock exchange (Effectenbeurs), 27, 29, 37, 118, 120, 137, 171, 225–7; official price list, 226
Amsterdamers, 115–16
Amsterdamsche Courant, 29–30, 36–41, 121, 141, 143, 150–1, 153, 163
Amsterdamsche Effectenpryslist, 18, 227
Anderson, Adam, 51, 62, 76, 89, 105
annuitants, 92, 94–7, 100, 109
annuities, 5, 10, 13–15, 18, 28, 38–9, 46, 51–3, 71, 77, 91–4, 96–101, 111, 113, 128; fixed-term, 92; irredeemable, 94, 97–101, 105–6, 109, 117; life, 90, 92; long, 91–3, 97, 99, 102; New South Sea, 53, 127n; perpetual, 8, 59, 90–1, 117; redeemable, 93–4, 97, 99–101, 117; short, 97, 100, 102; South Sea, 90, 102, 117, 147; term, 90, 92, 96; Three Per Cent, 57; transferable, 53
annulment of debts, 226
Antwerp, 5, 7, 10, 187
arbitrage, 165–9, 175, 178
Ashton, T. S., 67, 69, 79, 169–71, 221; Ashton effect, 67, 72, 78, 104

Asia, 118–19, 125, 129, 131, 136, 138–40
asiento, 52–3
assignats, 183, 191, 195, 198–200
Assurance of Ships, 54
Austria, 184, 196, 210, 226
Austrian Netherlands, 183–4, 215, 229
Autoregressive Moving-Average (ARMA) models, 81–3, 85–7, 148–50, 168, 174–6, 178

balance of payments, 190, 192
balance of trade, 221
Baltic trade, 131, 205
Baltimore & Ohio Railway, 174
banco, 7, 195
bank notes, 69–70
Bank of Amsterdam, 195, 198; *see also* Wisselbank
Bank of England, 12, 15–16, 23, 28–9, 38–9, 43, 46–7, 49, 51, 53, 59, 78–9, 83, 86, 89–94, 97, 99–101, 104, 106–8, 110, 112–13, 115, 117, 126–31, 142–4, 146–8, 150, 152, 155–7, 160, 175, 181, 184, 191, 194, 196–7, 199–202, 205–6, 210–11, 214, 217
Bank of England stock, 83–4, 86–7, 113–14, 116, 150, 155, 161, 170, 231–57
bankers' annuities, 93
Banque Generale, 73
Banque Royale, 62, 69–73, 75
Baring, Alexander, 180, 187
Baring firm, 186–8, 218, 225
Barnard's Act (1734), 150, 152, 154–5
Batavia, 135–6, 139
Batavian Republic, 27, 171, 226
"bears," 16, 22, 35, 224–5
Benfield, Paul, 183–4, 223
Bengal, 128, 136
beta coefficients, 57, 59–61, 127
billets de banque, 69–70, 74
billets-livre, 73
bills of exchange, 5–8, 10, 67, 69, 72, 78,

271